The Origins of Free Verse

The Origins of Free Verse

H. T. Kirby-Smith

Ann Arbor

THE UNIVERSITY OF MICHIGAN PRESS

*This book is dedicated
to the memory of Douglas Bush
and to my students
in English 570, "The Structure of Verse,"
at UNCG.*

First paperback edition 1998
Copyright © by the University of Michigan 1996
All rights reserved
Published in the United States of America by
The University of Michigan Press
Manufactured in the United States of America
⊗ Printed on acid-free paper

2001   2000   1999   1998   4   3   2   1

A CIP catalog record for this book is available from the British Library.

Library of Congress Cataloging-in-Publication Data

Kirby-Smith, H. T. (Henry Tompkins), 1938–
      The origins of free verse / H.T. Kirby-Smith.
         p.   cm.
      Includes bibliographical references (p.).
      ISBN 0-472-10698-8 (hardcover :   alk. paper)
         1. American poetry—History and criticism. 2. Free verse—History
      and criticism. 3. English language—Versification. 4. English
      poetry—History and criticism. 5. Imagist poetry—History and
      criticism.   I. Title.
      PS309.F7K57   1996
      811.009—dc20   96-4457
                                                                CIP

ISBN 0-472-08565-4 (pbk : alk. paper)

I do not sing the old. My new is better. New is King Zeus;
of old Chronos ruled. Away with the old Muse.
—Timotheus (446–357 B.C.)

The mind of man naturally hates everything that looks
like a restraint upon it . . .
—Joseph Addison

Je dirai que la réminiscence du vers strict hante ces
jeux à côté et leur confère un profit. [I will say that the
reminiscence of the regular line, close at hand, haunts these
diversions and that they benefit from this.]
—Stéphane Mallarmé

. . . those influential traditions of early English prosody
which form points of departure, at least, for any indigenous
rhythms and forms which may emerge.
—Hart Crane

One might also say that, in their attitude towards art,
the formal verse writer is a catholic, the free verse writer
a protestant.
—W. H. Auden

Preface

Early in 1763 James Boswell attended a gathering hosted by Alexander Montgomerie, Tenth Earl of Eglington, and afterwards confided to his journal that the company was so distinguished that he felt "most amazingly bashful and stupid." The conversation ranged widely, and at one point Boswell recovered sufficiently to join in.

> My Lord mentioned poetry. Sir James said it was just personification, animating every object and every feeling, and that measure was not necessary. Erskine agreed with him. I maintained that personification was only one requisite in poetry, and that measure was absolutely necessary, without which it ceased to be poetry and must be denominated some other work of the imagination. (124–25)

Behind this discussion was the recent publication of "Ossian," James Macpherson's purported author for his supposed translations from Celtic originals of ancient heroic poetry. The immense vogue that this production enjoyed led some of its readers to consider whether English prosody (or French or German for that matter) had not been on the wrong track all along—whether emulation of Greek and Roman meters, especially in epic and tragedy, might not give way to rhythmically articulated prose, dispensing with measure, and make possible an authentic natural expressiveness. With Dr. Johnson's dogged exposure of the whole thing as a fraud—although even now there remain a few last-ditch believers in Ossian—the idea lost credibility. Except for Blake, no important Romantic poet in England was affected by this fashion, though the authenticity of "Ossian" was an article of faith for Emerson and Thoreau and appealed to Matthew Arnold's repressed Romantic nature. Wordsworth positively rejected it. But Boswell's conversation, and others like it at the same time, might well be considered among the earlier discussions of free verse in English. Translated to the present moment, it might not be too fanciful to hear Sir James speaking for "Language" poetry, while Boswell sounds like an apologist for New Formalism.

In 1755 Johnson's dictionary had defined "personification" as "prosopopoeia; the change of things to persons." But in the jargon of mid-eighteenth-century critical theory personification (when used as a critical term) was more than just a rhetorical device; it encompassed the imaginative and metaphorical activities of the poetic imagination—the more subjective and unaccountable side of poetry. Even as the poetic *uses* of personification became more abstract and schematic, the *concept* of personification took on new depths. Personification in Johnson's "The Vanity of Human Wishes" descends to, "Around his tomb let Art and Genius weep." But the concept, as used by Joseph Warton among others, anticipated Coleridge's theory of the secondary imagination, extending to the poet creative powers analogous to, or even superseding, those of God. Personification implied that the artist possessed a power that made it possible to transform nature—not merely to imitate it. Among other things, this was an early instance of a Romantic reaction against the depersonalizing effect of Newtonian physics, a reassertion of the importance of the human point of view and an overreaching claim for the capacity of the human imagination to remake the material universe for its own purposes. As M. H. Abrams argued, "[I]n literary criticism the valid animation of natural objects, traditionally treated as one form of the rhetorical device of prosopoeia, or personification, now came to be a major index to the sovereign faculty of imagination, and almost in itself a criterion of the highest poetry" (55).

Personification in this sense seems roughly comparable to, or at least anticipatory of, the organic self-projection of Charles Olson, while Boswell's contention "that measure was absolutely necessary" sorts well with the views of Yvor Winters and other twentieth-century formalists. *Personism* in fact was a term coined and employed by Frank O'Hara to describe his own practice—and O'Hara's work is not only a successor to Olson's, but is surely an immediate precursor to Language poetry, whose authors are the most recent proponents of what is completely unaccountable in poetry and whose exponents regularly hark back to O'Hara and Olson. Some critics, too, speak of "personalism" as a quality found in much later twentieth-century American poetry. In the opposite direction we find Timothy Steele declaring his formalist affiliations in the title of his book, *Missing Measures,* placing the emphasis on regular meters and forms and deploring their absence.

The Ossian dispute may be forgotten along with the jargon of eighteenth-century criticism, but in the twentieth century no literary topic has proved more divisive than free verse. Division begins on the issue of whether free verse exists, and among those who admit its existence the question is whether it is a good idea. The only area of agreement, shared by many whose literary politics differ sharply in other respects, is that no one knows what free verse is. For my purposes that limited consensus is worse than none at all, since the aim of this study is to identify various kinds of free verse and to explain how they originated.

The best policy would be to neglect the issue altogether. Any sensible person in the year 1690 would have been well advised not to join in the now largely forgotten Battle of the Ancients and the Moderns, or to treat it with diffident aloofness as Dryden did. What we really need is a satirist of the stature of Swift to lay the whole thing to rest, as Swift did that earlier debate with his *Battle of the Books,* but it seems unlikely that Garry Trudeau will take it up. In the absence of such a solution we can try to establish the grounds of disagreement. By doing that, and by changing the terms of the discussion slightly, we may see more clearly the precise points on which the argument hinges.

My treatment is mainly historical. It is not within the scope of the present study to consider at length other theoretical attempts to account for free verse. Although I have discussed various comments by Eliot and Pound, to give adequate attention to their ideas and those of Amy Lowell, Richard Aldington, John Livingston Lowes, F. S. Flint, William Carlos Williams, Yvor Winters, Charles Olson, Timothy Steele, and others, to bring the formal versus free debate up to date, will require an additional book. In other words, this is more a study of the history of free verse itself than an attempt to present, adjudicate between, or synthesize theoretical statements *about* free verse, important as these may be. A rationale for separating the treatments of the subject, as I have, is that much free verse, including many of the varieties that have flourished in this century, had already been written before anyone thought to theorize about it. It would be disingenuous to pretend that one can write about free verse without espousing a view of it, though, and it would be best if I admitted that T. S. Eliot's comments, particularly as restated by others such as Theodore Roethke and Hugh Kenner, seem reasonable to me.

In treating American free verse it is worthwhile to consider a political analogy. The American constitutional system retains many principles of English common law but prohibits titles of nobility and discourages the formation of a class system. In similar fashion, American poetry is simultaneously beholden to and in revolt against its British antecedents. American poetry has oscillated between Anglophilic gentility and, on the other hand, forms of expression that reflect the coarseness of the frontier, the harshness of immigrant experience, or the fact of terrible economic inequalities. American free verse often does imply a rejection of the falsities of established social conventions, or a preference for informality. The authenticity of the individual voice is valued above the cultivation of an elevated style or the mastery of metrical norms. The poet may put on singing robes, but they are more likely to be homespun, buckskin, or jeans than the vestments of an ecclesiastic, an academic gown, or a tuxedo.

Yet the discarding of convention is itself a context for a poem. The best free-verse poems take advantage of the tension between tradition and revolt, working contrapuntally to the accentual-syllabic context—dressing down rather than up, and sometimes cross-dressing. But too many poems printed as free verse are simply devoid of rhythmic interest—as are, indeed, too many poems in accentual-syllabic meters.

There has never been any advance in prosody that did not in some sense build upon the achievements of earlier poets. To say this is not to argue that every prospective poet needs to be put through the wringer of learning to identify and scan numerous varieties of verse, nor that sound poetic theory is a prerequisite for the composition of good poems. Actually the opposite is true: much contemporary writing of many kinds is spoiled by critical theory, by the application of presuppositions to the writing of poetry. But poets from John Keats to Elizabeth Bishop, and from Emily Dickinson to Ted Hughes, have prepared themselves to compose poems by immersing themselves in poets who preceded them. The best writers of free verse, such as H.D., Eliot, Pound, Williams, and Levertov, have all understood conventional accentual-syllabic meters. Contemporary free verse owes its very existence to earlier varieties of poetry; the spontaneous generation of poems ex nihilo is no more likely than the spontaneous generation of worms in the Nile mud. Why should not the continuity of poetries seem as miraculous as some supposed divine intervention or inner enlightenment? The second sentence in Jonathan Holden's "The Free Verse Line," the lead essay in *The Line in Postmodern Poetry,* asserts sensibly, "Generally, the most accurate and efficient way of accounting for the lineation in good free verse composition is in terms of how the line alludes to and plays off our expectations regarding traditional, patterned prosodies" (Frank 1).

For most reference sources, accounts of free verse remain frozen as first enunciated in England between 1908 and 1916. Opening an entry in the fifteenth edition of the *New Encyclopaedia Britannica,* for example, is "free verse, poetry organized to the cadences of speech and image patterns rather than according to a regular metrical scheme." Without reading farther, we know that we will soon encounter the names of Ezra Pound, Amy Lowell, and the rest of the Imagists. Failure to consider carefully the whole question of free verse is most obvious in the concluding sentence of the *Britannica* article, which asserts, "[T]he versification [!] of [W. C.] Williams and [Marianne] Moore most closely resembles that of the *vers libre* poets of France." This is so completely untrue as almost not to be worth refuting; French vers libre often retained rhyme, which Williams almost never used, and Moore often composed in strict, though arbitrarily chosen, syllabic meters. As T. S. Eliot correctly maintained, it was *his* practice that most nearly resembled the French. Williams, with his animosity toward Eliot's and Pound's reversion from American to continental values, would have been livid at hearing his poetry described in a way that made it resemble theirs.

The *Britannica* entry is misleading in several other ways, but to persist in this critique would be merely peevish. The point is the extent to which literary history at the end of the twentieth century still accepts the beliefs of the Imagists as to the nature and history of free verse and credits them with its invention. Similar assumptions have long persisted on other matters; there are those who continue to assert that Wordsworth's ideas in the preface to *Lyrical Ballads* originated with him, and that he was the first to compose in his characteristic ways, when he was just as thoroughly a culmination of preexisting Romantic modes as Pope was of the neoclassical. Every student of Wordsworth should read the poems of William Whitehead (1715–85), who was poet laureate when Wordsworth was a child and in whose nature poetry occur many lines that reappear in modified form in Wordsworth. As Yeats did a century later, Wordsworth succeeded in assimilating many motifs and modes from the century that preceded his, and this accounts for his preeminence among his contemporaries. Great originality in literature often consists of inspired assimilation—not always, but often. I will be making the argument that the strength of Whitman's style was a consequence of his blending biblical phrasing, elements of opera, Ossian, and the rhythms of public oratory, and that his spontaneity and freedom, while authentic and original, is another example of a capacity for appropriation and transformation.

With the Imagists several disparate concepts came together at a time and in a way that suggested a radical shift in poetic priorities, and the resulting movement benefited from Amy Lowell's money, connections, and skills as a publicist. They attracted attention much more quickly than had Wordsworth and Coleridge a hundred years earlier; the Imagist anthologies made money for their publisher and their authors, and the introductions supplied by Lowell and Aldington achieved a combined *succés d'estime* (though not with Ezra Pound) and *succés de scandale.* Many examples of what Pound called "Amygism" have permeated reference sources; besides the *Britannica,* they may be found in entries on "cadence" and "free verse" in the Merriam-Webster and Random House dictionaries, and under "Free Verse" in the venerable Thrall and Hibbard *Handbook to Literature.* These definitions continue to give the impression that free verse had a metric of its own, quite independent of accentual-syllabic prosody. I hope to show that it does not.

All attempts to discover or invent an internally consistent scansion or form for free verse are misguided, except to the extent that certain kinds of free verse partially preserve scansions from the tradition that they are departing from. To say this is to disagree radically with William Carlos Williams and Yvor Winters; to take exception to some views held by T. E. Hulme, F. S. Flint, and Amy Lowell; and to propose modifications to remarks by others, including Pound, Ford Madox Ford, Richard Aldington, and Eliot. All these in their discussions contributed to a more exact understanding of what occurs in free verse, and their areas of common ground are more extensive than one might imagine. But no single theory is a complete or even adequate account. Like the Rum Tum Tugger, free verse "will do as he do do / And there's no doing anything about it"— when it comes to scansion.

The greatest difficulty in the way of our understanding of free verse is the extreme polarization of those schools of poetry in which metrics is an issue. Among those whom one can loosely call neoclassicists or formalists, whether old or new, discussion is usually limited either to the rejection of free verse or to an attempt—usually advanced with querulous insistence—to force some scansion on it; among organicists, for whom all poetry is an enthusiastic adventure, there is no pretense of rationality. Both extremes also have their sacred texts and their sacerdotal personages. On the one hand are those among whom no utterance by Charles Olson, whether critical or poetic, may be referred to except with reverential deference; for the New Formalists, on the other hand, the name of Yvor Winters seems too sacrosanct to be pronounced. Here, and even more so in my subsequent study, I have presumed to treat both these figures as fallible and their writings as open to question.

The discussion that follows presupposes, as a point of departure, a good knowledge of conventional accentual-syllabic metrics and an acquaintance with some of the terminology of prosody. Anyone who knows Paul Fussell's *Poetic Meter and Poetic Form* should not have any problems; in some sense my study is an expanded footnote to the pages devoted to free verse in Fussell's revised edition. I am aware of the strictures that T. V. F. Brogan applies to Fussell, finding him too interested in poetic expressiveness and accusing him of substituting "urbanity" in place of "rigor"; and I know that to others he has seemed an apologist for a sterile formalism. Such is the consequence of aiming at a reasonable centrism. But no better all-purpose introduction to prosody for the general reader has ever been written. The best short definitions for terminology seem to me those found in the *Oxford English Dictionary*. For more extended discussion *The Princeton Encyclopedia of Poetry and Poetics* is the most reliable guide. Also, I have written a computer tutorial program (MS-DOS, IBM-compatible) entitled *Prosody,* which provides basic instruction in metrics and metrical terminology. This may be copied and used without license and is available by writing to me at the English Department, University of North Carolina at Greensboro, Greensboro, NC 27412, and also through electronic file transfer (FTP) upon inquiry at my e-mail address, which is kirbys@fagan.uncg.edu.

At this point I would like to thank the staff and administration of UNCG's Jackson Library, present and past, for their continual assistance, and for never seeming to notice how much was going into my library study and how little was coming out. Noel Kirby-Smith, Jane Gutsell, and Heidi Czerwiec provided the most help and advice on my manuscript, but I have turned to numerous colleagues, friends, research assistants, and students for suggestions. Those who responded most helpfully include Donald Darnell, Gail McDonald, Russ McDonald, Alan Shapiro, Sheldon Pacotti, Marcia Cox, Margaret Muirhead, Eric Weil, James East, Kathleen Bulgin, Elizabeth Chiseri-Strater, David Scott, Mary Elder, Marcel Gauthier, and Lissa Brannon. Leigh Palmer pointed me in some especially useful directions, and an ongoing e-mail dialogue with her has constantly stimulated and sharpened my views on free verse. I have benefited from numerous casual hints and suggestions from others. I am grateful to the English Department at UNCG for lightening my course load to two courses for one semester, making possible a much speedier completion of this project, and to UNCG for a one-semester paid leave of absence that allowed time for proofreading and indexing of this book and for final preparation of the companion volume, *Beyond Free Verse*.

Acknowledgments

I am grateful to the following for permission to reproduce copyrighted material: Margaret Walker Alexander for permission to quote from: "For My People," originally published in *For My People,* Yale University Press, copyright © 1942 by Margaret Walker Alexander, reprinted in *This Is My Century: New and Collected Poems,* University of Georgia Press, copyright © 1989 by Margaret Walker Alexander; New Directions Publishing Corporation for permission to quote from "Marriage" by Gregory Corso in *The Happy Birthday of Death.* Copyright © 1960 by Gregory Corso. Reprinted by permission of New Directions. "The Dog" by Lawrence Ferlinghetti in *A Coney Island of the Mind.* Copyright © 1958 by Lawrence Ferlinghetti. Reprinted by permission of New Directions. "Oread" by H.D. in *Collected Poems, 1912–1944.* Copyright © 1982 by The Estate of Hilda Doolittle. Reprinted by permission of New Directions. "The Return" by Ezra Pound in *Personae.* Copyright © 1926 by Ezra Pound. Reprinted by permission of New Directions. "Flowers by the Sea" and "The Attic Which Is Desire" by William Carlos Williams in *Collected Poems, 1909–1939,* volume 1. Copyright © 1938 by New Directions Publishing Corporation. Reprinted by permission of New Directions; Leigh Palmer for permission to use her translation of "Solo de Lune" by Jules Laforgue, translation, "Lunar Solo," copyright © 1995 by Leigh Palmer; Penguin Books USA Inc. for permission to quote from: "Noah Built the Ark," from *God's Trombones* by James Weldon Johnson. Copyright 1927 The Viking Press, Inc., renewed © 1955 by Grace Nail Johnson. Used by permission of Viking Penguin, a division of Penguin Books USA Inc.

Contents

Chapter 1

Some Preliminary Issues

When we talk about free verse we usually assume that we are talking about poetry of the twentieth century. Scattered instances from earlier times may be pointed out: besides crediting Whitman for breaking the new wood, as Ezra Pound put it in "A Pact," it is common to mention Blake's prophetic books, "Dover Beach" and other poems by Arnold, and some experiments by W. H. Henley and Stephen Crane. But such references usually imply that before 1900 free verse was a freak and that its sparseness and its failure to take hold as a prevalent mode prove the rule that earlier centuries were completely dominated by conventional accentual-syllabic scansions and fixed forms. Among many American poets and scholars, in particular, the assumption is that such visionary gleams of free verse as may be found in past centuries are mere prefigurations that were finally fulfilled after 1900, or at best made possible an increased receptivity to the experiments of the Imagists early in this century. This is, on the whole, a correct view; at no time before this century had anything identifiable as free verse been a dominant mode for poetry. Simultaneously it is worth pointing out that a surprising amount of free verse, much more than most people imagine, did get written in earlier centuries.

Discussions of contemporary free verse are mostly contentious and dogmatic, and lively debates have been going on for more than eighty years. In some form or another argument began three hundred years ago. The controversy did not become central to the discussion of poetry, however, until free verse and Imagism emerged simultaneously as parts of a program aimed at overthrowing Victorian standards and, in particular, at revoking Lord Tennyson's poetic peerage. Agitation of the issue, which began in England about 1908, soon spread to the United States. Amy Lowell in her Imagist collections and Harriet Monroe in *Poetry* magazine opened their pages to discussion of the new prosody; vigorous exchanges also appeared in avant-garde journals such as the *Little Review, Others,* the *Egoist,* and the *Poetry Review.* The scribes and Pharisees of formalism, convinced that the new movement was a sign of decadence, were answered by those who identified free verse with cubist and futurist styles of painting and who celebrated perpetual iconoclasm as a way of ensuring originality. Edwin Arlington Robinson and Robert Frost refused to have much to do with free verse, contributing their famous one-liners ("I write badly enough as it is" and "like playing tennis with the net down," respectively). T. S. Eliot took the middle ground, justifying his and Pound's metric by arguing that what they were doing was not really free at all but was disciplined by a previously acquired mastery of regular meters. William Carlos Williams periodically defended his own practice or attacked that of die-hard formalists and of the high modernists as well; manifestos from his friends and followers among the Objectivists, the Black Mountain school, and the Beat poets kept the issue alive into the 1940s and 1950s. Yvor Winters, having executed an abrupt to-the-rear march in 1928, authored a body of criticism that aimed at a new justification for accentual-syllabic meter. Of Winters in his later years, following his reversion to strictly formal verse, Lawrence Ferlinghetti said to me in 1963, "It's just fine if you want to write sixteenth-century poetry."

Battle lines were drawn again in the War of the Anthologies, when the publication of *New Poets of England and America* in 1957, edited by Donald Hall, Robert Pack, and Louis Simpson, was answered in 1960 by Donald M. Allen's *The New American Poetry.* Poems in the former mostly stuck to accentual-syllabic meters, with astonishing numbers of villanelles, sestinas, sonnets, and rhyme royal stanzas; the latter included amazing amounts of Whitmanian anaphora. Robert Lowell, with memorable directness and simplicity, characterized the opposing sides as "cooked" and "raw." A parallel development occurred about a decade later. *Naked Poetry* of 1969 and *New Naked Poetry* of 1976 (both edited by Stephen Berg and Robert Mezey) provoked a delayed response in *Strong Measures: Contemporary American Poetry in Traditional Forms* in 1985, edited by Philip Dacey and David Jauss. Finally, in the 1980s, appeared the sharply opposed developments known as Language poetry and New Formalism, both of which set themselves against the informal, personal, "voice" poetry that had become the most widely published mode of that period and both of which eschew the confessional mode, though for opposite reasons. Most poets who have moved amphibiously between free and fixed (Stevens, Auden, Roethke, Bishop, Robert Lowell, Mona Van Duyn) have preferred to do rather than to describe or theorize, so that the debate has mostly been carried on by those who have a turf to defend or a program to advance.

The chief obstacle to a rational discussion of free verse is a common—though not universal—assumption that it is independent of any established prosody. This autonomy has been achieved, it is argued, by simply breaking free of the trammels of convention—or else by the invention of some new principle of scansion. Some poets have believed free verse to be a newly established *system,* which is actually regular, or should be, if only we could discover or invent the basis of its regularity; the problem is that no one has ever been able to articulate the principles of free-verse scansion in a form that is widely acceptable. But the belief persists in some quarters that there must be a discoverable pattern in free verse if someone with a sufficient grounding in "poetics" will only step forward to say what it is. Even poets who rejoice in iconoclasm are usually unwilling to believe that their own practice is anarchic, and others have been confident that they have discovered some new principle of regularity, some new line complete with identifiable feet and a viable scansion.

On the one hand, therefore, we have a naive organicism—frankly egoistic, romantic, and personal—that looks to the nature of the poet and builds on Coleridge's idea, anticipated by certain eighteenth-century theorists, of organic form. Not only is the poem's form a natural and concomitant growth with the poem's substance, but both are projections of the poet. The poem's form, then, may be discovered by taking the measure of the poet. Studies of the poetry of Charles Olson (and of that line of poets for whom Olson's essay, "Projective Verse," is a critical landmark) nearly always work on this assumption. As Michael McClure put it in the "Statements on Poetics" in Donald M. Allen's *The New American Poetry:*

> I write and make no/few changes. The prime purpose of my writing is liberation. (Self-liberation first & hopefully that of the reader.) The Bulk and its senses must be freed! A poem is as much of me as an arm. Measure, line, etc. is interior and takes an outward shape, is not pre-destined or logical but immediate. I no longer have interest in the esthetic rationales of verse. (423)

Opposite to the organicist approach is the effort to identify a free-verse foot, an attempt that falls back, consciously or unconsciously, on the sixteenth-century efforts to accommodate English to Greek and Latin grammar and prosody. This artificial method (of the Renaissance prosodists), when applied to the intrinsically accentual nature of the English language, eventually resulted in the accentual-syllabic compromise. Twentieth-century foot-based theories of free verse assume that once we know what the foot is we can work out the larger patterns objectively and dignify the poem with a rationalized scheme. Those who think this way forget that much English poetry from 1550 to 1900 grew metrically out of a deliberate attempt to contrive an artificial series of feet, and often a regular syllable count, that was not natural to English, much as early grammars for English attempted to impose cases and tenses derived from the classical languages. Certain contemporary poets—whether New Formalists or old formalists—whose knowledge of English poetry begins with Thomas Wyatt, with a glance back to Chaucer, remain—wilfully, it seems to me—unaware of the essentially accentual quality of English meters and obsessed with a desire to prove that an iambic *foot* is the most "natural" rhythm for English, rather than a concept imported from classical studies. They neglect what Coleridge, Hopkins, Hardy, Dylan Thomas, Robert Lowell, Ted Hughes, Anne Sexton, Seamus Heaney, and many other poets have already recovered for us, and they revert to a metrics much like that of George Gascoigne.

Both organicists and extreme formalists share a tendency to treat questions of metrics as absolute issues. Disputants seldom remember that in English this hybrid meter is a historical and cultural accident, in large part a consequence of the Norman Conquest, which established an enduring French presence in English poetry just as it did in English vocabulary. Chaucer began by translating French poetry into what he intended to be French meters. Wyatt began by counting syllables. Authentic meters in Germanic languages, uncontaminated by imitation of either Romance languages or the classics, were accentual and not syllabic. The important principle in the heroic poetry in those languages is the presence of four strong stressed syllables per line. There are no feet; there are only the four stresses and an indeterminate number of unstressed syllables. Over the centuries English-speaking poets have adapted themselves so completely to accentual-syllabic prosody that it has indeed become natural to many poets to use it. The widespread acceptance of *accentual-syllabic* to designate the compromise between stress and syllable counting, a compromise that has dominated poetry in English for four hundred years, argues a general recognition of the origin of this meter. But extremists will not accept this; for them, such meter is taken as an absolute standard that one is either for or against. Metrical rebels insist that the older meters are totally artificial, while reactionary neoclassicists, paradoxically attempting to enforce their own version of organicism, introduce arguments to prove that the iambic pentameter is altogether natural—that the iamb is equivalent to a heartbeat, and that the pentameter is a breath unit. If this is true, then the hearts of Swedes must beat backward, since their typical rhythms are trochaic, and all actors who perform Shakespeare must be endowed with abnormal vital capacities, since they often recite several lines in a breath. Even those who do not care to take sides may still tacitly accept accentual-syllabic meter as an absolute—which one sometimes employs and sometimes eschews. Most good poets resign argumentation of these matters to the pedantry of minor-league academics—if I may put it that way, in the same spirit as Dr. Johnson when he defined *lexicographer* as "a harmless drudge."

Despite the contentions of neoclassicists or ultraformalists, there is a sense in which anyone who objects to the artificiality of accentual-syllabic meter is taking a reasonable point of view. Yet why should artifice *not* be synonymous with art? The execution of a work of art in any medium has something unnatural to it. Mineral-based paint pigments, tubas, oboes, violins, the positions of classical ballet, or even the movements in modern dance—none of these is "natural." There is something contrived and to some extent forced in the use of regular iambs, trochees, or anapests. It is part of the poet's artistry—or *artificiality* in the older, nonpejorative sense—to make a succession of such units seem altogether natural, or, if not natural, graceful.

But the attempt to devise a free-verse foot to replace the earlier units—whose nomenclature was borrowed from the classics—is, it seems to me, completely misguided. Even in the most regular accentual-syllabic metrics exact identification of individual "feet" is often problematic and leads to controversy; the patterns are often ambiguous, unlike the Greek and Latin models on which they are based, which were much more definite. Agreement on the existence and identity of such units in free verse seems impossible. The odd thing is that it is those who are most contentious, inflexible, and dogmatic in their scansions of accentual-syllabic meters who are most likely to insist that there is indeed a definite free-verse foot or that free verse can be scanned using conventional feet. As I have said, they resemble grammarians who try to discover in English all the features of Latin and Greek.

I hope to show that in any case the indivisible unit for free verse is the line, and that in good free verse the entire line plays against expectations implicit in an entire metrical tradition. Such an argument will seem, to prosodic Jacobins, too reverential toward received conventions; but even those who claim to abandon tradition completely will admit that there was a tradition to be abandoned. The work of even the most rebellious poets acquires significance in part by its very rejection of the tradition, even when it claims to be discovering or returning to a more natural or authentic practice.

My treatment of free verse, then, will be mainly in terms of what it *is not*. I realize that the refusal to offer a positive definition may seem an evasion of the issue and that my arguments may seem circular; in reply I would point out that all definitions are ultimately circular and tautological—even mathematical ones. I invite anyone who disagrees with this statement to open a dictionary and attempt to pursue any definition to a point of certitude; while the process may lead to a clearer apprehension of terminology, you often come back around to the word you started with. Definitions can only be pragmatic, not absolute. Articulated speech may be the most godlike part of human nature, but language is human, not divine; it grows out of life and experience and does not precede or create that experience. Words, as poets from Chaucer to Eliot have reminded us, tend to slip out of place; rather than offering a succinct definition of free verse, therefore, I will hope that some understanding of its nature and origins will arise out of a protracted discussion.

A useful analogy to the problem of describing precisely what occurs in good free verse is the "three-body problem" of celestial mechanics. Given the masses, velocities, and distances of two objects moving in the fields of one another's gravity, it is simple to calculate what their orbits will be. But once a third body is introduced, the orbits assume a complexity that defeats precise analysis. It is easy enough to grasp how, in a star cluster such as the Pleiades, hundreds of stars are moving in paths that are mutually interactive and determined by gravitational acceleration, but it is beyond any mathematical method to predict the orbits—though a column in the August 1994 *Scientific American* reports that the problem can be circumvented by advanced statistical methods. In the best free verse, it seems to me, rhythmical laws are at work that are more elaborate extensions of the simpler, intralineal meters described by conventional scansions. But scansions are helpless, or of only minimal use, to describe exactly what occurs in the free-verse line, and attempts to rely on statistical occurrences, while of some validity, make extremely dull reading.

Communal usage determines the meanings of most words, and for most people *free verse* means poetry without a scannable pattern. Anyone who claims to have discovered a precisely definable free-verse *foot* must share honors with that remarkable personality and great philosopher, Thomas Hobbes, who repeatedly squared the circle. We know intuitively that there must be a square containing the same area as a given circle, and we know intuitively that some sort of rhythmic effect is occurring in good free verse, but anyone who claims to have demonstrated it objectively is probably in competition for an academic chair on the flying island of Laputa.

Hovering between organicist and scansionist theories, though closer to the former, is the notion of a *cadence* that is special to the poem or poet. Sometimes cadence seems to mean the natural speech rhythms of the language, but more often the idea is that it is an instinctive pattern that each poet imprints on the language. Cadence may consist of characteristic segments that resemble informal or variable feet—or it may be the inimitable personal rhythm of the poet. Pound's version of this, which was the aural equivalent of Eliot's "objective correlative," required that there be a rhythm that was exactly appropriate to the emotion at each point in a poem. Amy Lowell, Richard Aldington, and Williams (who eventually dropped it) all tried to do something with the concept of cadence, which originated among English poets with F. S. Flint and Ford Madox Ford. Apparently Ford believed that he had put it into practice in his own verse. Cadence, as we shall see, had already been invoked by French writers of vers libres and prose poetry. The term still finds its way into definitions of free verse. Writing in 1914, Richard Aldington argued, with a lack of subtlety that T. S. Eliot found nettling, and in terms that sound much like John Milton's objections to the use of rhyme (in the preface to *Paradise Lost*):

> For the essential difference between free verse and accented verse is just this: the old accented verse forced the poet to abandon some of his individuality, most of his accuracy, and all his style in order to wedge his emotions into some preconceived and sometimes childish formality; free verse permits the poet all his individuality because he

creates his cadence instead of copying other people's, all his accuracy because with his cadence flowing naturally he tends to write naturally and therefore with precision, and all his style because style consists in concentration, and exactness which could only be obtained rarely in the old forms. (351)

I should admit at this point that I do not subscribe to any of the cadence theories except that of Pound—and as reiterated and somewhat extended by Theodore Roethke when he wrote, happily subordinating the idea of "breath" to the poem and its subject, "It was Lawrence, a master of this sort of poem (I think I quote him more or less exactly) who said, 'It all depends on the pause, the natural pause.' In other words, the breath unit, the language that is natural to the immediate thing, the particular emotion" (83). One can see what Pound and Roethke were up to because many of their poems do employ cadences that communicate elusive emotions with unparalleled sensitivity—but these rhythms, or cadences, are subordinate to the poem; they are not intended purely as an expression of the poet's personality; they are also delicately contrapuntal to accentual-syllabic meters. Pound in particular retained that quality which used to be called "aesthetic distance," whereas most of those who speak of cadence imply that it is personally determined. Roethke was aware of rhythm as something that could be learned, assimilated—"I take this cadence from a man named Yeats," he says in "Four for Sir John Davies"—though as he pointed out himself, he was actually taking his cadence from the Renaissance poet Davies. But to most who evoke it as a criterion, cadence means something personal, idiosyncratic, and inimitable. The personal rhythm requires unusual typography to record it—and to a great extent, what began in this century as cadence theory has modified into a justification for idiosyncratic typography—or has led to claims that typography can transcribe cadence.

Some students of poetry in the 1990s therefore assume that there must be an entirely new, but as yet unformulated, key to the metrics of each poet whose work has become fashionable, even when they are unable to specify exactly what this may be. We are expected to discover how, in Aldington's words, the poet "creates his cadence" and to chart the "natural flow" of the poetry, accommodating ourselves to the "breath" or to the poem-as-appendage theories of Olson and McClure. Or if we cannot chart it, we are expected to acknowledge with reverence our own limitations and to take on faith the ineffable presence of an organic rhythm. But those who assert the existence of such a cadence cannot explain what it is; they may claim to hear it and they may talk about it, but they are unable to describe it qualitatively, let alone scan it. My treatment will not rescue them from their bafflement since it is not possible to invent explanations for something that is not there; much contemporary poetry simply lacks aural patterning. It may resemble Pound on the page, but not to the ear. Whatever a poetic foot, rhythm, or cadence may be, it is not something perceptible to the eye alone, and much contemporary poetry is typographical and not rhythmic—and the typography does not really transcribe a rhythm.

William Carlos Williams may have believed that his variable foot and triadic line restored auditory measure to the poem, and Charles Olson may have believed that his lines were a transcription of his breathing, but the most important function of their lines is to give the poetry a visual dignity or a visual sense of excitement—in so doing working out some of the earliest Imagist prescriptions for poetry. In the poetry of Williams there is also a continual tension or syncopation of actual speech against discarded meter; he originally (and perhaps accidentally) composed the opening lines of "Asphodel" in iambic tetrameters, as Kenneth Burke pointed out to him (East: letter of 7 November 1955). But the triadic line itself has only a *visual* regularity. For Williams and Olson the elimination of predictable rhythm, especially the iambic rhythm, was equated with energy and freedom and their typographies asserted their claims to this freedom.

While rejecting the concept of the self-referential, personal cadence as a basis for a metric, as well as scansionist and organicist arguments, I agree with T. S. Eliot, Amy Lowell, Yvor Winters, and many others—including Pound and, at times, even Williams—who have realized, and who have said with differing degrees of explicitness, that successful free verse does achieve idiosyncratic effects by playing against the established accentual-syllabic tradition. As Hugh Kenner has put it—

most "free verse" implies regular verse. Behind it, as Eliot wrote sixty-four years ago, lurks the ghost of some regular metric. That ghost says, "I am in my singing robes. I am not disregarding norms, I am raising their ritual to a ritual still more arcane. If I use the twelve-tone row I remember Mozart. Hear my ancient voice behind this jagged page." Even Whitman's free verse says, "Remember the King James Bible, the Psalms; remember the catalogues in the Song of Songs." (*Historical Fictions* 240–41)

Kenner goes on to argue that William Carlos Williams syncopated his line divisions so as to throw our rhythmic habits even further off balance—a point with which I concur; it seems to me that what Williams did was tirelessly to evade in his metrics every hint of the European or British heritage, and that to readers immersed in that heritage (as Williams himself had been) these evasions are rhythmically significant. Williams and Amy Lowell shared—like many another reader of poetry before and since—an early infatuation with Keats and, subsequently, a horror of Longfellow's sentimental tediousness. Their aim became to *escape* such a metric. Too many imitators of Williams, of course, have simply aped his typography—somewhat as imitators of Tennyson, and earlier of Pope, thought it sufficient to observe regular scansions and to employ exact rhymes.

The concept of "haunted" verse originated with Mallarmé, from whom Eliot borrowed it. Sometimes, as in much of Eliot's early work, the residue or "ghost" of the tradition is visible within the poem; sometimes, as with the free verse of Robert Lowell or Roethke, the entire tradition provides or implies the background; and sometimes, as in many of Williams's poems, the poem's rhythm is itself an insistent rite of exorcism. Such an explanation may be instantly dismissed as reductive by some literary theorists whose intellectual fortunes depend on a naive and unexamined organicism, and by some academic celebrants of the immediately contemporaneous in poetry, but an explanation is not necessarily wrong just because it is simple. To say that Shakespeare's blank verse assumes as a norm a five-beat line is likewise a reductive explanation that allows at the same time for unlimited variations and that in no way restricts the possibilities of that line; to say that in good free verse the entire line is contrapuntal to the metrical conventions that preceded it is likewise a simple explanation that permits an even greater range of variation.

At this point I am assuming that there do exist varieties of poetry that are best described by calling them free verse and that the term can be justified on the same grounds as Dr. Johnson's remark when a definition of poetry was required of him, "Why, Sir, we all know what light is, but it is not easy to *tell* what it is." In some respects it is even easier to tell what free verse is than to tell what poetry is. Free verse, to succeed as poetry, *must depart in a distinctive and recognizable way from one or more conventions that have in the past governed the organization of the poetic line, or the stanza taken as a whole.* It is analogous, on an enlarged scale, to the familiar idea of metrical substitution, or expressive variation, which takes place *within* the accentual-syllabic line. To say this is, of course, immediately to invite controversy; those who consider that all aspects of poetry are intuitive and unaccountable—that there is nothing to it but the "nameless graces which no methods teach"—will insist that true free verse is a breaking loose from all constraint and, at the same time, a declaration of new laws. These are the true poetic Jacobins who would reset all calendars, redraw all political boundaries, and establish new forms of worship in one fell swoop—or those who announce a new dispensation according to which Whitman strode out of the wilderness, and Williams into the city, as prophetic harbingers for Charles Olson and for those poets who take "Projective Verse" as a sacred text. And as I repeatedly acknowledge, certain neoclassicists will assert that any poetry that is rhythmically successful must be constructed of identifiable feet of some sort. Again I acknowledge the circular and tautological progress of my arguments and wonder whether Ludwig Wittgenstein would speak up (or keep silent) in my defense.

G. S. Fraser, as I do, sees free verse as a continuum with other practices: "Much that is taken as free verse, or as breaking the old rules, is merely, in fact, an intelligent use of the great flexibility of the old rules" (72). But "the old rules" did not allow nine-tenths of a poem to consist of lines that fit no rhythmical template and that are rhythmically unlike one another. Free verse permits the line, taken as a unit, to escape predictability, and it extends the same liberty to the stanza or "strophe." An adequate understanding of the rhythmical effect of the line requires that we be aware of the conventions from which a given instance of free verse is escaping. Sometimes this is easy; some fugitives from the law stand out—like the two who were identified as criminals by the headwaiter at the "21" Club when they ordered martinis *after* dinner. Other deviations from accepted practice are more subtle. My procedure will be to distinguish as best I can the conventions that provide the points of departure, and to show how, by playing against the expectations generated by the conventions, free verse succeeds.

An unstated corollary of the assumption mentioned above is that not every piece of protoplasmic verbiage that sees print is free verse. There must be tension, counterpoint, syncopation of some sort. T. S. Eliot's "ghost" theory of free verse—of which more later—is echoed in Fraser's definition: "What I recognize as good free verse is verse which does not scan regularly but seems always on the verge of scanning regularly; which is neither strictly in pure stress metre, nor stress syllable metre, nor quantitative meter, nor pure syllabics, but which often seems to be getting near to one or other of these, perhaps attempting to fuse two of them, perhaps deliberately and abruptly alternating between one and another" (74).

The definition of free verse as poetry that deliberately steps *outside,* or plays against, a convention is analogous, as I have already said, to the variety amid uniformity that occurs *within* a single convention, as when by a delicate shift in the placement of the caesura Pope produces some effect of irony, reinforces some rhetorical pattern, or even imitates a physical action. In the latter case, the individual foot constantly departs from the standard iambic footprint. Successful free verse departs entirely from a line-determined (or stanza-based) metrical convention but presupposes that convention as a possibility. Even the most violent rebel against established order must admit that the order did exist, and that it remains a possibility—even if it is viewed as an archaic and repellent possibility. Prosodic conservatives may argue that to use the convention in this way is to abandon it and to deny its validity; J. V. Cunningham characterized this practice as "parasitic." But to make use of the condensed—some might say fossilized—energies of a well-established convention in no way saps the strength of that convention. When Victor Hugo's play *Hernani* (1830) opened with an enjambed Alexandrine, a riot broke out in the theater; but the Alexandrine survived. Hugo's line, despite its appearance of Romantic abandon, varied *within* the convention of that particular poetic line. Variation *outside* the poetic line can be as useful metrically as internal variation, though to conservative prosodists it may give the appearance of rejection rather than variation. *The Waste Land* did not accomplish the destruction of the iambic pentameter nor of any of the other meters that it systematically disrupted; its metrics seem to me saprophytic rather than parasitic, breeding lilacs out of the dead land. *The Waste Land* might be thought of as a compost heap.

When it works, free verse makes use of a convention in a profitable, though ironic, way. Stravinsky, as Ezra Pound and Amy Lowell realized, used musical conventions ironically; the rediscovery and publication of musical scores from earlier periods opened up possibilities for imitation

and parody—an extension of counterpointing much like what Pound
achieved in "The Return." Rather than liberating the poet and reader
from pedantic and constraining forms, then, each real advance in the
writing of free verse requires an appreciation of antecedent traditions and
to some degree actually affirms and strengthens the traditions.

To expect the reader to acquire, as Eliot did in *The Waste Land,* a
more finely discriminating ear for poetic rhythms through a familiarity
with Baudelaire and Gérard de Nerval (as well as with liturgical cadences
and Popean closed couplets among much else) is to aim at the extension
and refinement of civilized experience. But to require the reader to accept
on faith, or to search out with obsequious diligence, the "organic" and
personal cadence of a single poet and to submit to it seems to me an
expectation of servile barbarism. The counterpointing of convention
achieved by successful free verse certainly constitutes a challenge to and a
criticism of the convention, but is at the same time a tribute to the power
of the convention and a reaffirmation of it.

In making such an argument it is necessary to take exception to, or at
least to offer modifications of, texts of considerable authority. "The free-
dom of Pound's verse is rather a state of tension due to constant opposi-
tion between free and strict." So far, so good. But then T. S. Eliot went
on to say, in his essay collected in *To Criticize the Critic,* "There are not, as
a matter of fact, two kinds of verse, the strict and the free; there is only a
mastery which comes of being so well trained that form is an instinct and
can be adapted to the particular purpose at hand" (172). The spirit of
what Eliot says does not conflict with arguments advanced above, but his
way of putting it may reflect the caution with which free verse was
mentioned around 1915, when it sounded much like "free love" and was
attacked on moralistic grounds. But when a poem strays so far from
established pattern as to be no longer predictable, while assuming a
regular metric as an ironic possibility, it becomes useful to call what you
have free verse. Otherwise Eliot's statement supports the contention that
a preexisting convention makes free verse possible, and his later pro-
nouncements, in essays collected in the same volume, become virtually
identical with the arguments just advanced:

> The most interesting verse which has yet been written in our lan-
> guage has been done either by taking a very simple form, like the
> iambic pentameter, and constantly withdrawing from it, or taking

no form at all, and constantly approximating to a very simple one. It is this contrast between fixity and flux, this unperceived evasion of monotony, which is the very life of verse. (33)

We may therefore formulate as follows: the ghost of some simple metre should lurk behind the arras in even the "freest" verse; to advance menacingly as we doze, and withdraw as we rouse. Or, freedom is only truly freedom when it appears against the background of an artificial limitation. (34–35)

According to this description *The Waste Land* could not be ranked among "the most interesting verse," since, as I shall show, it contains passages that are amalgams of several meters, and rather than invoking the "ghost of some simple meter" is at times more like a convocation of banshees. Although one may still wish that Eliot had distinguished more clearly between ordinary metrical "substitution" and the more radical step taken by free verse, the point of view advanced here is fundamentally in agreement with his. As we shall see, by 1947 he was speaking of free verse without qualification or apology.

As if to second Eliot's views—though carried by his own vital nature somewhat in the direction of Olson—Theodore Roethke in his essay "Some Remarks on Rhythm" (1960) wrote:

For many *strong* stresses, or a playing against an iambic pattern to a loosening up, a longer, more irregular foot, I agree that free verse is a denial in terms. There is, invariably, the ghost of some other form, often blank verse, behind what is written, or the more elaborate rise and fall of the rhythmical prose sentence. (81)

The most successful free verse comes from poets who have mastered a formal metric of some sort to the point of being able to assume it as a possible "background of an artificial limitation." This statement, too, may provoke immediate objections. On the one hand, those who cherish the sanctity, even the divinity, of the poet, and honor the eighteenth-century doctrine of original genius, may feel that it expresses a schoolmasterish desire to rebuke the natural impulses of the born poet. Those who cherish the older meters and lament their demise will conclude that I have sided with the subversives. No wonder that when John Dryden took up the Ancient-Modern controversy, he chose to do it as a dialogue in four voices so that it was hard to tell exactly what side the author himself was on! Discussion of free verse, as I have already said, in some ways resembles that dispute. Nevertheless, and with the awareness that there is nothing very new in the idea, I would like to point out that the free-verse poets whose position in modern literature seems most secure understood conventional metrics. Williams and cummings started out by writing like Pre-Raphaelites; they knew very well what sort of poetry the readers of their own times had come to expect, and those expectations made possible their own prosperous iconoclasms. Ginsberg and Ferlinghetti were well informed about traditional accentual-syllabic meters and could have written them if they had chosen to do so, as could Denise Levertov.

Ignorance of metrics is a liability for any poet. A number of well-known contemporary poets who now compose in slackened measures at one time ground slavishly away at their rhymes royal and their sestinas in an attempt to latch on to the neoformalist movement that followed the Second World War. They abandoned that fashion when it began to seem unprofitable, and their imperfect and rather mechanical assimilation of metrics now shows itself in the limpness of their later work. (With the resurgence of New Formalism some of them are resuming their youthful stiffness.) But over the half-century from about 1915 to 1965 a great many successful poems were composed by poets who had the craft and the discipline to write as they chose, and who chose to write in such a way as deliberately to run counter to centuries-old metrical conventions.

If there is a prejudice in this line of argument, it is an anti-Platonic one, opposed to the presumption of insanity in the poet; I believe that, in much of what they do, poets understand what they are doing. Poets who claim not to know what they are doing make this claim with such vigor that one may suspect that their irrationality is programmatic. Students of poetry who exalt the Platonic view—that the poet is a mad person who writes in a state of irrational ecstasy—sometimes forget that this was given as a reason for denying poets citizenship in an ideal republic, for exiling them as disruptive lunatics—not for honoring them as vatic singers. Whitman put a lot of thought into achieving the spontaneity of his prophetic voice. Because he left a few poems in genteel British meters we know that Whitman forged an original metric with a clear awareness of what he was departing from. As with his personal pose as a "rough," even his barbaric yawp was more civilized than he let on. His free verse was crafted to appeal to anyone who had delighted in biblical cadences, even as it challenged and played against the mindlessly regular musicality of Poe or the self-consciously polished verses by the American imitators of Tennyson. The best poets in the Whitmanian line have likewise written with a clear awareness of the traditions against which they compose their work. Allen Ginsberg abandoned the Tate-like mannerisms of his earliest poems and consciously chose the Whitmanesque mode for "Howl"—though to imply that Ginsberg is not insane may be to invite a libel suit.

It is much more difficult to account for metrical effects in good free verse than in accentual-syllabic scansions, but it can at least be attempted, making use of the tools of earlier prosodies but applying them more flexibly and discursively. Or if that proves impossible, it is at least useful to recognize that in principle free verse should be understood in the widest possible metrical context and that the evaluation of it should not be left to uninformed guesses and hunches. Any poem in which the aural pattern is genuinely complex and significant will offer its readers rhythmic effects that can be discussed and on which some consensus can be reached, even if the best that can be done is to agree that, in Amy Lowell's words, it produces "syncopating experience."

Yet another stumbling block in the way of discussion of free verse is a reluctance to construct a taxonomy by which it may be classified. Perhaps it appears that anything so personal or so unpredictable does not lend itself to such grouping, and that each poem constitutes a single category. In dealing with accentual-syllabic poems (if we are talking about their prosody) we start with the foot and the line and continue through larger units (fixed forms and stanzas), terminating with lengthier genres (odes, epics, and poetic dramas). Free verse cannot be treated in the same way as these because—contrary to what some have contended—it is not, and never has been, built from equal numbers of definite rhythmical units. But the fact that the direction of any free-verse poem is prosodically unpredictable need not deter us from noting a number of ways in which poets who practice it achieve this unpredictability; that is, we may examine the ways in which poets engineer their lines and "strophes" so that they do *not* coincide with a pattern established early in the poem and maintained throughout, and so that they do *not* satisfy older prosodies. Practitioners of free verse who insist on the personal "voice" may not like to have pointed out the means by which they attain a presumed originality or authenticity. Opponents of free verse may not care to agree that any generalizations about so amorphous a thing are possible.

The genealogy of twentieth-century free verse in English is far more complex than anything said so far may suggest. There are at least four important ancestries to be taken into account. Despite the more free-wheeling developments in the second half of this century, which require that the authentic poet disown any literary predecessors whatever, it is essential to be acquainted with French free verse in order to understand the metrics of much British and at least some American free verse. For this reason I will quote extensively from both the poetry and the prose writings of French poets. On the other hand, the discussion will make little use of the vocabularies of contemporary literary theory; too often, American academics invent jargons as a way of compensating for, among other things, a lack of acquaintance with foreign languages and in emulation of the exact sciences. Other complexities in the origins of free verse appear as we consider the contribution of several models that were in turn based ultimately on Hebrew poetry. A third, and seldom noted, precursor is the *versi liberi* that Leopardi learned from his Italian ancestors and that English poets borrowed from Italian and practiced in the seventeenth century. And finally there is the phenomenon of "Pindarism," which first appeared in the seventeenth century and which continued through the nineteenth.

Beyond these four one can discover a great variety of minor models, from operatic recitative to the patter of the cabaret performer or circus barker. My argument is, however, that in every case the implied contrast with the accentual-syllabic standard is important—as in, for example, the pub conversation in *The Waste Land,* which terminates with a Shakespearean tag. In addition to these historically discernible lineages there are the dozens, even hundreds, of spontaneous and self-elected "voices" that issue in unpredictable ways and that belong to the class of the unclassifiable.

Varieties of free verse in English poetry have appeared and reappeared in a series of cycles that began in the late sixteenth century and continue at the end of the twentieth. Objections to such an assertion may be expected from those who consider that nothing that consists of, or that is very near kin to, regular iambic rhythm can be free verse. No matter how irregular the line lengths, the counterargument goes, the iambic beat is always there, even in the most nobly wild effusions, and this constitutes ipso facto proof that the poem is not free verse. As it happens, Abraham Cowley's actual practice in many odes dating from the mid–seventeenth century was quite spasmodic and the scansion of many of his lines problematic. But even if we allow the objection that most such irregular poems can be scanned as iambics (as many of the choruses in Milton's *Samson* decidedly cannot be), the English pseudo-Pindaric ode much resembles those nineteenth-century experiments in French vers libres that retained rhyme and that employed the convention of *vers pairs*. In those French poems, which were the most important models for Pound, Eliot, Amy Lowell, and many others, every line contains an even number of syllables (six, eight, ten, or twelve, usually). Meter and rhyme remain, but the convention of the exactly recurrent line or stanza is disrupted, leaving the poem free in one important respect and subject to the whim of the poet.

Yet those who are determined to polarize the discussion of free verse will not agree with me that certain poems that retain iambics are free verse; even some humane and good-humored poets may be hard to convince. I can imagine both Lawrence Ferlinghetti and Timothy Steele, for example, pointing to "Dover Beach" and exclaiming "Free verse? Ridiculous!" And, continuing to put words into their mouths, I can imagine putting to both of them the question, "Well, then, what form is it in if it's formal poetry?"—and both answering, though with opposite intention, "Iambics; ordinary, recognizable iambics." I would argue, however, that in "Dover Beach" and in many other poems, over several centuries, we see a clear disruption of expectations of a predictable metrical line, and that what we see in that poem is an important instance of free verse. In "Dover Beach" the disruption is surely functional, suggesting the chaotic moral landscape consequent upon the loss of religious faith, despite the apparent tranquillity of the actual evening. It also imitates the progress of the speaker's wistful ruminations and gives an even more vivid impression of an ordinary speaking voice than the most relaxed pentameter could. Arnold's practice anticipates Eliot's extreme dislocations in *The Waste Land,* and is an early example of what Yvor Winters inveighed against as "the fallacy of imitative form."

The earliest free verse in English, French, Italian, German, and many other languages occurred when the predictable line, or a pattern of unequal lines arranged in regular stanzas, disappeared. Historians of English literature have long recognized these disruptions as free verse. Tucker Brooke, who composed the chapter on the Renaissance in *A Literary History of England* (1948), wrote, "[A] considerable part of Cowley's early reputation and influence derived from the fifteen *Pindaric Odes,* in which he retained rime but otherwise approximated to what is now known as free verse" (Baugh 667–68). Early in this century, just at the time when the pages of the *Egoist,* the *Poetry Review,* the *Little Review,* and *Poetry* magazine were full of controversial pronouncements about free verse, Robert Shafer completed a scholarly study in which he asserted,

> Cowley in his *Pindariques* frankly discarded the stanzaic structure of Pindar's odes, and adopted instead a free form of verse that gave him greater liberty, as he thought, for the imitation of the "style and manner" alone of Pindar. This free verse had had its beginning in England as early as the last decade of the sixteenth century, and had been written in one form or another by many English poets between then and the middle of the seventeenth century. So that when Cowley used it in his *Pindariques* he used a form of verse already well known in England, and one that English predecessors had developed and made ready for him. (7)

Amy Lowell, in the preface to the 1916 volume of *Some Imagist Poets,* made even more extensive claims:

> The *vers librists* are often accused of declaring that they have discovered a new thing. Where such an idea started, it is impossible to say, certainly none of the better *vers librists* was ever guilty of so ridiculous a statement. The name *vers libre* is new, the thing, most emphatically, is not. Not new in English poetry, at any rate. You will find something very much like it in Dryden's *Threnodia Augustalis;* a great deal of Milton's *Samson Agonistes* is written in it; and Matthew Arnold's *Philomela* is a shining example of it. Practically all of Henley's *London Voluntaries* are written in it, and (so potent are names) until it was christened *vers libre,* no one thought of objecting to it. But the oldest reference to *vers libre* is to be found in Chaucer's *House of Fame,* where the Eagle addresses the Poet in these words:
>
> > And nevertheless hast set the wyt
> > Although that in thy heed full lyte is
> > To make bookes, songes, or dytees
> > In rhyme or elles in cadence.

What Chaucer really meant by "cadence" is far from certain, but it appears from the context that it may mean the looser accentual meters of middle English songs. Or this may reflect the medieval division of musical/poetic meters into *ars metrica* and *ars ritmica,* meters of the classical texts and meters of popular songs. No such compositions by Chaucer survive, and in any case such songs were certainly not comparable to the "personal cadence" called for by Ford Madox Ford, F. S. Flint, and Lowell herself. Yet her point is basically well-taken.

Although the ultimate origins of poetry may be lost in the mists of surmise and speculation, the general outlines of the beginnings of many types of free verse can be discerned through the fog. Long ago an international association of linguistic scholars instituted a rule that no papers were to be read on the origins of language itself because of the bitter controversies such papers provoked and because of the absence of provable facts. But one can always take up at a later stage—whether that should be the origins of the Romance languages or, turning back to prosody, the origins of free verse. It is not hard to demonstrate that free verse has repeatedly originated from the formal poetry that preceded it.

Free verse makes its appearance whenever a set of poetic conventions becomes sufficiently well established to be perceived by poets more as constraints than as opportunities. By *conventions* I mean formal patterns and genres that are recurrent and predictable; excluded is what some would now decry as the "convention" or "genre" of free verse itself. To claim that free verse can be a convention is to push too far the paradox inherent in the term. Free verse that has not achieved its freedom in terms of some preexisting convention is simply nothing: a prosodic vacuity. It does not signify. Poetry journals are jammed with these nonentities.

Historically, the appearance of free verse is preceded by a loosening and stretching of those conventions from which it finally departs. The longer the conventions have persisted, and the more ingenious this loosening and stretching, the more extreme and protracted is the final rupture. After a period of experimentation with free verse, there then follows renewed exploration in the direction of regularity and predictability. I do not pretend, of course, to have discovered an ideal Hegelian process and do not set up as a Toynbee of the iambs. But such a cycle is easy to identify in the period 1600–1700; reappears in some ways between 1750 and 1820; and recurs with surprising vigor between 1840 and 1880. In this century there have been so many revolutions and reactions, so many cycles within cycles, that to attempt to schematize them neatly would produce something like the later, most elaborate versions of the Ptolemaic system—and just as useless. But, as Wallace Stevens said in "The Pleasures of Merely Circulating," things do "go round and again go around," and it would be worth while to note the major evolutions since 1900.

One cannot hope, in illustrating the recurrent cycles of free verse, that everyone will agree that all the poems discussed really *are* free verse, although they seemed dangerously libertine in their own time—and later—and were denounced as such. I have already argued, and will demonstrate at much greater length, that *vers libres,* when the expression was used in France between 1830 and 1875, came to mean much the same sort of poetry that Cowley invented for himself in seventeenth-century England, and that others had written even earlier. Nevertheless, some will view as an absurd anachronism the assertion that Cowley wrote free verse, and even those who admit that the "Pindarique" is free may not be willing to agree that the earlier literary madrigal was in some respects a *madrigal* free-verse revolt against the constraints of the sonnet. Curiously the main opposition to the recognition of these earlier modes as types of free verse comes not from those who believe in the personal cadence or the organic form but rather emerges as the consequence of a pinched and parsimonious neoclassicism, an impoverished version of certain views held by Yvor Winters.

Yet it is true that the period 1590–1720 is not usually thought of as one in which open forms were a serious alternative. For one thing, the neoclassical style, complete with the heroic couplet, had already been grandly launched by Ben Jonson and others, who never lacked for admirers and imitators in the rest of the century. Even amid the civil wars the Cavaliers continued to compose their lapidary pieces. Then, in the next century, the authority of the Augustans came down squarely in opposition to the open poetry; acceptance of the closed heroic couplet as the norm gave the appearance of a happy victory of reason and order over "enthusiasm." Political events may have made their contribution; the English were certainly glad to leave behind them the regicidal excesses of the seventeenth century, agreeing with Dryden, "'Tis well an old age is out / And time to begin a new." And the "old age" had not only produced political disorders; in poetry there were numerous examples of the loose pseudo-Pindaric ode, and, even earlier, the literary madrigal. The crowning example of seventeenth-century free verse was Milton's *Samson Agonistes,* with its completely irregular choruses; here the iambic meter actually disappears. Even more irregular were the experiments using as a model those English translations of the Psalms that imitated Hebrew prosody—centuries before it occurred to Whitman to do the same thing.

The eighteenth century saw a continuation of the irregular ode,

Smart

though more extravagant departures such as Christopher Smart's *Jubilate Agno* tended to be ignored. "Ossian" proved a more notable diversion, but those who accepted the verdict of the "Great Cham," Samuel Johnson, discounted it. That century really was, as most people see it, a period of extended reaction, and free verse was even more rare a commodity than neoclassical couplets are today. To say this is not to revert to the old clichés about the "cold age of reason"; the emphasis for almost two generations of literary studies has been, quite properly, on the exceptions to that point of view, whether that means dwelling on the abnormalities or eccentricities of the major figures or taking note of the numerous and various subspecies of poetic art that flourished.

It is likewise commonplace to insist on the differences between British neoclassicism and the rationalism seen elsewhere, to note that on the European continent the cosmopolitan and humane "enlightenment" decayed into inner illumination and neurotic subjectivism as the century wore on—a decay best seen in Rousseau. Even Voltaire's engaging and witty assaults on unreason betray a confidence—which to some seems dangerous—in the unassisted intellect that is not too different from a Calvinist conviction of election or a Quaker reliance on Inner Light. The British enlightenment was never as confident in its irreligiousness as the French; indeed, we should remember that Pope remained a good Catholic, that Swift was an Anglican priest, and that Johnson's piety could almost be called notorious. Rationalistic philosophy never supplanted religion in England as it did in France, where it left a yawning emotional chasm into which enthusiasms of all sorts, including eventually a self-aggrandizing nationalism, readily flowed. This had its effects on prosody, at first mainly in France. In the nineteenth century one of these currents emerged as prose poetry and free verse of various sorts that even included patterns borrowed from Whitman.

prose poem
"9 cards
19thC

In America the most important consequence of enlightenment was not the French type of philosophe; Franklin had no program for a radical and destructive reformation of his country. Rather, in the usually Johnny-come-lately fashion of pre-twentieth-century American developments, enlightenment showed itself as the distinctly American form of Unitarianism that appeared toward the end of the eighteenth century and that was more agreeable to the settled commercial and professional classes on the American seaboard than was puritanical zeal. The American Romanticism—or Transcendentalism—that got under way in the 1830s was, as has often been pointed out, partly a reaction to the emotional impoverishment of that rationalized religion, and the most important consequence for American poetry was, of course, Whitman. This pattern of "rough" reaction to suave gentility has repeated itself several times since in America—in the populists, the Objectivists, the Beats, projectivism, and any current form of antiacademic poetry.

More free verse might have been expected of the English Romantic poets, given the prevalence of doctrines that encouraged freedom, self-expression, common speech, and originality. Revival of lyrical poetry, the ballad, and more elaborate older forms such as the Spenserian stanza, together with a newly sensed liberty to invent stanzas of one's own, was sufficient to absorb much of the poets' restless energy. For Coleridge and Wordsworth it was enough to revive the irregular ode; Blake remains the chief example of a thoroughgoing rebel in prosody for the period 1750–1820. More experimentation occurred later in the nineteenth century; Matthew Arnold rises as such a magisterial figure above the Victorian period that one seldom thinks of him as a prosodic radical, yet some of his poems—"Philomela" is a good example—are more free than Whitman's in that respect, as were poems by Coventry Patmore and W. H. Henley.

The more carefully one looks over the entire corpus of pre-twentieth-century poetry in English, the more examples one finds of poets who have achieved effects by disrupting conventions as well as by establishing them—and this includes the convention of the predictable poetic line. To say this is not to deny or minimize the immense change that did take place early in this century, when for the first time in history free verse became a common mode—whether it aimed at expressing a distinctly modern and avant-garde iconoclasm, or whether it was seen (especially in the United States) as allowing a democratically individual "voice."

The debate over free verse, from the eighteenth century to the present, has often come down to whether it ought to count as poetry at all. John Livingston Lowes, the first eminent literary scholar to attack the problem, had mixed feelings. He admired the clarity of Imagist writing, but on balance could not admit that there was any marked distinction between their rhythms and those of the more ornate Victorian prose stylists, such as Meredith and Pater. As a friend of Amy Lowell, he trod delicately, but concluded, "Vers libre is exploring the borderland between prose and verse" (281). T. S. Eliot asserted early on, and repeated with quiet modifications, the opinion that no verse could be genuinely free. But numerous pieces for which no internal prosodic rationale can be supplied have now taken their places in all anthologies of poetry that include the twentieth century. Some of them have been appearing now for sixty years or more. Inclusion is to some extent self-perpetuating, or may be due to the requirements of intellectual history as opposed to literary excellence; a lot of bad poetry stays in print for these reasons (as, for example, the opening cantos of Byron's *Childe Harold*). But the literate public in the end has some sort of say about what gets printed, read, and taught; and many poems in open forms fill the pages of anthologies; some could almost be called popular favorites. Even Yvor Winters, in a purely personal decision, retained free verse in his *Collected Poems,* long after he had rejected it as a method. So, as a practical matter, we may say that free verse has been accepted as a variety of poetry. I once heard a physicist describe economics as "a firm grasp of the obvious"; sometimes that is the best thing to aim at.

In his essay on education, "The Rhythmic Claims of Freedom and Discipline," Alfred North Whitehead argued the importance of alternating cycles of romance and precision to assure a healthy growth of a pupil's mind. A retrospective view of poetry in English reveals that since the early 1500s prosody has gone through a series of overlapping cycles that exhibit similar patterns of looseness and restraint. In my view the most exciting poetry has been written just at the point at which an excessively disciplined metric is in the process of being relaxed: in the earlier seventeenth century with Donne and the other Metaphysicals; in the early nineteenth century with Blake, Keats, and Wordsworth; and in the early twentieth century. But the claims of romance (which, oddly enough, often coincide with the application of theory to the writing of poems) sometimes become excessive. In the Pindarics of Cowley, some of the compositions of Coventry Patmore, or something like Charles Olson's *Maximus,* the poetry may well lose enduring interest, though it may attract a good deal of attention among contemporary literati who enjoy discussing the theory behind it. Cowley still appears in anthologies of seventeenth-century literature, as will Olson in collections of modern poetry, but after making time for Donne, Marvell, Herbert, Herrick, Milton, and ten or fifteen others, few readers care to attend to Cowley— as Pope was already saying nearly three hundred years ago.

The more formal poetry that has preceded or followed what I have called the "exciting" moments retains its attractions a little better. Dryden makes better reading than some of the more extravagant Metaphysicals, it seems to me. While Cowley's ode to Thomas Hobbes has never recovered its lost audience, "The Vanity of Human Wishes" continues to reward readers receptive to its rhetoric and its moral justice. And certain poems now thought of as examples of New Formalism—especially those by Brad Leithauser and Timothy Steele—will always attract new readers.

Donne went as far as it was reasonable to go in testing the expressive limits of prosody at his time; Cowley went too far. Keats and Shelley went somewhat further, but Southey (in his odes as poet laureate) and, later, Coventry Patmore, went too far. Tennyson's formal contrivances, however overingenious some of them may be, continue to make good reading. In this century the great innovators—H.D., Williams, Eliot, Pound, Moore, Stevens, and others—have given us another great cycle of prosodic romance, but some of their successors have tried to keep it going too long—or so it seems to me.

But I would not wish to argue unequivocally in favor of prosodic traditions that insist on a fundamental predictability; when conventions are forcibly imposed on the language (as with Gascoigne's blank verse, Cleveland's couplets, Longfellow's quatrains, Swinburne's hexameters) one is glad to welcome those who throw off the shackles of a moribund metric. "Knock the glass out!" I shout alongside Dr. Williams. Bring out the red wheelbarrow!

In any event, free verse does exist and is widely read and widely accepted, and it would be best to get on with the business of explaining how it really works, or, to start with, how it does not work. In achieving this there may be a certain degree of self-contradiction, of polemic employed to discourage polemic, much like the local militia that sallied forth in the midst of the English civil wars to fight Cavaliers and Roundheads simultaneously. But at least we will escape foolish consistency.

Chapter 2

The Problems of Organic Form

The momentous historical shift from the view that the making of a work of art is a supremely purposeful activity to the view that its coming-into-being is, basically, a spontaneous process independent of intention, precept, or even consciousness, was the natural concomitant of an organic aesthetics.
—M. H. Abrams

The inconsistencies and absurdities of supposed scansions of free verse are easy to point out, and those who invent such systems have few disciples even when, as with William Carlos Williams, the poetry itself has an enormous following. There is more to be said for Williams's variable foot than those who call it "the rubber inch" will allow, but given the fact that in traditional scansions one person's iamb may well be someone else's spondee or pyrrhic, depending upon the rhetorical interpretation of the line, agreement on which groups of syllables within a line constitute variable feet will not come easy. It was a great help to Williams to imagine that he had hit on a variable foot, just as it was a great help to Yeats to believe that the spirits had dictated answers to his cosmological questions. But almost no one tries to make systematic use of Williams's "foot," and nobody believes in Yeats's gyres and tinctures. It now appears that not even Yeats took them as seriously as used to be thought. Even more problematic than Williams's theory was the attempt that Yvor Winters made as a young man to diagram and justify his own practices, in the course of which he allowed all sorts of inconsistencies. In addition to these two, there have been other attempts to scan free verse by counting the incidence of feet such as iambs or anapests; something valuable may result from such studies, but most are tedious and pedantic.

It is true that the occurrence of unstressed articles, as well as un-
stressed monosyllabic prepositions that often precede English nouns,
does give the language a predominantly rising rhythm. In Swedish the
article follows the noun, and the poetic rhythms are therefore predomi-
nantly falling, making it as easy to construct a series of trochees in Swed-
ish as it is to trot out a line of iambs in English. But the entire concept of
scansion by feet is fundamentally foreign to any Germanic language, of
which English is one. Poets have made feet work for them in English, but
not because feet are natural to the language. To devise a free-verse foot is
to convert an absurdity—the conventional foot—into a monstrosity.

Much more difficult to deal with, because they offer much less
ground for objective discussion and many more openings for contentious
assertion, are theories based on some idea of organic form. A belief in
organicism, overt or implied, informs so much discussion of free verse
that my refusal to allow it as a basis for discussion may seem perverse. To
dismiss it requires arguments that may seem needlessly elaborate and
irrelevant to metrics. Organicism—as its name suggests—is an invasive
and rambling weed, pieces of which always survive and give rise to new
infestations. The remainder of this chapter will not serve to extirpate it,
but may open a temporary clearing so that we can get a clearer view of
how it takes root and flourishes.

The problem is that organicism thrives on the most fundamental
ideas and convictions that most human beings live by—the concept of
the immortality of the human soul, for example. Emerson's view, upon
which Whitman acted, was that poetry should proceed from, and take a
form that is dictated to it by, the individual soul of the poet rather than
any external model or authority. Even declared enemies of free verse are
loath to disturb or question such beliefs directly; indeed, most twentieth-
century neoclassicists are pious persons, unwilling to tamper with reli-
gious orthodoxies, such as the Catholic belief that at some point in the
course of human gestation an eternal soul comes into existence and takes
charge of the organism's destinies, guiding it with the assistance of ecclesi-
astical advice. Protestants transfer the authority from an external scrip-
ture and an external church and priesthood to the soul itself, but neither
Catholic nor Protestant—nor Jew, from whose religion both borrowed
the idea—feels inclined to question the existence of the immortal soul,
whatever its origins and responsibilities may be. In some ways free verse
is a natural, even inevitable, development from such convictions, which
are themselves the foundations of religious belief. The discussion that

follows will therefore stray somewhat away from questions that are strictly those of prosody and will consider deeply underlying preconceptions, treating them with a skepticism that may seem to border on impiety. I will begin, however, by sketching the origins of organicism.

From its beginnings in the eighteenth century, German transcendental philosophy engendered an organic and antianalytic conception of nature, and of art as a continuation of organic processes—an outlook that was passed on to the English by Coleridge and to Americans by both Coleridge and Emerson, among others. By the end of the nineteenth century organicism was accepted as a self-evident truth; even Henry James—with fastidious indirection—absorbed the idea of organic form into his criticism. Amy Lowell, Williams, Charles Olson, and many others reverted to some variety of organicism and used it to explain their abandonment of conventional meters.

Although the connection may not be immediately apparent, the concept of organic form is powerfully linked to the sense of individualism and special election, the sectarian spirit that characterizes American poetry nearly as strikingly as it does religion in America. From the earliest days of American colonization both doctrine and experience encouraged self-sufficiency in spiritual as well as material matters. Even the Church of England in the early 1600s was deeply tinged by Calvinism; in our own times few Anglicans remember Article of Religion number XVII (appearing in the *Book of Common Prayer*), which makes it part of their official doctrine to believe that "the godly consideration of Predestination, and our Election in Christ, is full of sweet, pleasant, and unspeakable comfort." By 1700 Calvinism had receded in the English church, but in America it—and other forms of dissent—reflected and in part determined the national outlook, including typically American views of poetry. Parallels between a Calvinist or Puritan sense of election and the self-assurance with which many American poets have followed the dictates of their inner promptings seem to me inevitable. Toward the end of his chapter "The Augustinian Strain of Piety," with which he opens *The New England Mind: The Seventeenth Century,* Perry Miller described it his way: "Supernatural grace is a work peculiar to the elect, which comes upon them with irresistible force, and depends upon no antecedent conditions or preparations. . . . There must be room in the universe for a free and unpredictable power, for a lawless force that flashes through the night in unexpected brilliance and unaccountable majesty" (34).

The effect of American sectarianism is to place heavy emphasis on distinct personal identity and on the priesthood of all believers; in poetic theory, it reinforces—and in fact anticipated—the Romantic insistence on the primacy of the poet's own personality, and on the poem as a testament of the personality. It follows that a poem will be an idiosyncratic production. Poets produce the sorts of poems that they do because of their individual natures—or, to put it in religious terms, because of the uniqueness of their souls. One might call it the "streaks of the tulip" theory, remembering how the eighteenth-century prejudice *against* all idiosyncrasy expressed itself in Imlac's speech on the poet's duties in *Rasselas:* "He does not number the streaks of the tulip." In other words, the eighteenth-century view was that the artist or poet should neglect minute individual differences in favor of the general or representative, whereas the most common assumption now is that what counts is the individual and the particular—the "streaks" that mark the poem as the work of one particular poet.

Paralleling the sense of special election and the primacy of idiosyncrasy is what one might call the cult of the disenfranchised. Often this simply amounts to the self-pity that seems inevitable among human beings; would-be poets look back at the examples of Emily Dickinson and Walt Whitman and blame their own obscurity on whatever form of "establishment" they can identify—economic, academic, religious, or social. Countercultural poets have for decades been arriving at Harvard Square, finding their own work or works that they admire absent or underrepresented in the Harvard Coop and, now, even the Grolier Book Store, and returning home to air their grievances at such neglect. They rage against "mainstream" values that they suppose to be cultivated and protected at Ivy League universities, forgetting that not only e. e. cummings but even John Cage was invited to give the Norton Lectures, that Charles Bernstein's *Poetics* was published by the Harvard University Press, and that the philosophical patriarch of American crankiness, William James, held forth on that location for years—not to speak of Emerson. On the whole American universities suffer from a fear of being left behind by the avant-garde and from an excessive commitment to trendiness because of the suspicion, amply justified, that those who inhabit them are unimaginative. But the myth of marginalization of the avant-garde persists.

Part of the problem is the difficulty, in the United States, of being perfectly certain as to who is being elected and who excluded. There is no

Royal Academy, and even a Presidential Medal of Freedom seems to carry a less definite cachet than a knighthood. In poetry, there is the continuing suspicion—felt with great keenness by William Carlos Williams—that Americans never have found their own language, and the increasing belief in some quarters is that they never will. In any case, many poets begin with the assumption that the first step in being a poet is to make a break with whatever tradition can be identified.

The effort to make this break and to recover for the poet some kind of personal authenticity can be traced back at least a century and a half. Emerson, for example, found the "unexpected brilliance" mentioned by Perry Miller missing in the work of his own day, and in its place a tame imitativeness. As he said in the opening paragraph of his essay "The Poet," speaking initially of neoclassical aesthetics, "Their knowledge of the fine arts is some study of rules and particulars, or some limited judgment of color or form, which is exercised for amusement or for show. It is a proof of the shallowness of the doctrine of beauty as it lies in the minds of our amateurs, that men seem to have lost the perception of the instant dependence of form upon soul" (4). What Emerson had in mind was the derivative quality of most American art, which typically lagged thirty to a hundred years behind the fashions in England.

One can sympathize with his impatience with the shallowness and artificiality, the facile technical skills, of much that met the eye or ear in Emerson's time, and with his yearning for arts more genuinely rooted in the life of the new country. Even the best of American nineteenth-century landscape painting, and it is nothing to be ashamed of, is saturated with the old theories—the old aesthetic categories of the beautiful, the sublime, and the picturesque. In the early nineteenth century some American poets were still imitating Pope. Perhaps it was only overstatement for effect when Emerson spoke of the "instant dependence of form on soul"; perhaps his main intention was to insist on the proper claims of the individual American poet or artist that had, until then, been smothered by inherited and imported traditions. But this is the incipient stage of a concept that has come to dominate much twentieth-century thinking about poetry, and it may be well to question it at the outset—even to contradict it. The discussion that follows draws heavily on the naturalistic dimension of the philosophy of George Santayana, especially his *Realms of Being*. Implied here also is Santayana's far-reaching critique of American culture, found scattered through many of his volumes, faulting it not only for its "genteel tradition," but also for its crudeness. Santayana likewise repeatedly rebuked

Americans for a presumptuous subjectivism learned from Protestant theology and reinforced by German transcendentalism.

Bizarre as it may seem, then, to take up the concept of the human soul in a discussion of prosody, it is an impertinence that must be admitted. A settled, if unstated, conviction that the soul is a self-subsisting, immortal, entity is—for many poets—a powerful source of confidence in the validity of their formal preferences. And it was Emerson, after all, who brought it up—"the instant dependence of form upon soul." The problem posed by Emerson's statement results from the assumption of the existence of the individual soul independent of any circumstances to which it may find itself attached. This assumption was, I hardly need say, not only common among his contemporaries but is also an explicit tenet of many religious creeds, and colors the philosophies that often are extensions of those creeds. The aesthetics and criticism engendered by those creeds and philosophies have in turn affected the arts.

Leaving aside the ultimate issue of the soul's immortality, one may safely assert that in Western thought the *idea* of the individual and immortal soul does have a history; that the concept of the self-subsisting soul became especially important in the Romantic aesthetic theory; and that it is important to the composition of much free verse. The idea, originally Judaic, was reinforced and modified powerfully by the assimilation of Platonic philosophy into Christian theology. As Santayana put it, "[T]he Platonic and Christian tradition has come to identify the soul with a bodiless spirit, a sort of angel, at first neglecting and afterwards denying the biological functions" (329). With Plato the soul enjoyed considerable self-sufficiency, descending into matter and returning from it into some kind of heaven that, no matter how perfect, was, in Santayana's view, really a precursor to and a continuation of the existence of the soul on earth. The Platonic concept finds an exposition in Wordsworth's *Immortality Ode* that, however divorced it may be from Christian orthodoxy, appealed powerfully to Gerard Manley Hopkins because of its fundamental affinities with the Christian idea of the soul, among other things. Even Thomas Hardy acknowledged the tragic pathos of abandoning the consolations of continued existence in a heavenly afterlife, and Wallace Stevens—a lifelong reader of Santayana—held with difficulty to his own program of earthly satisfactions, "Things to be cherished like the thought of heaven." Less thoughtful poets, whatever other impieties their irreverence may lead them into, are unwilling to relinquish the prospect of immortality. Not for them the renunciation in Emily Dickinson's best poems, where immortality itself is another passenger headed gravewards in company with the poet, and where God manifests himself as a fly.

Santayana's naturalism is not, of course, the view of the convinced Platonist who hypostasizes properties of earthly objects into eternal "forms." Such a belief, which already appealed powerfully to a human craving for permanence and certainty to be found in some heaven of ideas, if not on earth, had added to it in the writings of Augustine a passionate religious emotion. The self-sustaining quality of Augustinian Platonism, suffused with the light of the convinced intellect, achieved a new intensity in Protestant theologies where belief in divine election tended toward self-election, or at least an extreme inner confidence that divine election had occurred. A secularizing of such beliefs helped to unseat eighteenth-century critical assumptions about the generality and universality of art by encouraging a concept of the artist as an autonomous creator. These notions—too briefly summarized here—are commonplaces of intellectual history, but most discussions of free verse do not even attempt to locate it within a context of intellectual history but rather discuss it as an absolute issue.

The exact relationships between the soul, the body, God, and the rest of the creation provide subjects for endless theological distinctions and wranglings, but the twin assumptions of immortality of the soul and its independence from matter remain unquestioned in most considerations of poetry. Such assumptions seem necessary in order to guarantee the ultimate importance of the poet and the poetry; in dedicating his anthology to Dylan Thomas, Oscar Williams felt it necessary to salute Thomas as "Immortal Soul." For both Plato and Emerson the soul animates the body, which is composed of matter. Matter itself is inert or even hostile to the intentions of the soul, according to such a view. "In man, and perhaps in other creatures, an evil fate had imprisoned some of these angelic souls in a natural body, and contaminated them with the vital principle—the old animal heathen soul—proper to such a body" (330). Santayana, in order to avoid the confusions implicit in the word, then chooses to treat the soul in two different ways—as a "psyche," by which he means something close to what we mean by *organism,* and as "spirit," by which he means "the actual light of consciousness," which the psyche makes possible.

But according to the Emersonian view, whatever the body, or person acting through the agency of the body, may do is an activity of the soul. The poem, then, originates as an activity of the individual soul;

using what we may now call the *metaphor* of organic form, the soul, by first creating the personality and body of the poet, puts forth poems as a tree puts forth flowers and fruit. (So far as I can tell, the absurdities of this point of view are entirely due to male poets, and I will therefore employ male pronouns for the rest of this paragraph and whenever the topic of organicist egotism is discussed.) The poet owes everything to the fact that he has, from all eternity, or at least from some special moment in his gestation, been endowed with the soul of a poet. Since it is an inevitable part of his nature to produce poems there may be some degree of irresponsibility in his writings. He may not even know what he is doing.

It must be emphasized that Emerson's views, though similar in some respects to Plato's, cannot strictly speaking be called Platonic. Even when in the *Ion* Plato calls the poet an inspired madman, or when in book 10 of *The Republic* he argues for the exclusion of all poets, including Homer, Plato thinks of the poet as a *conduit* for the utterances of the gods, or the Muses. The poet is not a God per se. The poet is an unconscious vehicle—and in addition to that produces imitations of imitations of reality. The poet is in the end a distraction. With perfect consistency, given these beliefs, Plato went on to argue that the poet was a disruptive force in an ideal republic and should be banned. Emerson escaped these consequences, simply announcing in "Self-Reliance" that "With consistency a great soul has simply nothing to do."

One of the main channels through which Germanic transcendentalism had reached Emerson was Coleridge, whom Emerson ranked as a philosopher on the same plane with Spinoza and Kant. In glancing at Coleridge's views it makes much sense to think in terms of a reaction against the anatomizing and classifying predilections of eighteenth-century criticism, and to see his writings as an effort to restore a sense of unity and vitality to literary performances that had indeed, in some respects, become too formal and calculated. As M. H. Abrams illustrates at length, quoting from numerous seldom-read letters and essays (167–77), Coleridge insisted that the animating principle, even of a crocus, was preexistent to and independent of the materials that the growing organism assimilated to itself. To explain growth in terms of physical laws, and to consider the organism in terms of its constituent parts, was, he felt, to impose a soulless and mechanistic system on the living substance of the universe, to anatomize it to death. Coleridge did not use this example, but one might think of how Alexander Pope had schematized the world in the rhyming couplets of his *Essay on Man;* to those who see Pope's metrics as mechanical and constricting his thinking also seems cold and analytical. Abrams offers a shrewd assessment of the ultimate implications of Coleridge's organicism:

> To substitute the concept of growth for the operation of mechanism in the psychology of invention, seems merely to exchange one kind of determinism for another; while to replace the mental artisan-planner by the concept of organic self-generation makes it difficult, analogically, to justify the participation of consciousness in the creative process. We shall see that, in some German critics, recourse to vegetable life as a model for the coming-into-being of a work of art had, in fact, engendered the fateful concept that artistic creation is primarily an unwilled and unconscious process of the mind. (173)

In questioning Emerson's idea of "the instant dependence of form upon soul," one must still admit that he had a point to make. But in issuing a call for self-assertion, for self-reliance, for a national identity and a national poetry, Emerson also encouraged an egotism that was evident even to him in Whitman's poetry. What Emerson initially intended as a metaphorical and rhetorical call for legitimate self-realization ended as authorization for egotism and eccentricity. The "instant dependence of form upon soul," if taken literally, means that the form of any work of art is idiosyncratic to that artist. Much work published as poetry at the end of the twentieth century is composed and accepted for publication on the assumption that its form owes everything to the poet's personality, soul, being, "voice," utterance, or self-sufficient inspiration. To disagree with this assumption puts one in danger of being judged by one's poetic and scholarly neighbors, of being subjected to the tyranny of public opinion that Tocqueville identified as a major liability of American democracy.

Should this be the truth about poetry—that it is intrinsically personal, privately inspired, and inevitably idiosyncratic—it is a truth not evident to poets of earlier times. Epic poems have arisen out of many cultures, and even when they bear the name of an individual author they are the result of a highly developed and long-cultivated tradition shared by both author (or performer) and audience. The same is true of songs and ballads. Even when poems have been treated as the personal property of the poet, until this century there has always been the expectation that the reader could share in the author's formal purposes. This did not limit the poet's ingenuity, but rather was a challenge to the poet to innovate formally as well as in other ways. Much contemporary poetry lacks any sense of accountability to the reader and, as natural consequence, is not much read, though the blame for this neglect is laid by poets on the ignorance of the reading public, somewhat as the pastors of shrinking congregations are apt to blame the faithlessness of the times.

Since, as I see it, some of the problem has to do with taking literally Emerson's metaphorical statement, I would like to substitute for this metaphor the natural facts, arguing that Emerson put it backward: form does not depend upon soul; soul depends upon form, among other things. Soul does not create itself but rather arises out of the organic and formal circumstances that brought it into existence. This is a naturalistic, even a materialistic, argument—the idea that soul, or individuality, supervenes upon biological form, but biological form is the necessary prerequisite, that the individual soul cannot be actualized without the agency of the underlying biological form. Consciousness, mental life, spirit, soul are real but unintended consequences of the material processes that create and sustain them. If soul were the *causative* factor, one might expect different souls to have very different bodies. As it happens, all our livers and kidneys are tolerably similar to one another. Personalities are infinitely diverse. Livers and kidneys make individuals possible, but individuals do not create their own innards. There are, of course, many human beings who are capable of believing that their bodies exist because of the activity of the soul and even the perceiving mind; a few of these even get into medical schools.

It may seem strange to depart this far—if only briefly—from a consideration of the rhythms of free-verse poems, but the grandiose claims of the organicists require a far-reaching refutation, if only because, if rightly understood, there is much truth in their point of view. As they insist, poetry does grow out of the organic circumstances that make it possible. The living biological organism must exist as the grounds of the individual human animal, and the social human individual must be brought into existence—must learn a language and acquire some cultural identity, and (dare one say it) *learn* to write poetry—before poems can be brought into existence. Such statements will fall upon the ears of born-again poets and their apologists, of course, with the same persuasiveness that papal edicts strike born-again Christians, and with the same acceptability that accounts of geological and biological evolution find among convinced fundamentalists. Nor will the mature transcendentally minded poet, who credits himself with his own existence, take kindly to the suggestion that theories of child development and education support the arguments advanced above and that his poetic personality is not something that he willed into existence. Calm consideration of biology and history ought to convince anyone that this is the actual order of things: mineral, protozoan, animal, human, civilized being, and poet. In each instance the formal grounding of the previous stage makes possible the next. The rich mental and emotional life that we think of as the soul grows out of the previous stages but does not create its own formal basis. Form makes possible individuality.

A true organicism, as applied to poetry, would argue that the idiosyncratic evolutions of successful free verse have likewise been possible only because of the vast groundwork of formal poetry in English. Free verse is in itself epiphenomenal to older meters, and this may account for the illusion that it is independent of them; but without the context, without— to use Eliot's metaphor—the arras from which the ghost emerges, free verse could not exist. Free verse separates itself from what produced it, but the relationship to its origins cannot be ignored, and the effects of free verse depend on an implied contrast, or difference, with what it *is not,* or rather, on what it came from and what it no longer is.

To argue in this fashion is to invite denunciations from formalists and organicists alike, both absolutists in their own ways, the most extreme of the former believing that they have looked into the mind of God and the most radical of the latter believing that they are the sole creators of their own experience—and both at times willing to forget that, as far back as we can see, poetry has been begotten by poetry, language by language. This absolutism is evident in the advice that Yvor Winters once offered a student. The student had written a poem and had submitted it for criticism. Winters told him that it was not bad, but that it lacked a last line that would make it much better. The author of the poem made several unsuccessful guesses and then asked what the line was. "You find it," said Winters. "It exists in the mind of God." I have elsewhere compared the school of poets that gathered around Winters at Stanford to the monks on the island of Iona, who kept the true faith secure while the Roman Empire tottered and fell to barbarian invasions. Contemporary Language poets seem to be trying to create their own worlds through the power of the word. Losing themselves in a domain of free association, they sometimes display an indifference to the feelings of those who inhabit regions beyond their ken. Although they seem to aim at the cultivation of finer shades of emotion and meaning, the movement constantly risks a descent into the self-conscious and jokey clubbiness of the inner circle.

Emerson's "instant dependence of form upon soul" proved valuable as a call to action—an appeal to the soul of America to discover itself—but it is not in the end sound aesthetics. Proponents of organic form who follow Coleridge and Emerson forget that in nature the individual is only one member of a species, and that even the most unusual species of organism can comprise an unlimited number of individuals.

Poetry arises out of human language and the life of the spirit much as the human spirit arises out of the circumstances—material, organic, and cultural—that make it possible. Poetry is not a solipsistic means of self-delight, nor the mad self-indulgence of a psyche that has persuaded itself that it is self-created and autonomous. Neither is it a Divine Pattern to be discerned by the attentive intellect. Poetry is a human utterance and in its ultimate intent is sociable—a "letter to the world."

The older genre theories of poetry were closer to a genuine organicism than the notion of the *poet* as a new variety of poem-producing vegetable. J. C. Scaliger long ago argued for this kind of biological analogy in his *Poetics* (3.96), published in 1561. There he listed among his rules for poetry the principle that a book should be subdivided into related parts just as nature composes an organic body; in this he gave a new twist to the doctrine of imitation, basing his comments on Aristotle, Horace, and other ancient sources. Latter-day organicism has something in it of a revolt *against* the natural sciences and even the natural world, an assertion that the growth of the spirit, equal or even superior in importance to the physical processes of the universe, occurs on its own without any particular indebtedness to those processes. There may even be the presumption that the spirit *causes* those processes to occur. This, I take it, is another aspect of what Charles T. Harrison meant when he once said that for the last two centuries we have been living in a period of fundamental heresy.

The appeal of the organic analogy as an answer to or a defense against the explanatory power of the natural sciences is, as I have already noted, at least two hundred years old, and owes much of its current authority to arguments originally advanced by Coleridge. In fact organicism is often treated as if it were exclusively a Coleridgean concept. In a study that is a continuation of this book I will examine Coleridge's ideas even more closely, but for the moment I take time only to acknowledge again priority of his claims and to quote one colorful assessment of his outlook:

> Indeed, it is astonishing how much of Coleridge's critical writing is couched in terms that are metaphorical for art and literal for a plant; if Plato's dialectic is a wilderness of mirrors, Coleridge's is a very jungle of vegetation. Only let the vehicles of his metaphors come alive, and you see all the objects of criticism writhe surrealistically into plants or parts of plants, growing in tropical profusion. Authors, characters, poetic genres, poetic passages, words, meter, logic become seeds, trees, flowers, blossoms, fruit, bark, and sap. The fact is, Coleridge's insistence on the distinction between the living imagination and the mechanical fancy was but a part of his all-out war against the "Mechanico-corpuscular Philosophy" on every front. (169)

So argues M. H. Abrams in a particularly eloquent passage in *The Mirror and the Lamp*. In American poetry, from Whitman's revulsion over the lecture of "the learned astronomer" to the countercultural assumption that science is to blame for our worst ills, we see a continuation of Romantic suspicion of the meddling intellect.

The tychistic disengagement of Language poetry is only the latest manifestation of a profound distrust of scientific systematization. For those affected by antiscientific prejudice, the eighteenth-century closed couplet—a good example being Pope's tribute to Newton,

Nature and Nature's laws lay hid in Night:
God said, *Let Newton be!* and all was Light.

—seems the epitome of heartless mechanism, while humane values can only reside in unreflective and aleatory free association of words and phrases. Adherents of a tychistic poetics, like those who espouse randomization in any art form, can only see formal patterning as a reductive elimination of possibilities. It never occurs to them that the formal pattern can itself be a guarantor of the accidental—that regular meters and rhyme patterns are an irrationally imposed template that can force a poet along paths of discovery that would never otherwise have been invented. This is an old and familiar argument, of course, and does not excuse those who traffic in what Pope called "the sure returns of still expected rimes." But it is important to insist that Romantic antirationalism (which is itself as intellectual as any other conviction) oversimplifies the purposes and effects of traditional poetic meter and form when it treats them as benighted or reactionary.

This excursion into religious and philosophical history has been necessary in order to place in the widest possible context certain assumptions that govern the composition of much free verse. That these assumptions are neither stated nor acknowledged by many poets is no argument against their existence. They are the unquestioned givens. To some extent they are part of what Bertrand Russell called, speaking of the philosophy of William James, the "subjectivistic madness" characteristic of our century. American political and cultural doctrine sanctifies individualism almost to the point of denying that we all belong to a single biological species. The emphasis is on individual identity far more than the shared ideals of a civilization. In saying this we should not forget that "shared ideals" have themselves been misused as instruments of oppression—that too often these ideals represent the currently empowered group. But recent comments by Arthur Schlesinger Jr. have pointed to the dangers to any world order of American exceptionalism when it is carried from religion and art into politics, but even if we restrict our attention to the arts, and to poetry in particular, the apotheosis of the individual is troublesome. If each person is a species, and particularly if he or she is a species of godlike artist, then what that person does, the fruits of any endeavor, must be idiosyncratic productions in order to be "authentic." Moralists in the 1990s are beginning to question "the ethics of authenticity" in American culture, and the concept of the idiosyncratic voice is also under attack by some who theorize about rhetoric. My arguments parallel these developments.

The effort to use the stamp of individuality as a guarantee of the authenticity of the work can defeat its own purpose, if that purpose is to speak with a messianic voice for all America. Even William Carlos Williams realized that a durable poetry requires that one lose oneself in the common language and common experience. The best-known term for the selflessness required of a great poet was coined by a Romantic: "negative capability." As Keats said, "A poet is the most unpoetical of anything in existence, because he has no Identity—he is continually in for and filling some other body." Keats's view was that the poet achieves self-fulfillment by losing self in the poem, an aesthetic version of "Whoever would save his life, must lose it." The problem with, say, Charles Olson, is that all his efforts went into being a poet; his individuality smothers his pages with lines whose justification depends solely on the fact that Olson produced them and that they are his and his alone, artifacts of his labored breathings. I realize that disciples of Olson would counter what I have just said by insisting that all his talk about "breath" was a kind of polemic, an argument for returning to the immediacy of the human voice; that his breath is not literal but rather a metaphor for that already metaphorical word, inspiration. But a scansion that satisfies the requirements of a single poet is no scansion at all. The effort to discover such a scansion may be worth making in order to prove this point, but there is no need to assume that because grandiose claims have been made there must be something to the claims.

The standard of measurement in certain kingdoms used to be the actual foot of the reigning tyrant. To accept any one person's breathing or breathlessness as a standard for a poem's form seems to me an unnecessary act of submission. To say this is not to argue the correctness of views that one might loosely call neoclassical. But there is no more need to glorify human limitations than there is to aim at a spurious conclusiveness and finality, to claim, in the words of Yvor Winters, "The final certitude of speech / Which Hell itself cannot unlock." Poems are inevitably human, imperfect, and fallible.

Chapter 3

Can Free Verse Be Classified?

While scansion of free verse is not possible, it does seem feasible to introduce and illustrate a provisional taxonomy for classifying free verse. Many free-verse poems do resemble one another in the particular ways that they escape or deviate from traditional meters. A little girl once organized a dog show in which there were three categories for entrants: big dogs, little dogs, and brown dogs. The show was a success, and perhaps my plan is at least as good.

Joseph Malof, in *A Manual of English Meters,* suggested some useful distinctions. Although I offer modifications to his scheme, Malof must be credited with being the first to devise a workable taxonomy for free verse and the first to show that this is a useful way to proceed. His book remains a classic on the subject of prosody. Malof's "phrasal free verse" is exactly what I designate at times by the same name, or which I call "phrase-reinforcing." His other categories I will mention below in conjunction with my own, pointing out how I differ from him.

One of these, however, I do not recognize at all—what he calls "cadenced free verse." I have already dealt briefly with the concept of cadence; what Malof has to say on the subject is essentially a summary of the Imagist views of free verse in general, especially as enunciated by Ford, Flint, Lowell, and Aldington. Malof also speaks of—and gives examples of—"accentual free verse"; in this, I think that he was influenced both by W. C. Williams's efforts to find a variable foot, and even more by Yvor Winters's experimental scansions.

Two of my own categories have already been identified. The most prominent is Whitman's biblical-anaphoric free verse, which derives mainly from rhythms of the King James Version of the Old Testament—though, as we shall see, there were other important sources. The King

James was in turn a loose equivalent of Hebrew poetry. In this century Whitmanian free verse appears not only in outright followers of Whitman (such as Ginsberg) but indirectly in the work of many others, including some African-American poets and certain feminist poets. Eliot, who found his own way back into the Scriptures, uses something similar, often modifying or disguising it cleverly. It is not an exclusively modern mode; Hebraic patterns appear in poems from the seventeenth and eighteenth centuries. Malof includes instances of this sort of free verse under the rubric of "prose-poetry," and also to some extent identifies it with what he calls "syntactic free verse." He discovers other sorts of organizational strategies based on syntax as well.

Next come the French terms for which *free verse* is now an incorrect translation: *vers libre, vers libres,* or *vers libérés.* Originally vers libres intended a loosening up of poetic structure into lines of irregular length (and was even applied to the flexible rhyme schemes of La Fontaine). Vers libres at first retained a certain regularity of syllabification and use of rhyming endings. A corresponding form of free verse is so common and characteristic in English that *vers-libristic* seems a good term to designate it. It appeared in English for the first time about 1590, when it was in part a spontaneous loosening of forms and in part a supposed borrowing from the Italian madrigal. It reappeared as the "Pindarique" in the seventeenth century, and again in the nineteenth century, following in some cases models in Italian and French poetry. The best example of this kind of free verse in English is "The Love Song of J. Alfred Prufrock." In its turn, "Prufrock" has become a model; Adrienne Rich's "Snapshots of a Daughter-in-Law" uses devices that filter down from the French through Eliot, and in addition imitates Eliot's loading of every rift with literary quotation. Malof identified this as "fragmented free verse," which works quite well as a description, but which does not recognize the importance of the French models for twentieth-century verse of this type. Since numerous examples exist from earlier times, however, Malof's term is a reasonable alternative to *vers-libristic.*

As free verse proliferated and blossomed in this century, there appeared several more strategies for determining its metrical irregularity. Many poems to this day, for example, use lines that parallel natural phrasal units; these can be called *phrase-reinforcing.* Here is a well-known example, by H.D., as printed in Amy Lowell's 1915 Imagist anthology (28):

OREAD
Whirl up, Sea—
Whirl your pointed pines,
Splash your great pines
On our rocks,
Hurl your green over us,
Cover us with your pools of fir.

A way of counterpointing the expectation of the natural phrase, however, is to interrupt it at an unexpected point; lines that do this may be called *phrase-breaking*. Here is an example from William Carlos Williams's *Collected Poems:*

FLOWERS BY THE SEA
When over the flowery, sharp pasture's
edge, unseen, the salt ocean

lifts its form—chicory and daisies
tied, released, seem hardly flowers alone

but color and movement—or the shape
perhaps—or restlessness, whereas

the sea is circled and sways
peacefully upon its plantlike stem

(1:378)

Notice that Williams's poem does not even stop definitely at the end. I will not pause here to explain at length the reasons behind the line breaks in these two examples. They have something to do with two varieties of perception: H.D.'s images swirl out at us like vortices on a Van Gogh canvas, while Williams's dissolve into blurred specklings reminiscent of Monet—and the patterning assists these two effects. The patterning also says to us: "Do not listen for regular rhythms! Suspend your requirements for aural equivalence! Use your eyes! *See* what I'm talking about!" The absence of scannable meter is intended to arrest our attention—not carry us forward upon hypnotic waves as we might have expected to be carried (by Longfellow, Swinburne, or Morris). In both these examples we see a studious avoidance of iambic meter; if T. S. Eliot's ghost of an established meter lurks behind the arras, H.D.'s and Williams's ghosts have faded into the light of day or have been nailed up in the attic.

It may be needless to introduce classifications that find application chiefly in the work of a single poet, e. e. cummings, but it does extend the list of possible violations to our expectations if we speak of *word-breaking* and *word-jamming* free verse. Examples of these practices may be found in every anthology that includes several of cummings's poems and hardly require illustration here. Facile imitators of cummings latch onto this aspect of his style, along with his lowercase spellings and abbreviations— but once in a while one encounters poems that use broken or jammed words in ways that do not seem derivative of cummings.

Finally there is the prose poem.

As a diversion I once invented learned words for these categories (*phraseotectic, phraseoclastic, logoclastic, logoplastic,* and *prosaic*), but to achieve the mystique of an I. A. Richards or a William Empson today it would probably be best to go the other direction and label the types the way physicists do quarks (i.e., "up," "down," "red," "blue," etc.). To revert to the dog-show metaphor, I realize that there may be some who will be disappointed that I have not more carefully distinguished, say, Airedales from Pekingese, and who will detect a preference for mongrels. Having recently read a book review, itself not at all recent, in which the writer went about his business like an efficient euthanist at an animal shelter, exterminating some fifty books of poetry and putting up one or two for adoption, I have a horror of such exact categories.

A feature common to all free-verse methods, or strategies, is the use of typographical arrangements that draw attention to the irregularity, or at least instill an awareness that the poem's appearance on the page is in itself a declaration of independence from metrical expectations. In earlier verslibristic poems this is less important; there, the unfulfilled background norm, usually iambic pentameter, appeals with such power to the ear that truncated lines are easily perceived aurally. But beginning with Imagism, especially as Imagist practice was affected by the antirhythmic dogma of T. E. Hulme, the line tended to be put at the service of the image, usually a visual image. Depending upon whether the image was static or dynamic, the line might be end-stopped or enjambed. Particular qualities of an image—color, texture, outline—might be emphasized by placing the modifying word at the end of the line; similarly, transitions in the nature of the image could be strengthened by ending the line with a verb or participle.

To a large degree this use of typography was a reaction away from

the hypnotic vagueness of poems like William Morris's "The Tune of the *NB.*
Seven Towers"; Yeats never abandoned his line to typography, but Ezra
Pound did his best to wean Yeats from the same evocative vagueness. To
insist on the imagistic content of language was to treat words more as
ideograms than as symbols for sounds; the language of the poem, then,
became a succession of ideograms for whose effect aural rhythm was of
minimal importance, at least for those who accepted Hulme's arguments.
Composition of free verse became in part an effort to *defeat* conventional
rhythms, in the interest of greater immediacies of other sorts. I shall
discuss the typographical aspect of free verse at greater length in a later
chapter.

If you examine the work of an unsuspecting free-verse writer, you
are apt to find that the poet, in a given poem, relies more on one of these
antirhythmic practices than on the others. But sometimes they are mixed
in the same poem, and to that degree they lose some usefulness as descrip-
tive tools, especially when mixture is as cunningly manipulated as it is in
The Waste Land. What they all have in common is that they run counter to
expectations of various sorts, or did, when they were first used.

These terms are not exhaustive and may not even be adequate, but
they are useful in pinning down certain poetic practices more exactly than
the all-purpose label *free verse* will do. It also is more sympathetic to the
poem, and especially to the reader, to focus on the common ground that
connects us with the poet: the words, syntax, and rhythms that we share.
It is more satisfying to make distinctions and identify recurrent habits in
the poems themselves than to accommodate ourselves obsequiously to
the quips, cranks, and wanton wiles of a poet. Despite the expectation of
various poets—from some of the earlier English vers-librists, such as
Edward Storer, to Charles Olson and beyond—that we permit each poet
a special "cadence," we need not allow ourselves to be dictated to in this
way. By exercising sufficient ingenuity one may invent a system that
seems to justify or explain almost any form of utterance by any person; in
that case, one operates on the assumption that the genius of the particular
poet is established beyond further question, that, like Mount Rainier or
Mount McKinley, his eminence of itself requires attention that would not
be bestowed on lowlier peaks. It seems to me preferable to aim at general
descriptive principles that cover many instances of free verse, and to try
to explain where they originated.

A major problem, in setting up classifications of free verse, is to
identify a sufficient number of such poems that have achieved widespread

approval by successive generations of common readers. There would be no point in deriving general principles from work that no one cares to read. To some degree the canon—whatever that may turn out to be—will have to take the place of the common reader in deciding which poems to consider. For my purposes, the canon largely consists of free-verse poems that were published prior to 1960 and that continue to be received into the major literary anthologies. In some cases, in order to retrieve interesting instances of free verse prior to 1800, I will evade the requirement of inclusion in an anthology. But twentieth-century anthologies, as it turns out, have done quite well at preserving earlier instances of free verse; one wonders if this may be an unconscious attempt at locating precursors to today's free verse, a consequence of Imagist metrics, or just a willingness to accept anything by a great name, such as Milton or Arnold, without bothering to wonder at its form or lack thereof.

Rarely is George Herbert's "The Collar" omitted from representative samples of his work; this poem, published in 1633, illustrates several of the points taken up in this chapter: it is an early example of free verse, it shows how a poet may play against established conventions to make a point, and it demonstrates the usefulness of identifying varieties of free verse. The foot scansion, of course, remains iambic, though with many substitutions. In this it somewhat resembles Milton's "At a Solemn Music," and it is similar in form to "Prufrock's" antecedents in Laforgue and Corbière, as well as Leopardi. Twentieth-century instances of this vers-libristic poetry are numerous and include a good number by Robert Penn Warren—and even Robert Creeley's "A Wicker Basket" (1959). As Herbert employs it, though, the very licentiousness of the form is made more evident because of the degree of real control that he exercises over his meters—and that, of course, is the gimmick: the subject of the poem is rebelliousness against the self-discipline required by his priestly vocation.

The fact that Herbert wrote only one free-verse poem might seem remarkable, and this could be used as an argument against its being called free; but he composed other types of experimental verse, including not only the well-known shaped poems, but some that incorporate additional varieties of ingenious patterning. Good free verse, although it makes a radical break with predictable lines and stanzas, is under the control of the poet. That control may be instinctive, intuitive, and unself-conscious, but as Eliot said, it comes of having mastered the rhythmic possibilities of the language.

THE COLLAR

   I struck the board and cried, "No more;
      I will abroad!
   What? shall I ever sigh and pine?
My lines and life are free, free as the road,
    Loose as the wind, as large as store.
       Shall I be still in suit?
   Have I no harvest but a thorn
   To let me blood, and not restore
What I have lost with cordial fruit?
      Sure there was wine
Before my sighs did dry it; there was corn
    Before my tears did drown it.
Is the year only lost to me?
    Have I no bays to crown it,
No flowers, no garland gay? all blasted?
    All wasted?
  Not so, my heart; but there is fruit,
    And thou hast hands.
  Recover all thy sigh-blown age
On double pleasures; leave thy cold dispute
Of what is fit and not. Forsake thy cage,
    Thy rope of sands,
Which petty thoughts have made, and made to thee
  Good cable to enforce and draw,
    And be thy law,
  While thou didst wink and wouldst not see.
    Away! take heed;
    I will abroad.
Call in thy death's-head there; tie up thy fears.
    He that forbears
  To suit and serve his need,
    Deserves his load."
But as I raved and grew more fierce and wild
    At every word,
  Methought I heard one calling, *Child!*
    And I replied, *My Lord.*

The line lengths are completely irregular and unpredictable. "My lines and life are *free,*" he declares! Rhymes are scattered randomly about, and line 13, "Is the year only lost to me?" does not match up with any other lines until we reach line 23, making it virtually independent. The whole thing is, of course, like so many of Herbert's poems, a display of angelic wit, of seraphic artifice. The very isolation of "me" as an unrhymed termination satirizes the egocentric impatience that caused this temper tantrum ("I," "me," and "my" have appeared in almost every line up to that point). Chafed by the restraint of the clerical collar, he bursts out in a metric that not only includes enjambments and jarring caesuras ("Sure there was wine / Before my sighs did dry it; there was corn / Before my tears did drown it") but one that violates the regularity of lines and stanzas as Donne never did. It introduces simultaneously images and themes of disorder; in the lines just quoted he is lamenting his failure to enjoy profane pleasures, the cakes and ale of carnal communion, deconsecrating the Host in his imagination.

Because of the speaker's spiritual submission at the close of the poem, as well as the appearance of rhymes, some may not wish to allow this poem to take its place as a specimen of vers-libristic poetry, even though the lines remain insubordinate to the end. Some may feel that free verse is not supposed to be as carefully crafted as this. And, of course, the whole thing is a parody of itself, a sort of self-imitation, such as the thinning down of the poem in "Easter Wings," and the joyous ascent of both poetic lines (literally, on the page) and spirit in the second stanza of that poem. It is not possible to know how consciously Herbert used the fad of the literary madrigal when he concocted the irregularities of "The Collar" and to what extent he was aware of that antiformalist eddy in prosody out of which spilled Pindarism. But surely the continuing appeal of this poem is that it has captured in so many ways the human impulse to kick over the traces, and it does this through a display of irregularity. One might say that he has secularized his meter in expressing the impulse to evade his responsibilities. In any case, since free verse is always a relative thing, free in comparison to something else, we may allow that "The Collar" is, in the context of the English seventeenth century, when intricate but repetitive stanza forms were the standard, a free-verse poem.

But Herbert was far ahead of his time in this poem, as he was in other ways in others. Vers-libristic poems prospered for some decades (1660–1720) under the rubric of the "Pindarique," but did not take permanent hold in English until the nineteenth century; as we shall see, Wordsworth, Southey, Shelley, and especially Matthew Arnold saw the possibilities of such loosened structures. After 1900, numerous models provided by French *vers-libristes* authorized experiments by Eliot and, quite separately, by Amy Lowell and the other Imagists. A detailed analysis of "Prufrock" appears in another chapter, but the practice of connecting lines of irregular length with unpredictable rhyme patterns, and of suggesting a loose larger structure by repeated lines and leitmotivs, a method invented by Jules Laforgue, has been frequently found in English since 1915. Amy Lowell's "Patterns" is a prime instance; the phrases "I walk down," "I shall walk," "my brocaded gown," "the softness of," and several others occur over and over like bells of a fixed timbre in the background. The poem as a whole takes the convention of the Browning dramatic monologue and systematically defeats Browning's usual iambic pentameter, in so doing producing an irregular cadence that suggests the troubled gait of the lady whose prospective husband has been killed. In the abrupt outburst that ends the poem Lowell may have borrowed an effect from William Morris. The emphasis on sharp visual detail, however, marks it as the work of an Imagist, and the shape of the poem reflects Lowell's wide acquaintance with the French writers, whose poems she anthologized, translated, and commented upon in *Six French Poets*. She was at work on "Patterns," published in the 1916 Imagist anthology, exactly at the time that she was compiling that collection. As I shall explain in discussing Eliot, the rhythmic effect parallels what occurred in French when the *vers-libristes* abandoned the *vers pairs* (lines with even numbers of syllables—eight, ten, twelve) for lines that were not only irregular in length, but that also contained uneven numbers of syllables: *impairs*. "Patterns" is very long; I quote only the opening and the end:

> I walk down the garden paths,
> And all the daffodils
> Are blowing, and the bright blue squills.
> I walk down the patterned garden paths
> In my stiff, brocaded gown.
> With my powdered hair and jeweled fan,
> I too am a rare
> Pattern. As I wander down
> The garden paths.

My dress is richly figured,
And the train
Makes a pink and silver stain
On the gravel, and the thrift
Of the borders.
Just a plate of current fashion,
Tripping by in high-heeled, ribboned shoes.
Not a softness anywhere about me,
Only whale-bone and brocade.
And I sink on a seat in the shade
Of a lime tree. For my passion
wars against the stiff brocade.
. . . .
In Summer and in Winter I shall walk
Up and down
The patterned garden paths
In my stiff, brocaded gown.
The squills and daffodils
Will give place to pillared roses, and to asters, and to snow.
I shall go
Up and down
In my gown,
Gorgeously arrayed,
Boned and stayed.
And the softness of my body will be guarded from embrace
By each button, hook, and lace.
For the man who should loose me is dead,
Fighting with the Duke in Flanders,
In a pattern called a war.
Christ! What are patterns for?

Most surprising, however, is to discover a poem by Yeats from about the same period—"Broken Dreams"—which uses all the vers-libristic techniques; this was included in *The Wild Swans at Coole* (1917), a volume in which the improved crispness of image and diction of some poems reflected the tutelage of Ezra Pound, although this poem, for all its license of form, reverts to a Celtic Twilight dreaminess.

BROKEN DREAMS
There is grey in your hair
Young men no longer suddenly catch their breath
When you are passing;
But maybe some old gaffer mutters a blessing
Because it was your prayer
Recovered him upon the bed of death.
For your sole sake—that all heart's ache have known,
And given to others all heart's ache.
From meagre girlhood's putting on
Burdensome beauty—for your sole sake
Heaven has put away the stroke of her doom.
So great her portion in that peace you make
By merely walking in a room.

Your beauty can but leave among us
Vague memories, nothing but memories.
A young man when the old men are done talking
Will say to an old man, "Tell me of that lady
The poet stubborn with his passion sang us
When age might well have chilled his blood."

Vague memories, nothing but memories.
But in the grave, all, all, shall be renewed.
The certainty that I shall see that lady
Leaning or standing or walking
In the first loveliness of womanhood,
And with the fervour of my youthful eyes,
Has set me muttering like a fool.

You are more beautiful than any one,
And yet your body had a flaw;
Your small hands were not beautiful,
And I am afraid that you will run
And paddle to the wrist
In that mysterious, always brimming lake
Where those that have obeyed the holy law
Paddle and are perfect. Leave unchanged
The hands that I have kissed,
For old sake's sake.

The last stroke of midnight dies.
All day in the one chair
From dream to dream and rhyme to rhyme I have ranged
In rambling talk with an image of air:
Vague memories, nothing but memories.

Yeats, of course, sticks even closer to the iambic pentameter norm than does Eliot in "Prufrock." But the intention of the poem is to ramble associatively—an extension of the loose pentameter of Coleridge's conversation poems. And the modulations of rhythm, though much less pronounced than Lowell's, exhibit more variety than repetition; as Yvor Winters said in the end about free verse, "[T]he norm is perpetual variation."

As we shall see what makes possible this perpetual variation is the abandonment of the idea that a poetic line is constructed of subsidiary units—whether syllables, accents, or feet—and the assumption that the fundamental unit of the poem is the unpredictable line. I will argue, however, that to be successful, such variation cannot be directed at the whim of the poet in accordance with some voice, some personal predilection, some privately articulated and unshareable technique, some prompting of unpredictable and inimitable genius. The variation acquires significance to the extent that it runs counter to a preexisting expectation. The disappearance of such expectations and their replacement by anticipated amorphousness make genuine free verse all but impossible, leaving us—as we approach the end of this century—with literary journals filled with attenuated and enervated imitations of the undoubted earlier triumphs in that iconoclastic medium.

Chapter 4

The First Cycle

The history of prosody in the English Renaissance is for the most part an account of the gradual rediscovery of accentual-syllabic meter, which Chaucer's followers had been unable to preserve, and the establishment of metrical conventions that persist until the present moment. While it is customary to point out the increasing freedom with which these newly accepted norms were employed (as in Shakespeare's later plays, in Jacobean drama, or Donne's poems), it is not common to suggest that there was any radical disruption to the fundamental prosody, and very seldom does anyone speak of free verse when discussing the poetry of that time. In some respects our contemporary view remains close to that of the early eighteenth century, which recognized the progress of meter in the direction of smoothness and sweetness, and away from "gothic" irregularity. Yet as we shall see in this chapter, hardly had conventions achieved stability than counterconventions appeared, some of which were extreme enough to be considered as free verse.

Since the eighteenth century, every revolution in prosody has also been a revolution against outworn poetic diction or against "academic" language. Timothy Steele puts it the other way in *Missing Measures,* making a strong case that twentieth-century disdain for meter is the consequence of a distaste for Victorian artificiality and pompousness. At any rate, the two seem to go together. At the beginning of the sixteenth century in England, however, exactly the opposite situation prevailed. The language of much poetry was pedestrian, the meter so awkward that regularity was almost impossible, and the progress of longer poems interrupted by irrelevant and tedious asides; in reading them one has the impression of being cornered by someone who is ignorant, garrulous, vulgar, and possibly drunk. The sheer boisterousness of Skeltonics makes them a good read, but one does not examine them in hopes of uncovering seven types of ambiguity. Poetry has never come so close to answering Wordsworth's call for a language really used by actual human beings, though we may have again approached this ideal in the last quarter of the twentieth century.

When poets aimed higher, the results could be even worse. Stephen Hawes was at least aware of his limitations; in "The Excusation of the Author," appended to *The Pastime of Pleasure* (1506), he wrote—

> Unto all poets I do me excuse
> If that I offend for lack of science.
> This little book yet do ye not refuse,
> Though it be devoid of famous eloquence.
> Add or detray by your high sapience,
> And pardon me of my high enterprise,
> Which of late this fable did feign and devise.
>
> 　　　　　　　　　　　　　　　　(Rollins 65)

Since *The Pastime of Pleasure* is already six thousand lines long, it is best that Hawes did not compose what he considered a big book. The apology, unlike those of Chaucer on which it is modeled, seems in other respects an accurate description of his work, and one hopes that his humility was genuine.

Good poems existed in the fifteenth and early sixteenth centuries, but they were in the folk forms that had never lost currency, the ballad and the song. Chaucer had scarcely bothered to cultivate these common modes, leaving them for the outland populace to enjoy, along with alliterative poetry, while he naturalized meters and stanzas from French and Italian models. His felicity in these more courtly measures died with him. What sounds like auditory stupidity on the part of his would-be followers in the early fifteenth century, whose efforts were hopelessly awkward, may have been due to their confusion over the rapidly evolving pronunciation of English during the period 1300–1500. As sound-values shifted, and especially as the final *e,* a remnant of Anglo-Saxon grammatical inflection, disappeared, it became impossible to read Chaucer's text without relearning it as an earlier form of English. Chaucer may have invented a new prosody, but no one wrote a textbook to explain it or to explain how pronunciation of the language needed to be modified in order to read the poetry correctly.

But the song and the ballad survived, adapting to changes in pronunciation. When Thomas Wyatt (1503?–1542) set himself the task of composing a lover's lament to be accompanied on the lute, his main problem was to achieve a refinement of diction and an aptness of imagery that improved upon commonplace expressions, much as Du Bellay called for *illustration* of the French language. Wyatt's meters were there, ready-made and readily accepted, and he needed only to take care that the words fit the measures with a little more exactness than in, say, "Alisoun" or "The Twa Corbies." Tetrameters and four- or five-line stanzas, often with a refrain, came to him almost as naturally as speech itself. When he emulated the brevity of Italian or French "trifles" in these native measures, the result was a happily finished-off poem ("My Lute, Awake" or "Forget Not Yet," for example). Wyatt's difficulties began when he essayed something that could serve as the English equivalent of the ten- or twelve-syllable line from the Romance languages, possibly even something comparable to the classical hexameter. He did not stumble nearly as badly as did Alexander Barclay (1475?–1552) and others whose efforts at retrieving the pentameter were even more galumphing than those of some who aim at a contemporary "new formalism." But Wyatt's ineptness in the pentameter was evident even to his contemporaries. *The Norton Anthology of English Literature* has included, since its second edition, the original version of "They Flee from Me" together with the revised version (which was not an improvement) offered by Richard Tottel, his first editor, in 1557. Tottel smoothed the meter but spoiled the diction.

Surrey (1517?–1547) took more readily to the iambic pentameter, working so hard to learn from Chaucer that many of his lines are near-duplicates of lines found in *Troilus and Criseyde*. Sometimes Surrey was too ready to fill metrical voids with expletives such as "eke" (a meaningless expression when so used); it has occurred to more than one person to call this "eke-ing" out his lines. But at his best, especially in the blank verse of his translation of *The Aeneid,* he achieved a suavity that made this line a convincing possibility for heroic epic and drama. His blank verse may have been suggested by Italian unrhymed verse, but in any case Surrey is always credited with the invention of this, the most important medium for serious poetry in English.

The first cycle of free verse that occurred in our language was a reaction against this hard-won regularity of the iambic pentameter; even more against its use in rhyming poetry in general; and most of all against its use in the English sonnet. We will therefore continue to trace the ways in which iambic pentameter achieved sufficient predictability so that it began to seem an impediment to easy expression rather than a vehicle and occasion for graceful ornamentation.

In terms of sheer bulk, iambic pentameter saw its widest deployment and greatest rhythmic elaboration in Elizabethan and Jacobean drama, serving as the prosodic medium for as many as two thousand plays. By the 1580s it was ubiquitous, but when Surrey was working on his *Aeneid* (ca. 1545), one dramatist, Nicholas Udall, essayed a comedy, *Roister Doister,* in which he used a rough "tumbling verse" that was close to the doggerel found in some late medieval plays:

> Master Roister Doister will straight go home and die;
> Our Lord Jesus Christ his soul have mercy upon.
> Thus you see today a man, tomorrow John.
> Yet saving for a woman's extreme cruelty,
> He might have lived yet a month or two or three,
> But in spite of Custance, which him hath wearied,
> His ma'ship shall be worshipfully buried.

(5.6)

These lines are typical of efforts made by anyone whose ear has never been trained to the conventions of accentual-syllabic meters. The only way to interpret the line metrically is to allow a rough four-beat rhythm, probably a survival of the Anglo-Saxon alliterative line, to dominate; but even in those terms the meter is less musical than that of *Piers Plowman,* an alliterative measure current in Chaucer's own time. The *Roister Doister* passage resembles an ad hoc improvisation for an awards ceremony at a fraternal lodge—and like such a performance, its rough-and-ready rhyming served its purpose, for Udall and for many another sixteenth-century playwright. Shakespeare used tumbling meter in *The Comedy of Errors,* and Ben Jonson revived it as late as 1606 for comic effect, as the appropriate meter for an improvised performance-within-the performance in *Volpone* (1.2). There it approximates anapestic tetrameter, just as it had in *Gammer Gurton's Needle* (William Stevenson, 1563). Because the earliest comedies were authored by university-trained scholars, one wonders if they thought they were attempting something like a classical hexameter deliberately coarsened to make it appropriate to the rustic language and characters, or whether they were taking a holiday from Latin and Greek meters. In any event, tumbling verse is so inept that it constantly must be forced into some semblance of regularity by keeping the line delivery isochronic and coming down hard on the rhymes, the way that contemporary rap songs do.

English audiences were treated soon enough to regular meters. I cannot agree altogether with Swinburne that the first blank-verse play, Norton and Sackville's *Gorboduc* (1562), is pure metrical monotony, but the aim was regularity, and regularity is what its authors achieved; if that play were used to test a student's grasp of scansion, anyone who marked every single line as perfectly regular iambic pentameter would get a passing grade. Twenty-five years after *Gorboduc,* Christopher Marlowe could take the underlying pentameter for granted and play against it; picking a passage at random from *Tamburlaine the Great* (1588), we see:

> Awake, ye men of Memphis! Hear the clang
> Of Scythian trumpets; hear the basilisks,
> That roaring shake Damascus' turrets down.
>
> (4.1)

But the miracle of Marlovian expressiveness was reserved for the soliloquy at the end of *Doctor Faustus,* where the disrupted meter mirrors the desperation of the protagonist, especially since it follows immediately after a formal, almost stilted, exchange between the Good and Bad Angels that has concluded in rhyming couplets. The Bad Angel describes the torments of hell with the calm regularity of a mechanic adding up an astronomical bill for automobile repairs, and what had remained of Faustus's composure vanishes:

> Ah, Faustus,
> Now hast thou but one bare hour to live
> And then thou must be damned perpetually!
> Stand still, you ever-moving spheres of heaven,
> That time may cease and midnight never come;
> Fair Nature's eye, rise, rise again, and make
> Perpetual day; or let this hour be but
> A year, a month, a week, a natural day,
> That Faustus may repent and save his soul!
> *O lente lente currite noctis equi.*
> The stars move still, time runs, the clock will strike,

> The devil will come, and Faustus must be damned.
> O, I'll leap up to my God! Who pulls me down?
> See, see, where Christ's blood streams in the firmament—
> One drop would save my soul—half a drop! Ah, my Christ!
>
> (5.15)

In the last line quoted the meter, too, has vanished. But this is not free verse. As we shall see, Shakespeare disrupted his prosody in *King Lear* even more violently—but, in both plays, like the violence in the plots themselves, metrical chaos resolves into an orderly context. After Faustus is dragged screaming into the mouth of hell, where, in some performances, he is rent in pieces that are then ejected onto the stage, the "Chorus" reappears with the quiet moralizing lines, "Cut is the branch that might have grown full straight, / And burned is Apollo's laurel bough / That sometime grew within this learned man." We are back into perfectly metered pentameter. This is what we expected at the start of the play.

The progress of Shakespeare's dramatic prosody in the course of more than twenty years (ca. 1587–1610) epitomizes what occurred in poetry both on and off the stage between 1550 and 1620. His earliest identifiable plays—*The Comedy of Errors* and the three parts of *Henry VI*—exhibit a mechanical regularity enlivened (in *Comedy*) by patches of awkwardly exuberant tumbling meter. Within a few years (1590–1596) he achieved an easy, if still extremely regular, command of rhythm and rhyme and displayed his virtuosity in *A Midsummer Night's Dream, Richard II,* and *Romeo and Juliet;* each of these plays contains more rhyming lines than any others that he composed in their respective genres, ranging up to an astonishing 45 percent for *Dream.* From 1597 through 1605 there was a steady loosening of the metrical reins and a steady extension of the expressive possibilities of the pentameter line. Statistical compilations easily demonstrate this, showing much larger percentages of hypermetric and enjambed lines in the later plays. Some of these studies are unreadably dense with minute distinctions and are aimed mainly at dating the plays; George T. Wright's *Shakespeare's Metrical Art* (1988) provides as thorough and intelligent a discussion, it seems to me, as the subject will ever require.

Shakespeare's increasing disruptions of the basic meter culminate in passages that have been called free verse. Take, for example, Lear's speech:

> Ay, every inch a king.
> When I do stare, see how the subject quakes.
> I pardon that man's life. What was thy cause?
> Adultery?
> Thou shalt not die. Die for adultery? No.
> The wren goes to't, and the small gilded fly
> Does lecher in my sight.
> Let copulation thrive; for Gloucester's bastard son
> Was kinder to his father than my daughters
> Got 'tween lawful sheets.
>
> (4.5)

But as with *Faustus* we expect the restoration of order, and we get it, in Edgar's concluding speech:

> The weight of this sad time we must obey,
> Speak what we feel, not what we ought to say.
> The oldest hath borne most; we that are young
> Shall never see so much, nor live so long.
>
> (5.3)

The deficient and hypermetric lines of Lear's outburst represent metrically the vacuities and superabundances that alternate within his disordered mind. The iambs march on, though unheard except as a lunatic flutter and hum in the mad king's brain.

Jacobean drama also furnishes connections between the accomplished rhyming and metered plays of the 1590s and various kinds of seventeenth-century extravagance. To take only one example, Cyril Tourneur's *The Revenger's Tragedy* of about 1606 includes many extended passages composed of heroic couplets—but at the same time there are truncated lines that much resemble the literary madrigal and its more elaborate successor, the pseudo-Pindaric ode. The immediate metrical texture of the play is not that far removed from what Milton would do in "Lycidas," while the far-fetched tropes are comparable in their baroque curiosity to Donne and Marvell.

Evolution from initial awkwardness through ornamented regularity, and then from excessive polish toward deliberately roughened expressiveness, occurred in shorter poems as well as on the stage, and we now return to where we left off with Surrey.

Like Wyatt, George Gascoigne could turn a graceful song in tetrameters; unlike Wyatt, he so thoroughly subdued the pentameter as to take all the starch out of it:

> Alas my Lord, while I do muse hereon,
> And call to mind my youthful years mis-spent,
> That all my senses are in silence pent.
> My mind is rapt in contemplation ["play-she-on"]
> Wherein my dazzled eyes only behold
> The black hour of my constellation ["lay-she-on"]
> Which framed me so luckless on the mould.
>
> ("Gascoigne's Woodmanship" 89–95)

Gascoigne's lines date from about 1570; twenty years later Edmund Spenser wrote with equal smoothness, but with a richness of vocabulary, sound, and imagery that compensates for the metrical plainness, in this description of the House of Busyrane:

> For round about the wals yclothed were
>   With goodly arras of great majesty,
>   Wouen with gold and silke so close and nere,
>   That the rich metall lurked priuily,
>   As faining to be hid from enuious eye;
>   Yet here, and there, and euery where vnwares
>   It shewd it selfe, and shone vnwillingly;
>   Like a discoloured Snake, whose hidden snares
> Through the greene gras his long bright burnisht backe declares.
>
> (*FQ* 3.11.28)

But even as the poetry of the English Renaissance approached perfection in a splendidly varied predictability, another spirit was creeping in, making its appearance in the work of the same poet (Spenser), insinuating itself almost imperceptibly into the texture of two of the most mellifluous and harmonious poems ever composed. George Saintsbury, gazing ahead from his chapter on the Spenserian 1590s, wrote:

> Still more alone, and still more unmistakably, stand the *Prothalamion* and *Epithalamion,* the first of the great English odes, and to this day

[1906] two of the greatest experiments in that regularly or irregularly strophied arrangement which numbers among its triumphs the achievements of Milton and Dryden, of Gray and Collins, of Keats and Wordsworth, of Tennyson, and Arnold, and Mr. Swinburne . . . a very large part of that beauty is derived from the unerring modulation of the variously lengthened and shortened lines. (1:362)

Despite the lack of perfect symmetry in Spenser's marriage poems, one feels no temptation to refer to them as free verse; but the Italianate experimentation with the shortening of some pentameter lines to trimeters, however regularly repeated, provided the warrant for more radical freedoms claimed by Milton and by Abraham Cowley in the next century.

Almost Spenser's contemporary, Philip Sidney found another way to counter the incipient rigidity of the pentameter. Here for the first time it makes sense to connect the Protestant sturdiness of his character, the youthful romantic ebullience, with a distinctive "voice" whose urgencies and emphases animate his rhythms, as in these lines from sonnet 21 in *Astrophil and Stella:*

> Your words, my friend (right healthfull caustiks) blame
> My young mind marde, whom *Love* doth windlas so,
> That mine owne writings like bad servants show
> My wits, quicke in vaine thoughts, in vertue lame.

Are we all that far from Donne's "For God's sake hold your tongue and let me love" here, or when we read the famous opening line of 31, "With how sad steps, O moon, thou climb'st the skies"? Yet nowhere in the writings of Sidney is there anything that warrants our ingenuity in identifying it as free verse. Donne comes somewhat closer in "The Dissolution," where the breakdown of the metrical scheme imitates the separation of the beloved's body into its constituent elements. Also, Donne permits the Hebraic poetic phrasing of the Bible, as imitated in Anglican liturgy, to override the meter and stanza form in "A Litany." In this poem, although it is not free verse, he employs the phrase-breaking enjambments characteristic of William Carlos Williams three hundred years later, bringing the poem to the very edge of vers-libertinage, much as—we shall see—his sermons verge on poetry from the other direction:

Father of heaven, and him, by whom
It, and us for it, and all else, for us
  Thou mad'st, and govern'st ever, come
And re-create me, now grown ruinous:
    My heart is by dejection, clay,
    And by self-murder, red.
From this red earth, O Father, purge away
All vicious tinctures, that new fashioned
I may rise up from death, before I am dead.

Sidney also at one point had come close to free verse, borrowing, like Spenser, from the Italians. In the *Old Arcadia,* the character Basilius, "seeynge the Sunne what speede hee made to leave oure West, to doo his office in the other Hemisphere, his Inwarde Muses made hym in his best Musick singe this Madrigall." William A. Ringler's commentary on this passage identifies the poem that follows as a "non-Petrarchan type of madrigal" and says, "This appears to be the earliest appearance of the word and the type in English" (Sidney 408). Here, again, is Sidney— once more sounding much like a godfather to John Donne ("Busy old fool, unruly sun") in his "Madrigall":

Why doost thou haste away
O *Titan* faire, the giver of the daie?
Is it to carry newes
To Westerne wightes, what starres in East appeare?
Or doost thou thinke that heare
Is left a Sunne, whose beames thy place may use?
Yet stay and well peruse,
What be her giftes, that make her equall thee,
Bend all thy light to see
In earthly clothes enclosde a heavenly sparke.
Thy running course cannot such bewties marke:
No, no, thy motions bee
Hastened from us with barre of shadow darke,
Because that thou, the author of our sight,
Disdainst we see thee staind with other's light.

                                (80)

Since I will shortly be arguing the case that poems very like this can be considered as free verse, I would like to explain why I choose not to see Sidney's madrigal in that way. First, Sidney invented yet another song for the same character, in which he reproduced exactly the line lengths and the rhymes of this poem; it appears then that he was experimenting with *establishing* a formal convention, rather than departing from it. Second, the context of the prose tale, in which appear all sorts of other songs, miniature odes, epigrams, eclogues, and so forth, argues for the poem's being a minor embellishment rather than a radical departure. The later development of the secular masque allowed for a medley of forms, but that is no reason to consider the masque free verse; it is rather a collection of individual pieces. Each unit within the masque proceeds according to its own rules. *Within* a masque, of course, there may be irregular poems: madrigals, "odes," and songs that do furnish a semilibertine contrast to the more regular segments. That most such variants were set to music further complicates the question, since a composer often calls for a repetition of lines in the actual performance that makes the madrigal more organized than it appears when simply printed as poetry. My intention is to stick to a consideration of poems composed as freestanding works of verbal art, not as ancillaries to some other medium; for purposes of this discussion, *madrigal* always means a literary performance, though one that—like the sonnet— had originally been modeled on a song lyric and most of the examples of which actually did continue to be sung. The literary madrigal also separated itself from its origins as a song lyric, and in so doing permitted a free form of versification.

Exact identification of the literary madrigal as a form (or nonform) is not easy. Some varieties of fungus exist that seem plantlike but that exhibit animal behavior; the literary madrigal is like Falstaff's otter, neither fish nor flesh. As a consequence of the formation of madrigal societies in the past two centuries, as well as our awareness of its original signification, we think of it mainly in musical terms—and indeed collections of madrigals draw mostly from Renaissance songbooks, identified as such. But as French Rowe Fogle says in *A Critical Study of William Drummond of Hawthornden,* "Although originally the literary madrigal was primarily designed for a musical setting, many such poems were written for their own sake" (97). By 1590 three collections of madrigals (by Nicholas Yonge, William Byrd, and Thomas Watson) had appeared, containing translations from Italian, but also native English lyrics (in

Byrd's *Psalmes, Sonets, and Songs of Sadnes and Pietie*). This was only the beginning of the spate of songbooks that poured out over the next three decades, many of which included "madrigals," which in some instances came to mean short poems of indeterminate form, loosely imitated from Italian originals. While the popularity of the songbook as a source of lyrics to be set and sung to music continued into the early seventeenth century—meaning that most poems designated as madrigals were indeed intended to be sung—the form also insinuated itself into sonnet sequences, where, it is clear, it was seen as a literary performance independent of music.

In 1593 a collection appeared of which it might be said the title and author's name are more memorable than the poems it contains: *Parthenophil and Parthenope* by Barnabe Barnes, who evidently hoped to emulate Philip Sidney. In a way he surpassed Sidney, carrying youthful high spirits to the point of outrageousness. According to Thomas Nashe in *Have with You* (as quoted by Victor A. Doyno in his edition of Barnes), that colorful poet achieved notoriety by "getting him a strange payre of *Babilonian* britches, with a codpisse as big as a *Bolognian* sawcedge, and so went up and downe Towne, and shewde himself in the Presence at Court, where he was generally laught out by the Noblemen and Ladies." And according to Janet Scott: "Il ressemble à ces romantiques français de 1830, qui voulaient avant tout 'épater les gens'" (86). [He resembles those French Romantics of 1830 who wanted above all else to astonish ordinary people.] I nominate this free spirit, this proto-Romantic, Barnabe Barnes, as my candidate for the first free-verse writer in English, on the grounds that he abandoned the regular forms of his sonnet sequence and inserted literary madrigals that are quite unpredictable in terms of line length, number of lines, and rhyme pattern, and some of which even include unrhymed lines. Barnes anticipated by nearly a half-century those licenses in *Lycidas* that helped to provoke Dr. Johnson's censure. In "Madrigal 25," for example, the "rage" of the first line never pairs up:

> Whiles these two wrathfull goddesses did rage,
>   The little god of might,
> (Such as might fitter seeme with craynes to fight,
> Then with his bow to vanquish goddes, and kinges)
>   In a cherry-tree sate smiling;
> And lightly wauing with his motley winges,
> Fayre winges, in bewtie boyes, and gyrles beguiling,

And cherry garlandes with his hands compiling
   Laughing, he leaped light
Vnto the Nymph, to try which way best might
Her cheare, and with a cherry braunche her bobbed:
   But her soft louely lippes
The cherryes, of their ruddie rubye robbed:
   Eftsoones he to his quiuer skippes,
And bringes those bottles whence his mother sippes
   Her nectar of delight,
Which in her bosome clamed place by right.

                            (63–64)

A certain licentiousness of subject and manner accompanied the metrical freedom and made Barnes repellent to nineteenth-century scholars; John Erskine speaks of his "cold-blooded frankness, [which] seems nothing short of brutal" and states: "The so-called madrigals, odes, and elegies scattered through the series are nothing but irregular rime-forms and cannot be generalized" (143). I would, however, venture to generalize the literary madrigal as a free-verse alternative to the sonnet. The degree of rebellion here is certainly far less remarkable than what occurred early in the twentieth century because in the 1590s the weight of metrical tradition was much less burdensome and more easily thrown aside; to call the literary madrigal free verse is not to argue that the Elizabethan literary madrigal is only a step away from *Paterson,* but rather to identify the first instance of a resistance to received forms. The Peasant's Revolt of the fourteenth century did not produce the same results as the French Revolution, but it was a popular insurgency all the same; it is human nature to resist oppression. The earliest theorists of twentieth-century free verse, such as Amy Lowell and T. S. Eliot, did not hesitate to reach back to the Renaissance for examples, and it simply will not do to retort with huffy pedantry, "Well, it's iambics all the same," especially since in the most extreme case—in many of the choruses of Milton's *Samson Agonistes*— the meter no longer *was* iambic. Nevertheless, should anyone demand it, I am willing to concede that these earlier undulations of English prosody seem far removed from the groundswell that culminated and broke at the start of the twentieth century. But the oscillation is already evident between fixed and free forms.

   The sonnet itself, of course, has never been a perfectly fixed standard; the most restrictive definitions of it include two or more varieties, and when the major sonnet sequences were being composed in the 1580s and 1590s, which established it as a permanent metrical resource, it meant no more than "little song." The first sonnet in *Astrophil and Stella,* "Loving in truth, and fain in verse my love to show," contains fourteen lines, but they are hexameters, and the rhyme scheme is *abababababcdcdee;* the next sonnet is pentameter, but rhymes *abbaabbacdcdee,* and might as well be printed as a Petrarchan sonnet. Those that follow vary in other ways. Barnes regularly used fifteen lines, putting a rhyme royal seven-line stanza in place of a closing sestet. For most poets, however, the sonnet did come to mean a fourteen-line poem with a regular rhyme pattern and with lines of identical length. There was a certain charm in succeeding within these limitations; but there was also a certain tediousness in trying to do it time after time. The literary madrigal was a way out, and half the appeal of the literary madrigal was that it departed from an established metrical norm. It was still close enough in length to the sonnet to be recognizable as something that was *not* a sonnet or, if you will, a completely irregular sonnet. Edward Bliss Reed said, "In technique the sonnet and madrigal do not approach each other; the madrigal form was not a fixed one either in its rhyme scheme or in the number of its verses" (210). Precisely; the poetic form known as the literary madrigal can be designated as the antisonnet. It represents an escape from what had become a restrictive form; it was an avenue for less inhibited expression. But the very freedom of the madrigal presupposes an ear attuned to the pentameter line and to the regularly recurring rhymes of the sonnet. Put another way, the madrigal would lose much of its effect if it did not have an air of freedom to it. It owes some of this sense of freedom to the discipline of the sonneteers.

A better poet than Barnes, but likewise a quirky personality, was William Drummond, best known for having written down Ben Jonson's crusty assessments of their contemporaries when Jonson visited him in Scotland. Drummond composed many sonnets; F. R. Fogle's thorough study of these leads him to conclude that Drummond's treatment of the form bordered on the licentious and that his sonnets settle into forms that are not distinctly either English or Petrarchan. Most of them lead off with an *abba* quatrain as if they were headed south toward Italy, but most draw up in Shakespearean fashion, with a concluding couplet. Usually the rhymes of the first quatrain reappear in the second, in some form; the third quatrain is quite independent of both. In short, Drummond's handling of the sonnet is a good example of the way in which, in advance of, or accompanying, the appearance of free verse, we find poets taking increasing liberties with established conventions, experimenting and reaching for new possibilities. Drummond began composing poems about 1610, when, as Douglas Bush says, commenting on Shakespeare's sonnets in *The Complete Pelican Shakespeare,* "[T]he main vogue of sonneteering had long passed." In 1609 Shakespeare's sonnets had been published in full for the first time; if there were a way of rendering a rhyme scheme canonical, that ought to have been it. But Drummond, ensconced among his books and friends in Scotland, went his own way. And his own way also included not only idiosyncratic sonnets and madrigals, but an extension of the madrigal into something resembling an irregular ode. Here is a poem that appears in many anthologies of seventeenth-century poetry:

SONG 2
Phoebus, arise,
And paint the sable skies
With azure, white and red;
Rouse Memnon's mother from her Tithon's bed,
That she thy career may with roses spread.
The nightingales thy coming eachwhere sing:
     Make an eternal spring;
Give life to this dark world which lieth dead;
Spread forth thy golden hair
In larger locks than thou was wont before,
And, emperor-like, decore
With diadem of pearl thy temples fair;
Chase hence the ugly night,
Which serves but to make dear thy glorious light.
That is the happy morn,
That day, long-wished day,
Of all my life so dark
(If cruel stars have not my ruin sworn,
And fates not hope betray),
Which, only white, deserves
A diamond forever should it mark:
This is the morn should bring unto this grove
My love, to hear and recompense my love.

Fair king, who all preserves,
But show thy blushing beams,
And thou two sweeter eyes
Shalt see than those which by Peneus' streams
Did once thy heart surprise;
Nay, suns, which shine as clear
As thou when two thou did to Rome appear.
Now, Flora, deck thyself in fairest guise.
If that ye, winds, would hear
A voice surpassing far Amphion's lyre,
Your stormy chiding stay;
Let zephyr only breathe,
   And with her tresses play,
Kissing sometimes those purple ports of death.
The winds all silent are,
And Phoebus in his chair,
Ensaffroning the air,
Makes vanish every star;
Night like a drunkard reels
Beyond the hills to shun his flaming wheels;
The fields with flow'rs are decked in every hue;
The clouds bespangle with bright gold their blue:
Here is the pleasant place,
And ev'ry thing save her who all should grace.

Are we not, in 1616, halfway between the subliminal irregularities of Spenser's marriage poems and the loosened exuberance of Milton's "Lycidas"? Can we not hear simultaneously "And all the woods shall answer, and their echoes ring" and:

Bring the rathe primrose that forsaken dies,
The tufted crow-toe and pale jessamine,
The white pink and the pansy freaked with jet,
The glowing violet,
The musk-rose and the well-attired woodbine
With cowslips wan that hand the pensive head

                                             (142–47)

Drummond's library included sixty-one titles in Italian, and Milton may have read everything in print in that language. These headstrong British poets made over Italianate conventions into something that suited them better, into relaxed lines that better accommodated their enthusiasms. Leopardi's Romantic *versi liberi* of the 1820s were modeled on the Italian sources familiar to Drummond and Milton. Milton's love of freedom and Drummond's stubborn individualism mark them, too, as essentially romantic personalities who chafed at the bondage of rhyme.

In 1633 Milton composed two poems that are reminiscent of Drummond's "Phoebus Arise"; these are "On Time" and "At a Solemn Music." Whether he had Drummond's piece in mind or not, Milton was drawing from the same well of Italianate and Spenserian fluidity, adding a Jonsonian smoothness. As F. T. Prince argues in *The Italian Element in Milton's Verse,* "[T]he other two pieces of this period are indeed sufficiently Italianate, but they take as their basis an Italian form, the madrigal, which is less exacting than the *canzone,* and which Milton can develop with characteristic power" (63). Prince goes on to say, incorrectly, "Drummond of Hawthornden was the only poet writing in English who had closely imitated the madrigals and epigrams of Tasso and his followers." As we have noted, thousands of madrigals were composed, and many had been translations from Italian. Prince, perhaps following Douglas Bush's description in *English Literature in the Earlier Seventeenth Century,* defines the madrigal as "merely one stanza of a *canzone*—a stanza which was not repeated." This seems reasonable, but he continues in the same sentence, "and it shared with the *canzone* the metrical basis of hendecasyllables and heptasyllables which had proved useful in English verse." This last assertion not only fails to describe the English madrigal, which could contain lines as short as two or four syllables, but appears to forget that English iambics come in syllabic pairs and tend to come out in even numbers when added together. Prince qualifies this partially, saying, "The Italian heptasyllable found its theoretic equivalent in English in a line of six syllables and three stresses." When one examines "At a Solemn Music," one finds acephalous lines that actually *are* heptasyllabics, though each one retains four stresses: "Hymns devout and holy Psalms / Singing everlastingly." In neither this poem nor in "On Time" do we find unrhymed lines, though "With Saintly shout and solemn Jubilee" has to wait seven lines for "everlastingly" to tie it back in. If these are not free verse, they certainly dwell close to that frontier; as I have already said, *vers libre* has often designated poems that are more strictly patterned than Milton's poem:

ON TIME

Fly envious *Time,* till thou run out thy race,
Call on the lazy leaden-stepping hours,
Whose speed is but the heavy Plummet's pace;
And glut thyself with what thy womb devours,
Which is no more than what is false and vain,
And merely mortal dross;
So little is our loss,
So little is thy gain.
For when as each thing bad thou hast entomb'd,
And, last of all, thy greedy self consum'd,
The long eternity shall greet our bliss
With an individual kiss;
And Joy shall overtake us as a flood,
When everything that is sincerely good
And perfectly divine,
With Truth, and Peace, and Love, shall ever shine
About the supreme Throne
Of him, t'whose happy-making sight alone,
When once our heav'nly-guided soul shall climb,
Then all this Earthy grossness quit,
Attir'd with Stars, we shall forever sit,
    Triumphing over Death, and Chance, and thee O Time.

William Fitzgerald in *Agonistic Poetry* discusses the second poem, "At a Solemn Music," and calls it "highly Pindaric" (179). Although it is certainly true that Milton knew Pindar, and although these two poems in some ways resemble the pseudo-Pindaric ode popularized by Cowley, I cannot see in either poem the erratic progress, the frenzy, or the afflatus supposedly cultivated in that form. They are expanded literary madrigals. But they certainly do anticipate the even greater metrical license that Milton was to permit himself in later poems. As Saintsbury points out— "the prosodic forms of 'At a Solemn Music,' 'Time,' and 'The Circumcision' are chiefly interesting to compare with the choruses of *Samson* long afterwards" (2:212). F. T. Prince arrives at a similar view, saying that they point forward to *Lycidas* and the choruses of *Samson Agonistes*.

Before continuing with Milton it may be well to confront squarely the problems that arise in suggesting that any poetry that he wrote can be called free verse. The major obstacle may be that much twentieth-century free verse relies wholly or in part on typographical arrangement, whereas Milton's appeal—despite Samuel Johnson's description of *Paradise Lost* as "verses only to the eye"—is mainly to the ear. It does seem preposterous to establish a category that would include *The Cantos* alongside *Samson Agonistes*. But if we consider free verse as depending upon freedom from a preexisting norm, we may allow that Milton not only stretched the pentameter to new lengths but that, at times, he moved completely outside the line. In *Samson Agonistes* he opens the work by establishing iambic pentameter as a norm and then introduces truncated lines that, in many of the choruses, become self-contained units that no longer can be subdivided into iambic (or any other) feet. The line itself becomes the atomic unit of the prosody, as it did again 250 years later.

With Milton, however, arguments over prosody may mask disagreements over other issues. Those who wish to see Milton as a solid pillar of Christian orthodoxy, despite his defects of character such as the "surly republicanism" remarked by Dr. Johnson, will not care to see him connected in any way with twentieth-century heresy, prosodic or otherwise. For this reason Douglas Bush, alas, is not on my side, stating flatly of *Samson,* "The irregular lines are not free verse, they are patterns, new in their abundance and variety, of the syllabic metre Milton had always used" (418). Such an argument seems to me designed to distinguish Milton from twentieth-century prosodic heretics such as Eliot, Pound, and Williams—to bring him safely into the fold of Christian humanism and the great line of British poets from Chaucer to Tennyson who have raised accentual-syllabic metrical poetry to a level equaling ancient achievements in quantitative meters. That accomplishment makes poetry in English comparable to the corpus left by the Latin poets, and scholars who honor the great central tradition of accentual-syllabic prosody prefer to keep it separate from twentieth-century metrical apostasy. That means treating Milton as a traditionalist.

But others will wish to exclude Milton as a vers-librist on entirely different grounds. Anyone who is convinced that nothing earlier than Whitman matters as poetry will refuse to take any interest in Milton, seeing in him only another prehistoric rhymer. On the other hand, I believe, William Blake, who took a great deal of interest in Milton, would have been in enthusiastic agreement with the contention that

Milton wrote free verse, as would Shelley; but one fears that in making
common cause with these Romantics, however one may love many of
their poems, one becomes committed to other opinions that are funda-
mentally unsound.

If this discussion appears to be blurring irresponsibly the lines be-
tween poetic craft, personal temperament, and religious belief and opin-
ion, I would argue that for many readers of Milton these things fuse
indistinguishably. To recapitulate some varieties of opinion about Mil-
ton's person and doctrine, opinions that unfortunately, and somewhat
irrelevantly, affect views taken of his prosody:

1. Despite his defects as a person, Milton was a great champion of
   order and orthodoxy on earth and a great conservator of tradi-
   tion, and this was all to the good, and he could not therefore have
   written free verse.
2. Milton defended civilized values and generally used metered po-
   etry, and also he was a believing Puritan Christian, and this was
   all to the bad, and he could not possibly have written free verse
   because he was too stodgily conventional.
3. Milton was a great rebel, "of the party of the devil without
   knowing it" (Blake, Shelley, et al.). This was a good thing, and
   anything that demonstrates his willingness to disturb orthodoxy
   is all to the good, and everything he wrote was free verse, more
   or less.
4. Milton was an additional instance of northern European neo-
   Hebraism that expressed itself not only in the Reformation but
   also in the Romantic movement and as such was a menace to
   truly civilized values, including poetic meter. (This is an extrapo-
   lation from certain comments on Milton by George Santayana.)

It is hard to discuss Milton's prosody without becoming entangled
in these, or similar, issues. If, however, one can accept an apolitical and
agnostic use of *free verse* to designate poetry the form of which is unpre-
dictable, which achieves some of its effects by deliberately departing
from an established prosodic convention, and in which the line rather
than the foot functions as the fundamental prosodic unit, then one may
say that Milton at times wrote free verse.

A consideration of Milton's opinions and personality supports this
view. His writing of free verse, if we can allow that term, is quite in

keeping with his advocacy of divorce, his defense of free speech, his belief in free will, and his general cantankerousness. Promotion of Milton as a free-verse writer might very well enhance his reputation in some quarters, much as—according to a dryly ironical remark once made by Douglas Bush to a class—the discovery that Wordsworth had an illegitimate child did his. An argument *ad doctrinam* may not be any more valid than one ad hominem, but it is a seldom-mentioned fact that in chapter 10 of *De Doctrina Christiana* Milton put the case, with a great display of biblical erudition and great cogency of argument, in favor of polygamy. I submit that a proponent of polygamy is capable of committing free verse. The appeal to authority makes a more legitimate argument, however, provided the authority is sufficiently respectable; there are still some scholars who would dismiss T. S. Eliot's criticism as "journalism," but the continuing appearance of his key essays on literature in anthologies appears to attest to their importance. In his 1947 essay on Milton— intended, in part, to atone for his strictures of 1936 and earlier—Eliot uses the term free verse without qualification or apology. He begins, in the passage quoted below, by quoting at length from Samuel Johnson's *Life,* and then adds his own reflections:

"The variety of pauses [says Johnson, speaking of *Paradise Lost*], so much boasted by the lovers of blank verse, changes the measures of an English poet to the periods of a declaimer; and there are only a few skilful and happy readers of Milton, who enable their audience to perceive where the lines end or begin. *Blank verse,* said an ingenious critic, *seems to be verse only to the eye.*"

Some of my audience [adds Eliot] may recall that this last remark, in almost the same words, was often made, a literary generation ago, about the "free verse" of the period: and even without this encouragement from Johnson it would have occurred to my mind to declare Milton to be the greatest master of free verse in our language. (*On Poetry and Poets* 180)

I have already mentioned more than once the irregularities of *Lycidas;* it will be more rewarding for readers to observe them themselves than for me to tabulate them here. Those who wish to deny the poem status as free verse may point out that it resolves itself at the end in a series of quietly modulated, rhyming pentameters, and may argue that anything that ends so is not free. Persnickety formalists may feel that

Milton has slighted his job by leaving many lines unrhymed in the body
of the poem. For reasons that were at least in part prosodic, neither Dr.
Johnson nor, in this century, Yvor Winters had any use for *Lycidas,*
sensing something artificial, insincere, and subversive about it. Robert
Frost knew it by heart, however, and loved to talk about it; Frost's closest
approaches to free verse use *Lycidas* as a model, as in the truncated lines of
"After Apple Picking." *Lycidas* will last.

    Samson Agonistes, too, will last, but its magnificence will reach a
smaller audience. One comes across many references to its famous cho-
ruses, but not many people read the play, even though the *Norton Anthol-
ogy of English Literature* includes it in toto. In support of the idea that it
includes something that could be called free verse, I will begin by citing
Samson's opening speech; after eighty highly expressive lines of blank
verse it departs into extreme irregularity, reflecting the disordered pas-
sion of Samson's outburst. The following passage begins at line 68 and
illustrates in a compressed way how free verse originates, first as a
roughening and stretching of a convention, and then as an abrupt and
total break from it.

> O loss of sight, of thee I most complain!
> Blind among enemies, O worse than chains,
> Dungeon, or beggary, or decrepit age!
> Light the prime work of God to me is extinct,
> And all her various objects of delight
> Annull'd, which might in part my grief have eas'd
> Inferior to the vilest now become
> Of man or worm; the vilest here excel me,
> They creep, they see; I dark in light expos'd
> To daily fraud, contempt, abuse, and wrong,
> Within doors, or without, still as a fool,
> In power of others, never in my own;
> Scarce half I seem to live, dead more than half.
> O dark, dark, dark, amid the blaze of noon,
> Irrecoverably dark, total Eclipse
> Without all hope of day!
> O first created Beam, and thou great Word,
> "Let there be light, and light was over all";
> Why am I thus bereav'd thy prime decree?
> The Sun to me is dark

And silent as the Moon,
When she deserts the night,
Hid in her vacant interlunar cave.

After Dalila's visit and departure, the Chorus tells Samson (beginning with line 1010):

It is not virtue, wisdom, valor, wit,
Strength, comeliness of shape, or amplest merit
That woman's love can win or long inherit;
But what it is, hard is to say,
Harder to hit,
(Which way soever men refer it)
Much like thy riddle, *Samson,* in one day
Or seven, though one should musing sit.

This vers libre is typical of all the choruses. But might not one take the argument that *Doctor Faustus* and *King Lear,* however disordered for expressive purposes by the crises of the plays, are not free verse because they resolve themselves at the end, and apply that argument to *Samson?* The conclusion of the play seems to argue otherwise:

All is best, though we oft doubt,
And ever best found in the close.
Oft he seems to hide his face,
But unexpectedly returns
And to his faithful Champion hath in place
Bore witness gloriously; whence *Gaza* mourns
And all that band them to resist
His uncontrollable intent;
His servants he with new aquist
Of true experience from this great event
With peace and consolation hath dismist,
And calm of mind, all passion spent.

If anything, the very last line is a perfect Greek dipodic dimeter; compare it with "A little onward lend thy guiding hand," the perfect English iambic pentameter that opened the play. How could we know that we would end this way?

Karl Shapiro's *Essay on Rime* is not an altogether reliable guide, but Shapiro's lines do provide one more opinion about Milton's irregularity:

> The chorus
> Of Milton's *Samson,* endlessly discussed,
> Flows by the count of ear and no more scans
> (But parse it if you can) than Hebrew.
>
> (128–31)

Should it be surprising to discover that Milton knew what he was doing? The essay that prefaces *Samson,* "Of That Sort of Dramatic Poem Which Is Call'd Tragedy," includes a much-quoted passage:

> [The] *Chorus* is here introduc'd after the Greek manner, not ancient only but modern, and still in use among the *Italians.* In the modeling therefore of this Poem, with good reason, the Ancients and *Italians* are rather follow'd, as of much more authority and fame. The measure of Verse us'd in the Chorus is of all sorts, call'd by the Greeks *Monostrophic,* or rather *Apolelymenon,* without regard had to *Strophe, Antistrophe,* or *Epode.*

As best I can judge, "Apolelymenon" is a transliteration of a Greek word that, as Milton uses it, means nothing more nor less than "free verse." In Liddell and Scott's *Lexicon,* the closest application of απολελυμενον is its use in rhetoric, where it means "without regular pauses." Milton appropriated it to describe his poetic practice, not finding any term from prosody that conveyed the degree of freedom he had exercised. I am not arguing that his use of the word here has to do with individual feet or the absence thereof, or even the poetic line. But much in the same spirit as Cowley had abandoned the true Pindaric form in favor of something looser, Milton clearly is declaring his freedom from the expectations of a regular form. He may well have had in mind the extreme irregularity of the dithyrambic poets, especially Timotheus (446–357 B.C.), whose productions were admired by Euripides. Sir Arthur Pickard-Cambridge, discussing objections raised by contemporaries of Timotheus to his style, wrote:

> A great part of the lyrics of Timotheus were *apolelymena*—free from the trammels of strophe and antistrophe, and so may have seemed to

old critics to be "twisting ant-runs," but this phrase is probably better explained by Düring as "tunes of a chromatic character." (50)

The models from Italian that Milton mentions are most likely *Il Pastor Fido* of Guarini and *Adamo* by Andreini. Arguments and examples provided by Prince in *The Italian Element in Milton's Verse* are perfectly convincing on this point and provide one more example of how an English poet could import looser forms from that literature in order to secure greater expressive license in his own language.

Detailed prosodic analysis of *Samson* inevitably leads to controversy. Robert Bridges spent twenty pages of *Milton's Prosody* trying to explain what went on there and in *Paradise Regained;* George Saintsbury took fifteen pages of his *History* answering Bridges. Gerard Manley Hopkins and Yvor Winters both took exception to Bridges. The terms of the argument are somewhat unclear; Bridges at least provided interesting tabulations of line variants that prove that the licenses of *Samson,* even in pentameter lines, go far beyond *Paradise Lost.* The effects in *Samson* depend on complex and scarcely definable counterpointing that Milton sets up against (not *within*) the iambic pentameter. These effects depend only partially on the adaptation of quantitative effects from Greek and Italian, and possibly something from Hebrew. It is no great step from the sustained enjambments and verse paragraphs of *Paradise Lost,* across the line into a practice that depends on total departure from the pentameter; a practice that assumes the possibility of a well-established metrical norm as a background or a foil, but not as an existing context. Analogies are always treacherous, but it seems to me that in the choruses of *Samson* Milton has done something like late quartets of Beethoven; he has stepped outside the conventions. To do this in a poem—to use the line rather than the foot as the unit for substitution—is to write free verse.

In a doctoral dissertation completed in 1916, which was subsequently published as *The English Ode to 1660: An Essay in Literary History,* Robert Shafer concluded with several chapters that further bolster my arguments. I would like to draw particular attention to Shafer's study because I see no evidence of its being cited in previous discussions of free verse, where it ought to have taken a prominent place. The date of Shafer's writing is especially interesting, since the debate on free verse was then under way in earnest, in *Poetry* magazine and in Amy Lowell's Imagist anthologies. Chapter 7 of *The English Ode to 1660* includes a section 3 entitled "English Free Verse from Spenser to Crashaw," and section 4, "Free Verse in Crashaw." The entire chapter is a carefully documented survey of irregular forms in English poetry, mostly from 1600 to 1660, which is provided as a background to Abraham Cowley's "Pindariques."

Shafer is even more ready than I am to discover free verse, saying of Spenser, "[H]e held to his scheme [in the marriage poems] so loosely that there is real reason for noticing both poems at the outset of an inquiry into the course of English irregular verse" (133). He draws attention to Drummond, as I have, and provides metrical notations of his literary madrigals that illustrate their great variety. He also points out poems by Donne and Herbert that I have found occasion to notice. There are metrical notations for poems by Quarles, Carew, Cartwright, and Vaughan that show differing degrees of variation from a stanzaic norm, and a description of twenty-four *Festival Hymns* by Jeremy Taylor, of which all but one are irregular. In section 4 Shafer describes numerous poems by Crashaw, insisting that, even in some that are not quite so irregular, "the principle of freedom is plainly present" (149).

Shafer's treatment of all these Metaphysical and devotional poets is very careful and thorough, and amply illustrates the degree to which manneristic distortion of meter, such as we see in Donne, progresses toward complete unpredictability. With the one exception previously mentioned ("The Dissolution") Donne writes in regular stanzas or couplets, as did Marvell, Herbert (except for "The Collar"), Herrick (with one or two minor exceptions), and all the Cavaliers. But with Donne, especially, the individual line is treated with great flexibility, and other poets went even further. These vers-libristic excursions noted by Shafer in other poets can then be seen as escapes from, and beyond, stanzaic composition, much as the literary madrigal escaped the confines of the sonnet. Crashaw is a remarkable example of this.

Of all seventeenth-century fads, however, the one that produced the most lasting effects in the composition of free verse was that initiated by Abraham Cowley with the publication of his *Pindarique Odes* in 1656. Because of Cowley's productions the word *Pindaric* came to signify a whole attitude toward poetry and continued to be used until the end of the nineteenth century to characterize poems that were free in spirit and in form. The fact that the term is no longer in common use, and the embarrassment that the whole phenomenon causes to neoclassicists, is no reason to neglect this important precursor to modern free verse. Pindarism requires a chapter of its own.

Chapter 5

"Those Monstrous Compositions"

We may use the benefit of the Pindaric way . . . where the
numbers vary and the rhyme is disposed carelessly.
—John Dryden

Almighty Crowd, thou shorten'st all dispute;
Pow'r is thy Essence; Wit thy Attribute!
Nor Faith nor Reason make thee at a stay,
Thou leapst o'er all eternal truths, in thy *Pindarique* way!
—Dryden, "The Medal"

A hundred years ago a term was still in common use to describe a poetic
manner in which enthusiasm and inspiration prompted a loosened form
or which seemed the authentic utterance of something primitive or an-
cient, whether a Hebrew prophet or a wild Celtic bard, or in which the
contemporary poet allowed himself or herself an unusual degree of li-
cense. *Pindarism* has long since faded from the critical vocabulary, but
Matthew Arnold used it and, with an appropriate degree of civility and
classical restraint, allowed it to affect the way he composed some of his
poems. In the period when Tennyson and Browning for the most part
elaborated predictable feet and scansions, *Pindaric* remained in use, hav-
ing survived Samuel Johnson's conversion of it into an expression of
opprobrium, to designate poetry that was formally unpredictable. In
fact, the fad of Pindarism lasted for almost three centuries.

To judge from the flood of completely irregular poems that saw
print after 1700 and that purported to be translations of Pindar, or Pin-
daric odes, or just "essays in the manner of Pindar," no Englishman had
understood how that Greek poet really composed. The true form of the
Pindaric ode can be described in less than one sentence: it contained one
or more triads, each of which consisted of two long stanzas, the strophe

and the antistrophe, which were identical; and a concluding stanza, or epode, which was *different* from the strophe but *the same form as all other epodes in the same poem.*

But when we look at what poets were actually writing in the earlier eighteenth century, we find almost nothing that is really Pindaric in form. Picking a poem at random from volume 3 of *Minor English Poets, 1660– 1780,* one turns up a piece by Thomas Yalden, a name unknown to the *Oxford Companion to English Literature,* and mentioned in no literary history. Samuel Johnson gave him a three-page biography in his *Lives of the Poets,* which is chiefly memorable for its definition of the word *wonder:*

> His [Yalden's] Hymn to Light is not equal to the other. He seems to think that there is an East absolute and positive where the Morning rises.
>
> In the last stanza, having mentioned the sudden eruption of new-created light, he says,
>
> Awhile th'Almighty wond'ring stood.
>
> He ought to have remembered, that infinite knowledge can never wonder. All wonder is the effect of novelty upon ignorance.

The poem of Yalden's that we are to examine, however, is one that, as Johnson said, is "of that irregular kind, which, when he formed his poetical character, was supposed to be Pindaric":

HUMAN LIFE.

SUPPOSED TO BE SPOKEN BY AN EPICURE.

IN IMITATION OF THE SECOND CHAPTER OF THE

WISDOM OF SOLOMON.

TO THE LORD HUNDSON.

A PINDARIC ODE.

Then will penurious Heaven no more allow?
  No more on its own darling Man bestow?
Is it for this he lord of all appears,
  And his great Maker's image bears?
To toil beneath a wretched state,
  Oppress'd with miseries and fate;

Beneath his painful burthen groan,
And in this beaten road of life drudge on!

(French 319)

The poem drudges on for a hundred more lines, in six stanzas that range in length from seventeen to twenty-four lines. Runs of two to eight tetrameters are interrupted by pentameters and by an occasional Alexandrine. The rhymes are sometimes couplets, sometimes quatrains (*abba*), with a few tercets for good measure. Only by chance does it run to six stanzas, as might have occurred in Pindar; another of Yalden's "Pindariques," entitled "The Curse of Babylon," consists of either seven or eight stanzas, depending on whether stanza divisions coincide with page breaks. The one thing that "Human Life" might have had to connect it with Pindar is quite lacking; in place of erratic transitions and poetic "fire" we find sentiments closer to Horace's authentic carpe diem, except that Yalden's epicurean speaker seems to favor champagne over Falernian, and more of it: "Then gay and sprightly wine produce, / Wines that wit and mirth infuse: / That feed, like oil, th'expiring flame, / Revive our drooping souls, and prop this tottering frame."

By 1700 Pindar had been available in print for nearly two centuries, a first edition having appeared in Venice in 1513. According to Robert Shafer, "[T]he more general characteristics of the structure of the Pindaric ode *were* clearly understood from the early part of the sixteenth century on, as we may see from any early edition of Pindar. That is, it was clearly known that these odes were constructed in a series of triads, with each triad containing a strophe and antistrophe, and an epode" (58). Ben Jonson had no difficulty in apprehending either the form or spirit of Pindar, inventing *turn, counter-turn,* and *stand* as equivalents for the triadic division, and grouping four such triads in "To the Immortal Memory and Friendship of That Noble Pair, Sir Lucius Cary and Sir H. Morrison." The third turn is often printed as an independent poem:

It is not growing like a tree
In bulk doth make man better be;
  Or standing long an oak, three hundred year,
  To fall a log at last, dry, bald and sere:
    A lily of a day
    Is fairer far in May,
  Although it fall and die that night,

It was the plant and flower of light.
In small proportions we just beauties see,
And in short measures life may perfect be.

Jonson executes the poem with a balance and restraint that is more
Horatian than Pindaric; but elsewhere he speaks of Pindar's "fire," mak-
ing clear that he saw that quality in the original. And even here there is
something about the performance that leads him to kick up his heels in an
uncharacteristic way. Many readers are struck with how he separates his
own name across the boundaries of third counterturn and stand; just
beyond that is something that Marianne Moore might have—in fact,
has—done:

Such truths as we expect for happy men;
And there he lives with memory, and Ben.

THE STAND
Jonson, who sung this of him, ere he went
Himself to rest,
Or taste a part of that full joy he meant
To have expressed
In this bright asterism;
Where it were friendship's schism
(Were not his Lucius long with us to tarry)
To separate these twi-
Lights, the Dioscuri;
And keep the one half from his Harry.

The period after "Ben" may seem to point to a line stop, but his name
appears regularly with a period, which only signifies that it is an abbrevia-
tion. But it is the splitting of *twilight* that is almost painfully witty,
converting it into something more like "two-light," suggesting the stars,
Castor and Pollux, as well as the mythological twins, perhaps even play-
ing with a false etymology for "Dioscuri." At any rate, the split word
imitates the close separation of two stars in an asterism.

The mystery is how, after Jonson's example, any English poet could
still mistake the meaning of *Pindaric,* at least as far as regards form.

Part of the explanation is that by the end of the seventeenth century poets were already so desperate to wriggle free of the increasingly end-stopped heroic couplet that they snatched at any name that carried the weight of ancient approbation and that seemed to allow more freedom, regardless of whether their use of that name really justified their own practice. English poetic measures never did correspond to ancient meters anyway; it was absurd to try to bundle Homer and Virgil into rhyming couplets, as Pope and many others did, and to pretend that the closed couplet was an equivalent to the dactylic hexameter. Since there could be no exact equivalence, why not take liberties in opening up forms as well as in restricting them unnaturally? The heroic couplet conveyed classical restraint; an irregular form might allow flashes of ancient genius to shine through. In some sense what we see happening in 1700 is the prosodic counterpart of T. S. Eliot's "dissociation of sensibility": couplets for thinking, Pindarics for feeling.

As we have already observed, the middle decades of the seventeenth century saw the composition of many poems in irregular stanza forms. Most of these also displayed a Metaphysical extravagance in vocabulary and imagery, and to that extent their prosodic freaks can be tolerated—or condemned—as one more aspect of that baroque "incorrectness" that was soon to be remedied by the smooth numbers and chastened language of Waller and Denham. Yet even those poets whose pursuit of a Virgilian or Horatian elevation anticipated the coming triumph of neoclassicism could yearn for more freedom than couplets or stanzas normally allowed. Since these clearly anticipate the freedom that was eventually licensed as Pindaric, it will be worth while to glance back again to that earlier time. Dating from the 1640s we have "A Reveille Matin, or Good Morrow to a Friend" by Mildmay Fane, earl of Westmoreland:

> As the black curtain of the night
> Is open drawn
> By the grey-fingered dawn,
> To let out light
> And bid good morrow to the teeming day:
> So let all darkened thoughts through sin
> Call in
> Their powers, that led them in a blindfold way;
> And roused up from security,
> Bring better fruits unto maturity.

For now the fragrant east,
The spicery o' th' world
            Hath hurled
A rosy tincture o'er the phoenix nest;
    And from the last day's urn
            Another springs,
                    And brings
With it a chareter too in its turn.
        So then by this new fire
Be goodness hatched, all wickedness expire.

Then as this prince of heat doth rise,
    In power and in might seem stronger
    Proclaiming that 'tis night no longer;
By vanquishing the witchcrafts of the skies,
        The spelly-vap'rous mists:
        So let th'enlightened soul
                Control
Our actions, that no further they persist
    To follow sense, whereby to invite
Ruin, the sauce t'unruly appetite.

            Thus now it's clear,
            Out of all question,
The world's unmasked, and all of veiling gone.
Phoebus triumphant o'er our hemisphere:
    Let us not therefore in disguise
            Seek, or bravado,
To shadow as if under maskerado
    So many faults and villanies,
    Knowing that he who made the light
Cannot himself be destitute of sight.

        But though his providence
            Did this beget,
        That suns that rise and set,
    And in appearance vanish hence;
Yet doth he claim for th'interest
            Of daylight's bliss,
            We slumber not amiss;

Whenas our light is borrowed by the west;
But the choice cabinet of the mind adorn
With contemplations may befit next morn.

The relaxing of metrical standards in this poem has not permitted a commensurate increase in its expressiveness. These measures do not rival the strained regularity in the stanzas of Donne, the modulated neatness of Herrick, or the taut muscularity of Marvell's tetrameters. The form, however, does furnish an additional example of how poets in the years 1630–1650 were trying to escape the confines of regular stanzas and, most of all, the couplet; Fane himself more commonly wrote in couplets. In the poem quoted above he achieves something close to Cowley's *Pindariques.*

Until 1656 those who composed in irregular stanzas did so, one might say, at their own risk; there was no model, either native or classical, no recognized genre. Not even the madrigal could serve as an example, since the madrigal contained no more than a single stanza. Available, at least, was the word *ode,* which in English practice had been applied to all sorts of middle-length poems, only a few of which had been modeled on the odes of Horace, and—as we saw—only one of which truly followed the practice of Pindar. But *ode* was more likely to appear in the title of a poem in regular meters and stanzas.

Nonexistent too, for the most part, was the spirit of the classical ode. In all of Pindar, and in some of Horace's *Odes,* the celebration of a public occasion, or at least the assumption of a public manner, distinguishes the poetry from other genres. The ode also has the purpose, especially in Pindar, of expressing, or even arousing, an excited state of mind appropriate to the occasion. Fulfilling all these thematic and emotional requirements is Milton's *On the Morning of Christ's Nativity* which—because of line 24 ("O run, prevent them with thy humble ode")—is commonly called the *Nativity Ode.* For Milton, no occasion of greater public significance, and no occasion calling for greater poetic enthusiasm, could be imagined than the birth of Christ, and the poem succeeds so well that among the various compliments paid it is that of calling it "Pindaric." The *Nativity Ode,* however, is Pindaric only in limited ways—certainly not in form. The stanzas of the two parts are quite regular, though some lines pose interesting problems in scansion. But the poem does point toward the pseudo-Pindaric, not only in its exalted diction, but also in the way that the "Hymn" section of the poem uses stanzas that are a roughened and highly expressive modification of the opening stanzas. One need go no further than the first three lines of the "Hymn" to illustrate this. Up to this point we have had regular pentameters, punctuated with concluding Alexandrines in the Spenserian manner; but then we launch into—

> It was the winter wild,
> While the Heav'n-born child,
>   All meanly wrapt in the rude manger lies.

How many beats do the first two lines have? The first is not very hard— the ambiguity is whether to put a stress on "It" or on "was," or in some way to share the stress between them. One way to read it would be—

> /   *   *   /   *   /
> It was the winter wild

Others will want to place a stress on "was" or try to get by with only two stresses. The only sure thing is that we do have six syllables to work with. But that security disappears with the second line. Even without an explicit apostrophe to determine pronunciation, "heaven" in Milton's time got only one syllable. I cannot help reading the line as if it were composed of an anapest and an iamb:

> *   *   /   *   /
> While the Heav'n-born child

But this cannot possibly be correct, as the rest of the "Hymn" makes it perfectly clear that in every stanza the first two lines contain three feet, or beats. Yet I hear only two in the line above—unless one places all three beats at the end of the line. And as a matter of fact the rough indeterminacy of the opening is pleasing. The rudeness of the lines is perfectly appropriate to the effect of suddenly launching in, even imitating the "wildness" of that winter. It implies the abruptness of Christ's entry into nature.

The purpose in dwelling for the moment on a poem that is definitely *not* free verse is to make the point once more that in the year 1629, when Milton composed it, there was at work a powerful impulse to open more possibilities of expression in poetry. At the same time, and even more markedly following the Restoration, it was clear that the closed heroic couplet, which gave the effect of classical balance and restraint, was going to be the norm for the most serious poetry. Jonson had long since shown what could be done with it in his poem on Shakespeare, the greatest tribute ever paid by one poet to another, unless one counts Virgil's adaptation of Homer as a tribute. In some sense the heroic couplet was simply the next step in the rediscovery of Chaucer's meter. But some poets were already uncomfortable with it, and Milton (earning Dr. Johnson's grudging acceptance) chose blank verse over the couplet for *Paradise Lost.*

Earlier I raised the question of why, at the end of the seventeenth century, no one seemed to know what a Pindaric ode really was. The answer is, *they did not want to know.* Pindar's name, the honor with which he had been regarded in antiquity, served as a license for writing pretty much as one pleased. One could feel comfortably neoclassical, inclining toward the ancients over the moderns in the quarrel burlesqued by Swift in *The Battle of the Books,* and yet spare oneself the labor of getting the rhyme word in at the end of every second pentameter line—or spare oneself clear-cut proof of one's ineptness in failing to make the couplet sound like a probable sequence of words. The impulse to write Pindarics as a way of escaping onerous requirements of the meter parallels the urge to imitate the free verse of Dr. Williams in this century, and there are other parallels, as we shall see.

And the later seventeenth century had its Dr. Williams. In his day, Abraham Cowley was much better known than Milton; unlike Shakespeare, he was buried in Westminster Abbey, next to Chaucer and Spenser, and his funeral set a record for pomp and splendor that has, for a poet, yet to be surpassed, perhaps anywhere on earth. Charles II himself said that Mr. Cowley had not left a better man behind him in England, and honorific pronouncements dropped from other dignitaries like apples in an autumn storm. In life, without claiming it for himself, Cowley had given every evidence of the kind of poetic genius looked for in the following century. He published his first book of poems when he was thirteen. From the same early age he was, in his own words, "such an enemy to all constraint, that his master never could prevail on him to learn the rules without book." This is quoted by Johnson in his *Life of Cowley,* and Johnson goes on to explain that Cowley *could* have learned the ordinary rules of grammar, but found he did not need to. In the course of his life Cowley tried almost every form and genre of poetry and seemed to succeed at all—even the epic. Johnson took the occasion of writing Cowley's biography to make his definitive pronouncements on Metaphysical poetry in general—and this provides additional proof of Cowley's range, since he could even be considered as a pupil in the school of Donne. Included in his stable of forms was the pseudo-Pindaric ode. According to Arthur H. Nethercot (1931), "He was the popularizer, almost the inventor, of the Pindaric or irregular ode; and he was therefore a liberal influence on versification. Although he also wrote and helped to develop the couplet, he would probably have been in the van of the *vers librists* if he had lived in the second decade of the twentieth century" (290).

Johnson's remarks on Cowley's Pindarics are much quoted. They provide a capsule history of the form by someone who lived two hundred years closer to the phenomenon than we do, and who not only had strong feelings about it, but whose comments had some effect on its fate. Johnson devotes several pages to this one topic, and anyone who wishes to enjoy a stern and uncompromising, but not altogether unsympathetic assessment, ought to read them. He begins—

> The Pindarique Odes are now to be considered; a species of composition which Cowley thinks Pancirolus might have counted in *his list of the lost inventions of antiquity,* and which he has made a bold and vigorous attempt to recover.
>
> The purpose with which he has paraphrased an Olympic and Nemeaen Ode is by himself sufficiently explained. His endeavor was, not to show *precisely what Pindar spoke, but his manner of speaking.* He was therefore not at all restrained to his expressions, nor much to his sentiments; nothing was required of him, but not to write as Pindar would not have written.

Johnson then proceeds to compare Cowley with the original, to blame Cowley for introducing Metaphysical conceits into a classic, and to fault him for absurd diction. After this he turns to Cowley's prosody—

> To the disproportion and incongruity of Cowley's sentiments must be added the uncertainty and looseness of his measures. He takes the liberty of using in any place a verse of any length, from two syllables to twelve. . . .
>
> It is urged by Dr. Sprat [friend of Cowley's and secretary of the Royal Society], that the *irregularity of numbers is the very thing* which

makes *that kind of poesy fit for all manner of subjects.* But he should have remembered, that what is fit for every thing can fit nothing well. The great pleasure of verse arises from the known measure of the lines, and uniform structure of the stanzas, by which the voice is regulated, and the memory relieved.

Sprat's remarks are of particular interest in connection with Timothy Steele's argument (in *Missing Measures*) that modern free verse emulates prose partly because of the authority of prose as a language of scientific exactitude.

Johnson continues—

> If the Pindaric style be, what Cowley thinks it, *the highest and noblest kind of writing in verse,* it can be adapted only to high and noble subjects; and it will not be easy to reconcile the poet with the critic, or to conceive how that can be the highest kind of writing in verse, which, according to Sprat, *is chiefly to be preferred for its near affinity to prose.*
>
> This lax and lawless versification so much concealed the deficiencies of the barren, and flattered the laziness of the idle, that it immediately overspread our books of poetry; all the boys and girls caught the pleasing fashion, and they that could do nothing else could write like Pindar. . . . Pindarism prevailed about half a century; but at last died gradually away, and other imitations supply its place.

Johnson continues for one more paragraph, in which he makes some allowances for "great comprehension of knowledge, and great fertility of fancy," but he cannot let the "Pindariques" go without one final ironic thrust, ". . . it may be said with truth, that no man but Cowley could have written them." As we shall see, Johnson's complacency in announcing the disappearance of the pseudo-Pindaric ode was not warranted. But long before Johnson's effort to put the final cachet of oblivion on Cowley his reputation had faded. "Who now reads Cowley?" asked Alexander Pope, adding, "Forgot his Epic, nay Pindaric Art, / But still I love the language of his heart." These lines are from the epistle "To Augustus," composed in the early 1730s, by which time Pindar's true form had been rediscovered and restored to him.

Among those who really know Pindar, and who really know Cowley, the consensus is that Cowley was too good a classicist not to realize, in 1656, how far his practice departed from his model. If that is true, then Cowley's own preface is misleading, asserting that "though the *Grammarians* and *Criticks* have labored to reduce his Verses into regular feet and measures (as they have also those of the *Greek* and *Latine Comedies*) yet in effect they are little better than *Prose* to our Ears." Cowley's first performance in this series of poems is a rendering into English, supposedly, of Pindar's "Second Olympique Ode." The result includes eleven numbered stanzas, and this makes it deliberately unlike the original in form. Cowley's contention that Pindar's meter has not been understood serves as an excuse for retaining nothing of the true form. And Cowley's own reputation, combined with that of Pindar, was enough to excuse almost any sort of irregularity in his subsequent imitators. The greatest poet of the age, so it was thought, had shown the way and set an example by translating one of the greatest poets of antiquity.

To say this is not, of course, to damn the intentions of "Pindarique" odes as poems. "*To Mr.* Hobs." is an elevated tribute to one of Cowley's contemporaries for whom, given the interdisciplinary jealousies assumed by the "two-culture" theory of the late Lord Snow in our century, we might not expect Cowley to have cherished much regard. Yet by "elevated" I do not mean that it is particularly readable or memorable; I reproduce it here in its entirety as an example of what has occurred in a previous age when a poet has substituted impulsively improvised measures of his own devising in place of an accepted convention. The principle of organization in Cowley's ode is not that far removed from what we see three hundred years later in Olson's *Maximus*. The ode, of course, retains the use of rhyme, but the rhythms in many lines are personal and spasmodic, and the theory of Pindarism even placed emphasis on afflatus, a passable precursor of Olson's "breath." In order to include one complete specimen of Pindarism, however tedious, I quote the poem entire.

TO MR. HOBS.
I.
Vast *Bodies* of *Philosophie*
I oft have seen, and read,
But all are *Bodies Dead,*
Or *Bodies* by *Art fashioned;*
      I never yet the *Living Soul* could see,
      But in thy books and thee.

'Tis only *God* can know
Whether the fair *Idea* thou dost show
Agree entirely with his *own* or no.
  This dare I boldly tell,
'Tis so *like Truth* 'twill serve our turn as well.
 Just, as in *Nature* thy *Proportions* be,
As full of *Concord* their *Variety*,
As *firm* the parts upon their *Center* rest,
And all so *Solid* that they at least
As much as *Nature, Emptiness detest.*

2.

Long did the mighty *Stagirite* retain
The *universal Intellectual reign,*
Saw his own Countrey's short-liv'd *Leopard* slain;
The stronger *Roman-Eagle* did outfly,
Oft'ner *renewed* his *Age,* and saw that *Dy.*
Mecha itself, in spite of *Mahumet* possessed,
And chas'ed by a wild *Deluge* from the *East,*
His *Monarchy* new planted in the *West.*
But as in time each great imperial race
Degenerates, and gives some new one place,
  So did this noble E*mpire* wast,
  Sunk by degrees from glories past,
And in the *School-mens* hands it perisht quite at last.
  Then nought but W*ords* it grew,
  And those all B*arb'rous* too.
It *perisht,* and it *vanisht* there,
The *Life* and *Soul* breathed out, became but empty *Air.*

3.

The *Fields* which answer'd well the *Ancients Plow,*
Spent and out-worn return no *Harvest* now,
In barren *Age* wild and inglorious lie,
   And boast of *past Fertilitie,*
The *poor relief* of *Present Povertie.*
  Food and *Fruit* we now must want
   Unless new *Lands* we *plant.*
We break up *Tombs* with *Sacrilegious hands;*
   Old *Rubbish* we remove;

To walk in *Ruines,* like vain *Ghosts,* we love,
   And with fond *Divining Wands*
      We search among the *Dead*
      For Treasures *Buried,*
   Whilst still the *Liberal Earth* does hold
So many *Virgin Mines* of *undiscover'd Gold.*

4.

   The *Baltique, Euxin,* and the *Caspian,*
And slender–limb'ed *Mediterrean,*
Seem narrow *Creeks* to *Thee,* and only fit
For the poor wretched *Fisher-boats* of *Wit.*
Thy nobler *Vessel* the vast *Ocean* tries,
        And nothing sees but *Seas* and *Skies,*
        Till unknown *Regions* it descries,
Thou great *Columbus* of the *Golden Lands* of *new* Philosophies.
Thy task was harder much than his,
For thy Learn'd *America* is
   Not onely found out first by *Thee*
And rudely left to *Future Industrie*
   But by thy *Eloquence* and thy *Wit,*
Has *planted, peopled, built,* and *civiliz'd* it.

5.

        I little thought before,
      (Nor being my *own self* so *poor*
      Could comprehend so vast a *store*)
    That all the *Wardrobe* of rich *Eloquence,*
      Could have afforded half enuff,
      Of *bright,* of *new,* and *lasting* stuff,
To cloath the mighty *Limbs* of thy *Gigantique Sence.*
Thy solid *Reason* like the *shield* from heaven
      To the *Trojan Heroe* given,
Too strong to take a mark from any mortal dart,
Yet shines with *Gold* and *Gems* in every part,
And *Wonders* on it grave'd by the Learn'd hand of *Art,*
      A *shield* that gives delight
      Even to the *enemies* sight,
Then when they're sure to lose the *Combat by't.*

6.

Nor can the *Snow* which now cold *Age* does shed
            Upon thy reverend Head,
Quench or allay the noble *Fires* within,
            But all which though hast *bin*,
            And all that *Youth* can *be* thou'rt yet,
            So fully still dost Thou
Enjoy the *Manhood,* and the *Bloom* of *Wit,*
And all the *Natural Heat,* but not the *Feaver* too.
  So *Contraries* on *Aetna's* top conspire,
Here hoary *Frosts,* and by them breaks out *Fire.*
A secure *Peace* the *faithful Neighbors* keep.
The'emboldned *Snow* next to the *Flame* does *sleep.*
            And if we weigh, like *Thee,*
Nature, and *Causes,* we shall see,
            That thus it *needs must be,*
To things *Immortal Time* can do no wrong,
And that which never is *to Dye,* for ever must be *Young.*
            (*Complete Works* 188–90)

I have retained Cowley's original typography on the assumption that the italicized words did carry additional emphasis. If so, a proper reading of the poem must require the sort of insistence, the dwelling on particular words with nervous urgency, that we hear in recordings of William Carlos Williams reading his own poetry. The paradox is that to open the form is also to open the poem to a greater variety of interpretive readings; the typography may be an effort to control these—and, as such, betrays a certain insecurity, a need to retain personal direction of the poem. In the end what one admires about Cowley's ode are his intentions. He recognized in his friend a doughty battler for a new direction in philosophy; Hobbes can certainly take his place in the pantheon with Descartes and Spinoza. Most literary effort expended on Hobbes in the seventeenth century went toward discrediting him, especially treatises penned by prelates of the Anglican Church.

Cowley also meant to add a noble new genre for the use of poets in English, and it is possible to argue that without the fashion that he established Wordsworth would have found no fitting vehicle for his *Immortality Ode,* nor Allen Tate for his "Ode to the Confederate Dead." But who would care to memorize "*To Mr.* Hobs."? In *The Oxford Dictionary of Quotations* Milton occupies thirteen pages and Pope six; Cowley, "The Muses' Hannibal," counts as his conquest three-quarters of one page, less than Crabbe or Crashaw.

Yet he is of great importance in tracing those currents in English poetry that drift toward free verse. Cowley's reverence for Hobbes may again recall to us his friendship with Thomas Sprat, poet and author of *The History of the Royal Society*. In the later seventeenth century natural philosophy was still a family member occupying a room in the same house with aesthetics. Cowley, as I have already noted, was much affected by the emphasis put on prose as a more reliable medium for the expression of the truth than poetry, and he apparently felt that, using the authority of Pindar, he could free English poetry from the constraint of regular metrics and thereby attain some of the flexibility of prose. Apologizing for Cowley's practice, in a passage that we saw Johnson referring to, Sprat said—

> But that for which I think this inequality of number is chiefly to be preferr'd, is its near affinity with Prose: From which all other kinds of *English* Verse are so far distant, that it is very seldom found that the same man excels in both ways. But now this loose and unconfin'd measure has all the Grace and Harmony of the most confin'd. And withal, it is so large and free, that the practice of it will only exalt, not corrupt our Prose: which is certainly the most useful kind of Writing of all others: for it is the style of all business and conversation. (Quoted in *Complete Works* lxi)

This new flexibility would permit new discoveries in poetry. In retrospect, such a concern may seem a quixotic attempt to put poetry and natural science on the same footing, one that, given the retention, and even encouragement, of extravagant language and imagery in Pindarics, never got very far. But the *theory* of loosened metric, as enunciated by Sprat, puts us on the road toward the prosodic revolution of the twentieth century, and even toward William Carlos Williams's dictum, "No ideas but in things." The tendency that Swift identified (inappropriately, as we now see) as a ludicrous failing of the Royal Society's efforts to make language more precise, and that he satirized in book 3 of *Gulliver's Travels,* has been revived in this century as literary doctrine.

Cowley's Pindarics were also a challenge to genre theory. The loose form, like prose, was to accommodate itself to any subject, and would not vitiate the subject by imposing the unnatural restrictions of a preconceived structure. This impatience with a too-constrictive form paralleled Milton's desire, expressed in the preface to *Paradise Lost,* to dispense with rhyme.

A consideration of the connections between Cowley's metrics and the beginnings of British empiricism and associative psychology would carry us too far from a central concern with prosody. But surely these developments, which were in some sense a secularizing of Protestant theology, do bear on the subject. The transformation of the Calvinist conviction of election into a certainty that one's inner preferences were absolute mental categories, with relations as definite as physical laws, encouraged a self-sufficiency in many things, including metrics. Building on Cowley's known admiration for Hobbes, David Trotter, in *The Poetry of Abraham Cowley,* offers convincing arguments to support his statement:

> The basis for that poetic lies, I believe, in the equivalence between Cowley's version of the Pindaric ode and the radical psychology developed by Thomas Hobbes, who, unlike the various theorists cited by Goldstein, knew Cowley well, possibly at Great Tew and certainly at Paris, during the years immediately prior to the composition of the *Pindarique Odes.*

And further on, Trotter says, "Cowley's interest in Pindar's inconstancy of argument is, I would suggest, equivalent to Hobbes's interest in discursion" (115–17).

The argument that Pindaric freedom corresponds to, or permits, a confidence in one's own prophetic voice finds support in a note that Cowley appended to Ode 34, "Chapter of the Prophet *Isaiah.*"

> The manner of the *Prophets* writing, especially of *Isaiah,* seems to me very like that of *Pindar;* they pass from one thing to another with almost *Invisible connexions,* and are full of words and expressions of the highest and boldest flights of *Poetry,* as may be seen in this Chapter, where there are as extraordinary Figures as can be found in any Poet whatsoever; and the connexion is so difficult, that I am forced to add a little, and leave out a great deal to make it seem *Sense* to us, who are not used to that elevated way of expression. (*Complete Works* 214)

As we shall see, there is an entirely separate line of free-verse poetry dating from the early 1600s, none of which I have yet touched upon, that drew upon the poetic books of the Old Testament. Cowley here identifies the spirit, though not the form, that animates that kind of free verse which originated in the prophetic enthusiasm of Hebrew poetry.

Most who admire Cowley's Pindarics are reluctant to extend their appreciation to his imitators; though he came after Cowley, Dryden should not be counted among these. Always quick to sense the advantage of new experiments, Dryden modified the new mode so completely as to make it distinctively his own, illustrating not what he had learned from Cowley but rather what Cowley should have done. "To the Pious Memory Of the Accomplisht Young Lady Mrs Anne Killigrew" (1686) proved in advance Pope's rule, "Those move easiest who have learned to dance." Dryden writes with great ease, and employs his newfound freedom to compose in great sweeps that carry him at times more than fifteen lines without a full stop, yet without straying into extravagance or absurdity. The degree of control is similar to that of Milton in *Lycidas,* but the even greater looseness of the form communicates a sense of personal engagement and affection missing in the latter. Dryden's other two Pindarics are quite specialized, both having as their occasion the subject of music, and both being written in such a way as to encourage their being set to music. Handel, among others, took the hint and turned them into small oratorios. I mean, of course, "A Song for St. Cecelia's Day, 1687" and "Alexander's Feast; or The Power of Musique" (1697). Both poems are tours de force, full of high-spirited diversion, and hardly count as examples of Cowleyesque poetry. Dryden, indeed, may have gone beyond Cowley; the use of the name Timotheus in connection with Alexander may be meant to suggest the dithyrambic poet (who in fact died before Alexander's birth). The extravagant and disorderly productions of Timotheus— which were called *apolelymena,* or nonstrophic—provided yet another example from ancient times that could license irregularity in modern verse.

Dryden excepted, the history of Pindarics after Cowley is the history of a form that had to wait more than a century to live up to its promise. George Saintsbury bragged of sparing his readers examples of Pindarics, and said of them that they "almost immediately 'made a school'; that they produced, during the last half of the seventeenth century and much of the eighteenth, some of the very worst verse (poetically, not always prosodically) to be found in the English language"

(2:340). It would be easy to assemble a hefty anthology of these poems, provided one were permitted the use of an optical scanner to read them into a computer memory. I had thought of providing a table of contents for such an anthology, with estimated dates for a number of examples that I have come across. In the end, even that seemed excessive. It will be sufficient to list the names of a number of poets with the number of Pindarics that such a casual survey has been able to assign to them, to prove the point that the period was rife with these productions. It is a shame to be so brief, since the titles are certainly worth reading, such as John Pomfret's "ON THE / GENERAL CONFLAGRATION, / AND ENSUING JUDGMENT. / A PINDARIC ESSAY."

Here is the list: Thomas Otway (1—extremely long); the Earl of Roscommon (1); John Pomfret (3); Edmund Smith (2); Thomas Sprat (3); the Earl of Halifax (1); Elijah Fenton (2); Thomas Yalden (3); William Somervile (2); William Broome (1); Isaac Watts (2); William Hamilton (2); William Shenstone (1); Robert Lloyd (3); William Falconer (1); Thomas Morrison (1); Matthew Prior (3). Anyone who has heard of more than three or four of these poets is very well read in English poetry. Yet this list is only the bare beginning of a complete catalog of published "Pindariques."

It belongs rather to a survey of the ode than of free verse to record the eventual fate of the Pindaric, which was to be reregularized. William Congreve, Ambrose Phillips, and others provided arguments and examples to recover the original structure, and after that anything invoking Pindar's authority had to follow the correct form. For a while (ca. 1740–1780) there was a lull, as those who cared to cultivate the Pindaric assiduously composed in strophes, antistrophes, and epodes. But the pseudo-Pindaric, gradually assuming the name of *irregular ode,* never quite died out, and the form was there waiting for Wordsworth and Coleridge. Also, the term *Pindaric* stuck as a synonym for loose and expressive composition, only dying away toward the end of the nineteenth century.

In its heyday the pseudo-Pindaric provided a subterranean current of metrical irrationality that ran, like Coleridge's sacred river in "Kubla Khan," beneath the neoclassical symmetry that arched above. At times Pindarism spilled over into other channels; some performances labeled as Horatian odes extended prosodic liberties to that genre, employing *short* irregular stanzas. We are often reminded that the eighteenth century was not really a homogenous period, but the true extent of its variety is seldom comprehended. Rummaging around in the minor poetry reveals almost perfect continuity between 1660 and 1798, and Pindarism provided an important link between the two dates. Instead of Augustan canons of taste, one finds preserved in various kinds of minor poetry every sort of previous lyrical mode—even the use of Metaphysical conceits, which had come to seem in bad taste to most critics. Sometimes when the forms seem more regular, the poetics of sensibility, of Romantic melancholia, and of landscape poetry modify the subjects as insensibly as did Gothic-revival architecture or picturesque landscape gardening. Such modes are continuous from the "antic pillars massy proof, / And storied windows richly dight" of Milton's "Il Penseroso" through the medievalized passion of Pope's "Eloisa to Abelard," and continue with the collections of owls, ivy, ruined towers, and moonlight of the poetry of melancholic sensibility. The only difference was that after 1798 all these came into the foreground of English poetry. There was never anything in English literature remotely comparable to the French Revolution in politics. Cowley's mid-seventeenth-century "Pindariques" had long since licensed the form of the *Immortality Ode* when it appeared.

I have begged the question of whether the fad initiated by Cowley really was a form of free verse. John D. Jump, a sensible scholar if there ever was one, thinks it was not: "Since his lines are metrical, and since they rhyme, he cannot be considered a writer of free verse like Walt Whitman, Ezra Pound, or D. H. Lawrence" (15). I am glad that there is no comma after the word "verse" in that sentence, because I find that I am entirely in agreement with what it says, so long as the phrase that follows restricts the sense so as to imply "that variety of free verse *written* by Whitman, Pound, and Lawrence." Cowley's free verse belongs to an entirely different species from that by any of those three, except for a few pieces by Pound. Whitman, other than a few poems in conventional meters, wrote nothing but biblical-anaphoric free verse; Lawrence resembled Whitman in some poems, and in others used phrasal verse. Pound was all over the place, but did not do much with pure vers-libristic poetry of the French type, in the sense that I have described and defined it. Cowley's practice *does* resemble that of the late-nineteenth-century French *vers-libristes;* it is also close to what Matthew Arnold did in "Dover Beach" and to Francis Thompson's "The Hound of Heaven"— both of which are distant lineal descendants of Cowley's odes. I would argue (again) that "Pindariques" meet the criteria of free verse because they are unpredictable and because they were a reaction against confining forms: ingenious but regular stanzas and the closed heroic couplet. Early seventeenth-century Pindarism also laid emphasis on the necessity of erratic poetic genius; it assumed that the poet spoke with a distinctive and prophetic voice; and (as Sprat argued) it called for innovative technique based on the freedom of prose.

Others agree with me, more or less. James G. Taaffe speaks of "His leisurely experiments in free versification" (60). Cowley's biographer, Arthur H. Nethercot, wrote:

> The choice of a "free" verse form he was not much concerned with, since many poets in England and France, from Spenser to Crashaw and Corneille and Racine, had used irregular metrical effects and rhyme schemes. Even though both he and Sprat felt called upon to defend his prosody for its "near affinity with prose" and to warn readers that the lines, like Pindar's, might seem rough if not pronounced, accented, or elided correctly, he was still more concerned with a theory of translation which he had evolved. (136–37)

In 1876 Edmund Gosse composed an essay on Cowley in which he asserted, "In publishing these odes Cowley performed a dangerous innovation; nothing at all like these pompous lyrics in *vers libres* had hitherto been attempted or suggested in English" (*Seventeenth Century Studies* 214). This quotation is remarkable not only for what it says about Cowley, but also because the use of *vers libres* predates the earliest citation in the *OED* (including the revised second edition) by more than twenty years and proves that the term was already in use in England by the last quarter of the nineteenth century. When Gosse wrote this he could not have been aware of all the other experiments in free verse that preceded Cowley's, but we might expect him to have thought of Milton's irregular poems.

Robert Shafer makes the strongest case of all:

> The metrical structure that Cowley affected was frankly "impulsive." He wanted for himself, as we shall see, perfect freedom in writing these poems, and so adopted a structure that would leave his inspiration as free and untrammeled by considerations of form as possible. The essential characteristic of this system was, then, its absence of restraint, its "superiority" to all rules. In practice it meant simply that Cowley left himself free to rime his lines as he pleased, throughout a poem, to make each line of whatever length he pleased, and to make

each of his stanzas just as long or short as convenience or caprice might dictate. It was, in fine, what we call free or irregular verse that Cowley used. In such verse the amount of freedom actually exercised may vary almost infinitely, while the principle of unlimited license behind it remains ever the same. (128–29)

I cannot help being aware that to a narrow-minded neoclassicist, for whom Dryden's "Alexander's Feast" is an embarrassment, the suggestion that anything that found favor anywhere in the Augustan period could be considered as free verse will seem anathema, as indeed the Pindaric itself seemed to Johnson. But many literary histories certainly show a willingness to consider it in that light.

Shafer's introduction of the word "impulsive" allows one more connection between free verse, as it emerged in the seventeenth century, and Romanticism, both English and American. We may think of Wordsworth's "One impulse from the vernal wood / May teach you more of man," and of Emerson's insistence upon the need to rely on impulse, an insistence that Perry Miller identified with the Calvinist sense of the immediate presence of God within oneself. With that connection we may resume a chronological survey of free verse, turning to Romanticism—as always, with Romanticism, not certain precisely what it is we are turning to.

Chapter 6

From Romantic Afflatus to Victorian Contraption

Of free verse in the Romantic period one would expect a multitude of examples. Rebellion was in the air, and Romantic doctrine encouraged innovation, individual expression, liberation from every sort of restraint, oddness, idiosyncrasy, the language of ordinary speech, organic form, inspiration, resistance to authority, adventurousness, spontaneity, self-assertion, superiority of the artist to any law—and so continues the familiar recitation. Given these articles of faith, the works of free verse are surprisingly few.

In the 1740s William Collins had, in his own peculiar way, contributed to the restoration of true Pindaric form, sticking his epode in the middle, between the strophe and antistrophe; but he also kept the irregular ode going in "The Passions: An Ode for Music." By the beginning of the nineteenth century the irregular ode had been in use so long as hardly to qualify as free verse, however unpredictable the line lengths and the placement of rhymes; more radical experiments were needed to give the effect of running counter to convention. I have already pointed to Wordsworth's *Immortality Ode* as a continuation of the irregular forms of the previous century, as were Coleridge's "Ode on the Departing Year" and "Dejection: An Ode." "Kubla Khan," though sometimes cited as an example of free verse because of the apparent organic expressiveness of the meters, is actually a tightening up of that form, achieving a bardic exhilaration and sublimity that earlier poets had hoped to attain in emulating Pindar. In America, where styles in the arts still took decades to cross the Atlantic, it was close to the middle of the century before irregular odes on the British model appeared, composed by Emerson and Melville, who drew on examples from other literatures as well. Frederick Goddard

Tuckerman's "The Cricket" likewise belongs to this genre. Irregular odes by others had appeared in the pages of the *Dial* (1840–1844). The spirit of the times was at least not inimical to the free-form ode. Rather than being discarded as a contemptible instance of "incorrectness," as it had been by more conservative eighteenth-century critics, it became the vehicle for some of the Romantic period's most memorable works, first in England and then in America.

Iambic pentameter continued to prosper, though under a new rhythmical dispensation. Among the earlier of the pre-Romantics the pentameter remained almost as strictly decasyllabic as in the most polished of Dryden's or Pope's couplets. But the lines begin to stretch a little at the seams, even as early as 1726, the date of publication of James Thomson's *The Seasons*. Enjambments—not as vigorous as Milton's, but nevertheless assertive of the poet's right to pause where it suited, not where the meter dictated—crept back in. Also, words that strict neoclassical practice would contract to two syllables, indicating the syncope by printing an apostrophe for the omitted vowel, were allowed to expand toward trisyllabic pronunciation. For example, take these lines from Thomson's *Winter*—

> Thro' the hush'd Air the whitening Shower descends,
> At first thin-wavering; till at last the Flakes
> Fall broad, and wide, and fast, dimming the Day,
> With a continual Flow. The cherish'd Fields
> Put on their Winter-Robe, of purest White.
> 'Tis Brightness all; save where the new snow melts.
>
> (229–34)

At least two of these lines are strongly enjambed by the separation of subject and verb. More remarkable, though, is the absence of explicit syncope (which would have been indicated by an apostrophe) in "whitening" and "wavering"; also, the more conventional synaeresis of "continual" into three syllables, rather than four, is just a little doubtful. It will not do to oversimplify by saying that the meter is being opened up so as to imitate and express more accurately the details of the winter landscape. In the lines above the "continual flow" of the heavy snowfall accumulates with the help of the enjambments, but in fact the "flow" of the line is interrupted at exactly that point. What occurs is more subtle: the phrase "With a continual flow" occupies the position of three feet— or six syllables, allowing for the synaeresis; but there are really only two stresses. The rhythm is blurred and evened out. Or so it seems; comic examples invented by both John Crowe Ransom and J. V. Cunningham warn us against overingeniousness in finding rhythmic equivalents for meaning, and if one substitutes "With a perceptual flaw," the original effect evaporates. Literal meaning is essential. In any event, the fluidity of the metrics does not interfere with description of a cumulative process in nature. With equal caution we may approve the opposite effects further on in Thomson's *Winter:*

> With the fierce Rage of Winter deep suffus'd,
> An icy Gale, oft shifting, o'er the Pool
> Breathes a blue Film, and in its mid Career
> Arrests the bickering Stream. The loosen'd Ice,
> Let down the Flood, and half-dissolv'd by Day,
> Rustles no more.
>
> (722–27)

The lines seem to freeze up in the middle, especially when all the "r" and "c" sounds abruptly cease following "Career / Arrests the bickering Stream." Imitative form this may be, but Ovid did it in the *Metamorphoses* eighteen hundred years earlier, and there are even intraline examples of it in the poetry of Yvor Winters, who invented "the fallacy of imitative form."

As long as the poet remains focused on the subject, the form subserves a larger purpose even as it mimics what it describes; it is only when form is intended to be expressive of the poet's own state of mind, or personality, that it verges toward what (allying myself with F. R. Leavis temporarily) I would call Romantic, or organic, heresy, as it did many years later in Shelley's "Ode to the West Wind" (1819):

> Thou on whose stream, mid the steep sky's commotion,
> Loose clouds like earth's decaying leaves are shed,
> Shook from the tangled boughs of Heaven and Ocean,
>
> Angels of rain and lightning: there are spread
> On the blue surface of thine aëry surge,
> Like the bright hair uplifted from the head
>
> Of some fierce Maenad, even from the dim verge
> Of the horizon to the zenith's height,
> The locks of the approaching storm. Thou dirge . . .

One has to break off because there is no convenient stopping point. Further on, the personal symbolism of the wind, which he assumes to himself as an expression of his own turbulent feelings ("Be thou me,' impetuous one!"), becomes explicit; this subjective overreaching was already evident in the confused and inconsistent imagery with which "Ode to the West Wind" opens, and on account of which Leavis dealt with Shelley very harshly. I recognize the justice of Leavis's strictures, but I continue to enjoy reading the poem; one cannot justify fireworks as enduring art, but they are nevertheless satisfying.

I do not, of course, introduce "Ode to the West Wind" as free verse—only as something that goes far beyond the quietly variegated rhythms of what one might call the "picturesque pentameter," examples of which we saw above and which are found in poems that treat subjects and use imagery typical of the late-eighteenth-century cult of the picturesque, as Wordsworth did in "Tintern Abbey." Shelley instead aims at the sublime, in the eighteenth-century sense: an evocation of the wild, the uncontrolled, the terrifying—effects that J. M. W. Turner carried even further in his paintings. Shelley's poem illustrates the radical disruption of the pentameter, more violent than Milton's practice even though Shelley retains a strict and elaborate structure based simultaneously on terza rima and the sonnet. For most Romantic poems, this was a more than sufficient degree of freedom—the freedom to dissolve and combine, to innovate, to revive, to stretch to new limits the accentual-syllabic meter. Simultaneously the poets introduced all the other violations of Augustan proprieties—in vocabulary, self-revelation, unrestrained emotion, exotic locales, altered states of consciousness, and so on.

To return to something closer to the pre-Romantics: Wordsworth may not have succeeded in limiting himself to "the real language of men," but when he wrote "Tintern Abbey" he certainly did his part to restore to the iambic pentameter line a more conversational rhythm. Also, he purged the worst of eighteenth-century diction from his poetry, much as Pound and Williams set out a hundred years later to clean out Victorian usages.

> Five years have past; five summers, with the length
> Of five long winters! and again I hear
> These waters, rolling from their mountain-springs
> With a soft inland murmur.—Once again
> Do I behold these steep and lofty cliffs,
> That on a wild secluded scene impress

Thoughts of more deep seclusion; and connect
The landscape with the quiet of the sky.

In this opening verse-paragraph of "Tintern Abbey" we see enjambments that could seem violent except that they have the opposite effect of quietly linking one line to the next, often employing the verb/object connection that we saw in Thomson. This occurs in three of the first eight lines. Of the first fifty lines, more than half are completely enjambed, lacking any punctuation at all, and most of the rest end with commas. The disappearance of end-stopped lines was radically liberating for Wordsworth's poetry; he hardly needed to take it any further in the direction of prose. With this line he could ramble freely along the shores of Lake Windermere, and cross the Alps with such ease that he scarcely knew what he had achieved.

Coleridge, whose capacious mind with difficulty held to a single purpose, succeeded even better with recurrent enjambments; the first ten lines of "The Eolian Harp" avail themselves of but one comma as a line ending. But his greatest achievement in combining associational psychology with a relaxed metric is "Frost at Midnight." One line leads quietly to another, as one thought leads to another, until we return to the "secret ministry of frost" with which it opened. Again, I am not providing instances of free verse, but rather explaining why Coleridge required no additional freedom; both he and Wordsworth found sufficient license for their metrics in the loosened pentameters of pre-Romantic eighteenth-century poems. In "Frost at Midnight" Coleridge had in mind the ruminative progress of such poems. Even such a protogothic poem as Robert Blair's *The Grave* (1743) could have provided a rhythmical model:

The Wind is up: Hark! how it howls! Methinks
Till now, I never heard a Sound so dreary:
Doors creak, and Windows clap, and night's foul Bird
Rook'd in the Spire screams loud: The gloomy Isles
Black, plastr'd, and hung round with Shreds of 'Scutcheons
And tatter'd Coats of Arms, send back the Sound
Laden with heavier Airs, from the low Vaults
The Mansions of the Dead. Rous'd from their Slumbers
In grim Array the grizly Spectres rise,
Grin horrible, and obstinately sullen
Pass and repass, hush'd as the Foot of Night.
Again! the Screech-Owl shrieks; Ungracious Sound.

(32–43)

Now of course Coleridge's poem is quite devoid of superstitious terror, and the beauty of "Frost at Midnight" is that the witching hour has become a moment of affectionate reminiscence and gentle optimism. Nevertheless, the pace is like that of *The Grave:*

> The Frost performs its secret ministry,
> Unhelped by any wind. The owlet's cry
> Came loud—and hark again! loud as before.
>
> (1–3)

and—

> Inaudible as dreams! the thin blue flame
> Lies on my low-burnt fire and quivers not;
> Only that film, which fluttered on the grate,
> Still flutters there, the sole unquiet thing.
> Methinks its motion in this hush of nature
> Gives it dim sympathies with me who live.
>
> (13–18)

Other instances of leisurely enjambments may be found throughout those writings called pre-Romantic, licensing Wordsworth's and Coleridge's practice well in advance. Examples include William Somerville's *The Chace* (1735); and even more remarkably in Mark Akenside's *The Pleasures of the Imagination* (1744) and Joseph Warton's *The Enthusiast: Or the Lover of Nature* (1744). One can also mention John Brown, Thomas Warton, and William Mason. In all of these one sees clear prefigurations of "Tintern Abbey," *The Prelude,* and Coleridge's conversation poems. Take, for example, these lines from *The Pleasures of the Imagination:*

> O ye Northumbrian shades, which overlook
> The rocky pavement and the mossy falls
> Of solitary Wensbeck's limpid stream;
> How gladly I recall your well-known seats
> Belov'd of old, and that delightful time
> When all alone, for many a summer's day,
> I wandered by your calm recesses, led
> In silence by some powerful hand unseen.
>   Nor will I e'er forget you, nor shall e'er
> The graver tasks of manhood, nor the advice

Of vulgar wisdom, move me to disclaim
Those studies which possess'd me in the dawn
Of life, and fixed the color of my mind
For every future year.

(3.19–32)

Compare this with one of the best-known passages from *The Prelude:*

Ye Presences of Nature in the sky
And on the earth! Ye Visions of the hills!
And Souls of lonely places! can I think
A vulgar hope was yours when ye employed
Such ministry, when ye through many a year
Haunting me thus among my boyish sports,
On caves and trees, upon the woods and hills,
Impressed upon all forms the characters
Of danger or desire.

(1:464–72)

This easygoing metric proved so accommodating that—when added to the exciting possibilities of the revived ballad, the songlike lyric, and the irregular ode—neither of the "Lake Poets" felt the need to extend their explorations further in the direction of prose. The quietly variegated pentameters lent themselves to the pursuit, in poetry, of that mode of Romantic perception called the picturesque, which found its analogue not only in paintings of rural scenes—with or without Gothic ruins, owls, or moonlight—but also in landscape gardening and travel literature. Buried in the quotation from Wordsworth are the other categories—"danger" associated with the sublime, and "desire" with beauty—which for him were the dual aspects of nature. A hundred lines further on he says even more explicitly—

Nor sedulous as I have been to trace
How Nature by extrinsic passion first
Peopled the mind with forms sublime or fair,
And made me love them . . .

(1:544–47)

When sublimity was the goal of the Romantic poet, there was more likelihood of departure into genuine free verse, though even there the

pentameter could serve, as in Shelley's "Mont Blanc" and in Words-
worth's description of the scene from atop Mount Snowden. Such expres-
sive freedom, harking back to Milton's blank verse, was as exhilarating
for the Romantics as the total abandonment of iambics would be for the
Imagists; nothing further was needed.

Coleridge, it is true, experimented with a new metrical principle in
Christabel, and one might see in his attempt to revive a four-stress meter,
with an indeterminate number of unaccented syllables, something closer
to a native English tradition and therefore closer to natural speech. In the
preface to that poem he wrote:

> I have only to add that the meter of *Christabel* is not, properly speak-
> ing, irregular, though it may seem so from its being founded on a
> new principle: namely, that of counting in each line the accents, not
> the syllables. Though the latter may vary from seven to twelve, yet
> in each line the accents will be found to be only four. Nevertheless,
> this occasional variation in the number of syllables is not introduced
> wantonly, or for mere ends of convenience, but in correspondence
> with some transition in the nature of the imagery or passion.

One wants to ask Coleridge how he got four stresses out of the fifth line
in the poem: "How drowsily it crew." The concept of the "unrealized
beat," an unheard continuation of a well-established rhythm, will take
care of it, but one would like to hear what Coleridge himself would say.
Here are the five opening lines—

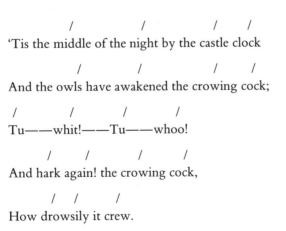

'Tis the middle of the night by the castle clock

And the owls have awakened the crowing cock;

Tu——whit!——Tu——whoo!

And hark again! the crowing cock,

How drowsily it crew.

But on the whole Coleridge sticks closely to his plan. The question is whether this takes us in the direction of free verse, and I believe that it does. It anticipates the theorizing about cadence by Ford Madox Ford, Amy Lowell, and William Carlos Williams, and it also looks forward to T. S. Eliot's revival of Anglo-Saxon rhythms as a norm around which his line can oscillate and from which it can finally depart, especially in *Murder in the Cathedral*. The comment about "correspondence with some transition in the nature of the imagery or passion" ties meter with the notion of organic form, and of form as determined by an accommodation to the speaker's voice. Also, the evident interest in experimentation with technique—recall that Coleridge was the first to use that word in English—may make us think of various Poundian pronouncements.

Of Keats and Byron I have little to say. For Keats, passion, imagery, subject, and meter fuse so indistinguishably, and delight in the resources of meter is so evident, that for the moment one accepts all the Romantic dogma about genius and simply submits oneself to what Keats achieved. In Byron we see a Romantic personality whose metrics are neoclassical. Even his adaptation of the Spenserian stanza in *Childe Harold* and the enjambed lines of *Manfred* seem no advance on eighteenth-century models. *Don Juan* connects *Hudibras* with Gilbert and Sullivan, but this, of course, is the most formal of formal poetry, replete with comic triple rhymes. Free spirits and free verse do not necessarily go together.

Because the rhythmical prose of James Macpherson's "Ossian" (1760) resembles biblical phraseology more than anything else, I will return to it at greater length in the next chapter where I consider the long line of poems in that manner. Macpherson's Celtic hoax, however, also affected the writing of accentual-syllabic meters in the early part of the Romantic period, inspiring first of all Frank Sayers, who produced poems in a form that George Saintsbury called "rhymeless Pindarics." I draw heavily on Saintsbury's authority at this point, because the poems of Sayers have disappeared from print and as a subject of critical discussion; as with other free-verse writers whom I have taken up, this may serve as cautionary information regarding the durability of such experiments. Saintsbury identifies names in Sayers's work as Ossianic, and says, "I have no doubt that the immense influence of Macpherson had a good deal to do with his rhymelessness" (3:41n). He quotes a sample chorus from *Moina,* a "British tragedy":

Hail to her whom Frea loves,
    Moina, hail!
When first thine infant eyes beheld
    The beam of day,
Frea from Valhalla's groves
Mark'd thy birth in silent joy;
Frea, sweetly smiling, saw
The swift-wing'd messenger of love
Bearing in her rosy hand
The gold-tipt horn of gods.

Dark, dark is Moina's bed,
On earth's hard lap she lies.
Where is the beauteous form
    That heroes loved?
Where is the beaming eye,
    The ruddy cheek?
Cold, cold is Moina's bed,
And shall no lay of death
With pleasing murmur soothe
Her parted soul?
Shall no tear wet the grave
    Where Moina lies?
The bards shall raise the lay of death,
The bards shall soothe her parted soul,
And drop the tear of grief
    On Moina's grave.

                        (Quoted 3:40n)

Sayers composed these lines about 1790. To judge from a short defense
that he wrote of the practice, he thought that Milton's choruses in *Samson
Agonistes* warranted his own practice. Saintsbury thinks that Sayers's
lines are just chopped-up Miltonic blank verse, an accusation similar to
the opinion of those who think of William Carlos Williams as hashed
Whitman. A note on Southey in Samuel Chew's section of *A Literary
History of England* states that "Sayers in turn derived the form from
William Collins who, however, had used it in the ode *To Evening* with far

more delicacy and within manageable limits" (Baugh 1161). I find this hard to accept; it is quite clear that Collins meant to compose an English Horatian ode, and he does it very successfully; what Sayers does hardly resembles this, though he may have considered the lack of rhyme in "To Evening" a useful precedent.

A slightly better known example of short-line free verse is Robert Southey's *Thalaba the Destroyer,* a piece of Middle Eastern neoprimi-tivism that he composed in 1801. Southey explains his prosody in the preface to the fourth edition:

> The dramatic sketches of Dr. Sayers, a volume which no lover of poetry will recollect without pleasure, induced me, when a young versifier, to practise in this rhythm. I felt that, while it gave the poet a wider range of expression, it satisfied the ear of the reader. It were easy to make a parade of learning, by enumerating the various feet which it admits: it is only needful to observe that no two lines are employed in *sequence* which can be read into one. Two six-syllable lines, it will perhaps be answered, compose an Alexandrine: the truth is that the Alexandrine, when harmonious, is composed of two six-syllable lines.
>
> One advantage this metre assuredly possesses,—the dullest reader cannot distort it into discord: he may read it prosaically, but its flow and fall will still be perceptible. Verse is not enough favored by the English reader. Perhaps this is owing to the obtrusiveness, the regular Jew's-harp *twing-twang,* or what has been foolishly called heroic mea-sure. I do not wish the *improvisatore* tune, but something that denotes the sense of harmony, something like the accent of feeling,—like the tone which every poet necessarily gives to poetry. (4:7)

Section 40 of the fifth book of *Thalaba* provides a good example of Southey's practice:

> The undefended youth
> Sprung forward, and he seized
> Mohareb in his grasp
> And grappled with him breast to breast.
> Sinewy and large of limb Mohareb was,
> Broad-shouldered, and his joints

Knit firm, and in the strife
  Of danger practised well.
Time had not thus matured young Thalaba;
  But high-wrought feelings now,
 The inspiration and the mood divine,
Infused a force portentous, like the strength
  Of madness through his frame.
Mohareb reels before him; he right on,
  With knee, with breast, with arm,
   Presses the staggering foe;
   And now upon the brink
  Of that tremendous spring,—
There, with fresh impulse and a rush of force,
  He thrust him from his hold.
  The upwhirling flood received
  Mohareb; then, absorbed,
  Ingulfed him in the abyss.

              (4:156)

Samuel Chew was very hard on Southey for writing this way:

> Southey's choice of meter in *Thalaba* was ill-advised. The rimeless
> lines of varying lengths, contracting and expanding according to no
> discernible principle of either sense or form, seem but so much prose
> chopped up indiscriminately; the reader is constantly looking for a
> pattern that is not there. . . . Even so, Southey was in this matter a
> precursor, for where he failed later poets, managing more subtly the
> cadences which distinguish free verse from prose, have succeeded.
> (Baugh 1161)

Chew's comment itself, dating from the late 1940s, is of historical inter-
est, showing how widespread the concept of cadence was then, however
poorly defined the concept may have been.

  Southey is sometimes said to have abandoned free verse at the same
time as his political views turned more conservative, but in "Ode Written
during War with America, 1814," one encounters the earliest totally ir-
regular ode that I know of, with no rhyme at all and fourteen stanzas that
contain lines ranging from dimeters to pentameters. He wrote several
others at about the same time, and I have found no reference to the

unusual form of any of these, which ought to count as milestones in English prosody, in Saintsbury or anywhere else. In honor of improved Russian-American relations I will quote from Southey's "Ode to His Imperial Majesty, Alexander I., Emperor of All the Russias."

> Rear high the monument!
> In Moscow, and in proud Petropolis,
> The brazen trophy build;
> Cannon on cannon piled
> Till the huge column overtop your towers!
> From France the Tyrant brought
> These instruments of death
> To work your overthrow;
> He left them in his flight
> To form the eternal record of his own.
> Raise, Russia, with thy spoils
> A nobler monument
> Than e'er imperial Rome
> Built in her plenitude of pride and power!
> Still, Alexander! on the banks of Seine,
> Thy noblest monument
> For future ages stands—
> PARIS SUBDUED AND SPARED.
>
> (3:192)

When he was eighteen years old, Shelley tried out free verse as well as atheism. According to Mary Shelley, "[T]he rhythm of *Queen Mab* was founded on that of *Thalaba*" (340). The earlier sections are in free verse, but much of the poem sinks back into Miltonic blank verse. This verse paragraph from canto 8, "The Fairy," is a good example:

> Joy to the Spirit came.
> Through the wide rent in Time's eternal veil,
> Hope was seen beaming through the mists of fear:
> Earth was no longer Hell;
> Love, freedom, health, had given
> Their ripeness to the manhood of its prime,
> And all its pulses beat
> Symphonious to the planetary spheres:

> Then dulcet music swelled
> Concordant with the life-strings of the soul;
> It throbbed in sweet and languid beatings there,
> Catching new life from transitory death,—
> Like the vague sighings of wind at even,
> That wakes the wavelets of the slumbering sea
> And dies on the creation of its breath,
> And sinks and rises, fails and swells by fits:
>> Was the pure stream of feeling
>> That sprung from these sweet notes,
> And o'er the Spirit's human sympathies
> With mild and gentle motion calmly flowed.

(282)

Not all the lines of *Queen Mab* are as easily scannable in iambics as these, but most are. Though he later condemned this poem ("I doubt not but it is perfectly worthless in point of literary composition"), Shelley has confirmed the earlier steps taken beyond the irregular ode, abandoning rhyme altogether.

Shelley also made an important contribution to free-verse doctrine in *A Defence of Poetry:*

> An observation of the regular mode of the recurrence of this harmony in the language of poetical minds, together with its relation to music, produced metre, or a certain system of traditional forms of harmony of language. Yet it is by no means essential that a poet should accommodate his language to this traditional form, so that the harmony which is its spirit, be observed. The practice is indeed convenient and popular, and to be preferred, especially in such composition as includes much form and action: but every great poet must inevitably innovate upon the example of his predecessors in the exact structure of his peculiar versification. The distinction between poets and prose writers is a vulgar error.

Shelley continues extending the bounds of poetry to include a great portion of his favorite reading ("Lord Bacon was a poet"), even the Greek historians. In this we see a continuation, on more subjective grounds, of the position advanced by Sprat in defense of Cowley, that verse gains in flexibility as it approaches prose. One would like to ask Shelley if "Kubla Khan" would be as effective without its incantatory tetrameters; or if the meter of *Christabel* might not have been partly responsible for the hallucination that he experienced upon hearing it read aloud.

In Shelley's emphasis on the great poet's "peculiar versification" we may also see an adumbration of "Voice of the Bard" theory of poetry—to borrow a phrase from Blake, to whom we now turn.

If my treatment were strictly chronological, I would have taken up William Blake at the beginning of this chapter. In discussions of historical trends, as in life, Blake remains at the fringes of English Romanticism, for the most part out of touch with his contemporaries, and scarcely read until discovered in midcentury by the Pre-Raphaelites. It is hard to distinguish between accidents, random personal malice or exploitation by others, and Blake's cranky self-sufficiency in explaining his obscurity; but the last of these surely helps to explain his poetry. Another reason that I have not made Blake central to this period is that he is a prime exemplar of the Hebraic-prophetic mode of free verse, and I wish to treat that separately in the following chapter. Also, his rebelliousness could carry him in more directions than one; he was a radical innovator in the way that he used *regular* iambs, trochees, and anapests, together with some of the most skillfully executed trimeters and tetrameters in the language. One can, as with all poets, find advance hints of Blake's *regular* versification in eighteenth-century oddments, not to speak of songs and nursery rhymes. He was determined to go against sanctioned authority, whether it was Joshua Reynolds and the Royal Academy, or whether it was the iambic pentameter, and he could rebel by tightening up as well as by loosening.

Blake did, of course, employ the iambic pentameter, in some of the short lyrics, such as "The Little Black Boy," as well as in the pseudo-Shakespearean *King Edward the Third*. One of his most interesting free-verse experiments, though, teases that meter until it unravels:

TO THE EVENING STAR
Thou fair-hair'd angel of the evening
Now, whilst the sun rests on the mountains, light
Thy bright torch of love; thy radiant crown
Put on, and smile upon our evening bed!
Smile on our loves, and, while thou drawest the

> Blue curtains of the sky, scatter thy silver dew
> On every flower that shuts its sweet eyes
> In timely sleep. Let thy west wind sleep on
> The lake; speak silence with thy glimmering eyes,
> And wash the dusk with silver. Soon, full soon,
> Dost thou withdraw; then the wolf rages wide,
> And the lion glares thro' the dun forest:
> The fleeces of our flocks are cover'd with
> Thy sacred dew: protect them with thine influence.

The first line is a tetrameter, or seems to be until one reads the second. At that point the ear questions whether "evening" might not have been meant to carry three syllables, which it never does in earlier poetry—and hardly ever does now. The strong enjambment of "light / Thy bright torch," with its internal rhyme, also confuses the issue; Milton never enjambed in that fashion until he wrote *Paradise Regained,* since to do so tends to destroy the meter altogether. But if we seem committed to looseness by the first two lines, we must immediately abandon even that certainty because of the ten-syllable regularity of "Put on, and smile upon our evening bed!" Here "evening" reappears in its perfectly definite two-syllable form. Well, then, so it *is* iambic pentameter. "Smile on our lives and while thou drawest the" is ten syllables—but wait! End a line with an article? Unheard of—until William Carlos Williams did it more than a century later. But at least the syllable count is correct. Or is it? "Blue curtains of the sky, scatter thy silver dew"—that's twelve syllables. And so it goes to the end, skirting the pentameter, flirting with ten syllables, then turning away. Among other things the poem is the earliest (ca. 1775) phrase-breaking free verse that I know of, separating article from noun, preposition from object. Not even the choruses of *Samson Agonistes* do that.

Several other poems in *Poetical Sketches,* published in 1783, exhibit some of the same features: "To Summer," "To Autumn," "To Winter," "To Morning," and others. It may be piling one oxymoron atop another to speak of "classic free verse," but these poems of Blake's illustrate exactly how free verse can prosper by presupposing the possibility of regularity—in this case, the loosened blank verse of the later eighteenth century—and stepping outside or beyond the convention. "To the Evening Star" would lose much of its interest as a poem if there were nothing for it to be *different* from. Anyone who argues that Blake did not know what he was doing and that I am apologizing for juvenile ineptness will have to explain Blake's competence in regular meters dating from the same time. I would no more doubt Blake's command of prosody than I would his ability to see angels.

In Tennyson and Browning the Romantic enthusiasm for experimentation in prosody continued, even as the personal voice of the poet disappeared. To say this is not to question how genuine Tennyson's grief was when he composed the individual segments of *In Memoriam,* but I do mean to point out that the technical feat of transforming envelope-quatrains of tetrameter into a medium to convey that grief—and much else—is the work of a poet, not a stricken mourner. Even more remarkable is the control of the meter in "Tears, Idle Tears." And in most of his poetry, Tennyson is the disengaged artisan, accomplishing the most remarkable aural effects to be found in English poetry. Browning is crude in comparison, but his poetry, too, is a collection of experiments with almost every possible combination of feet, line lengths, and stanza forms. The work of both these poets is the polar opposite to free verse, and I would argue that between them, they seemed to have so thoroughly exhausted the possibilities of accentual-syllabic metrics that the only thing left to achieve originality—besides servile imitation—was to try some sort of free verse.

In his early twenties Tennyson did compose a rather irregular piece, "The Sea Fairies," which he later expanded into "The Lotus Eaters." The second poem is a dazzling display of poetic engineering that takes the Spenserian stanza and accomplishes its disintegration in the course of the poem; this parallels, of course, the demoralization of the drugged sailors. The case could be made that this is a sort of free verse, a precursor of *The Waste Land.* My view is that "The Lotus Eaters" never steps outside the form that it is exploiting, the Spenserian stanza, though it does distort it to the point that it could not be recognized. I realize that Yvor Winters, were he alive to pronounce upon this, would say that "The Lotus Eaters" presents its subject without evaluating it, and that the metrics should be part of the moral evaluation. He might argue that the metrics destroy the poem, or that the lack of moral evaluation destroys the metrics. To which would I nod respectfully, and continue to include the poem on my syllabus. It is a wonderful example of Victorian gimcrackery, but it is not free verse.

Irregular stanzas can certainly be found in Tennyson. There is "Eleanore," and *Maud* is full of them. He composed a good old-fashioned irregular "Ode on the Death of the Duke of Wellington." But in all these he draws back from innovations introduced by Southey and Shelley.

In Browning there is even less that remotely qualifies as free verse. I think of the madrigal when I see the irregular stanzas of "Home Thoughts from Abroad," because of the Italian context of that poem. But there seems to be no impulse anywhere in Browning to commit the ultimate grotesquerie of abandoning regular meters and rhymes. For a poet who practiced and celebrated robust self-assertion, who disdained tame perfection, and who enjoyed throwing into doubt Victorian proprieties and even moralities, his reluctance to take this step is odd—one additional reason to join with Ruskin in calling him the literary puzzle of the nineteenth century.

Matthew Arnold is also a puzzle, but in his case the enigma is why he *did* write free verse. George Saintsbury tried to ignore this inconvenient fact in his *History,* which discusses "The Forsaken Merman" without noting that it is free verse, and which does not even make reference to "Dover Beach." Others, such as "Philomela," are presumably included in those poems that he calls "attempts, especially in rhymeless measures, are as little happy as they are new" (3:261). This comment occurs not in the discussion of Arnold, but in connection with some of the minor poets with whom he has grouped Arnold; Saintsbury makes much the same point that I have, that Tennyson and Browning seemed to have done everything possible, and all that was left was free verse. I would also argue that there was, in Matthew Arnold, a buried vein of Romanticism, suppressed in much of his poetry after "Tristram and Iseult" (which was itself partly done in *Christabel* meter), and that this impulse emerged in his prosody.

However it occurred, there is no question that "Philomela" is free verse:

PHILOMELA
Hark! ah, the nightingale—
The tawny-throated!
Hark, from that moonlit cedar what a burst!
What a triumph! hark!—what pain!

O wanderer from a Grecian shore,
Still, after many years, in distant lands,
Still nourishing in thy bewilder'd brain

That wild, unquench'd, deep-sunken, old-world pain—
Say, will it never heal?
And can this fragrant lawn
With its cool trees, and night,
And the sweet, tranquil Thames,
And moonshine, and the dew,
To thy rack'd heart and brain
Afford no balm?

Dost thou to-night behold,
Here, through the moonlight on this English grass,
The unfriendly palace in the Thracian wild?
Dost thou again peruse
With hot cheeks and sear'd eyes
The too clear web, and thy dumb sister's shame?
Dost thou once more assay
Thy flight, and feel come over thee,
Poor fugitive, the feathery change
Once more, and once more seem to make resound
With love and hate, triumph and agony,
Lone Daulis, and the high Cephissian vale?

Listen, Eugenia—
How thick the bursts come crowding through the leaves!
Again—thou hearest?
Eternal passion!
Eternal pain!

Other poems that may count as free verse, though some make much more use of rhyme than "Philomela," include "The Voice," "Stagirus," "Parting," "The Strayed Reveler," "Early Death and Fame," "Dover Beach," "The Youth of Man," "A Summer Night," "The Buried Life," "The Future," "Epilogue," and parts of *Merope* and *Empedocles on Etna*. There are also Arnold's experiments with a rhymeless line that is either a sort of trimeter or some kind of dipodic rhythm ("Memorial Verses" and "Rugby Chapel"). With no explicit explanation from Arnold of the models for his metrics in these, one imagines that he had read Wordsworth's *Immortality Ode* and knew Southey's experiments, and that he combined these suggestions with the sorts of passages from Greek drama that Milton drew on. Those of his contemporaries who comment on the form of

Arnold's irregular poems speak vaguely of "Pindarics." Saintsbury thinks he did Southey one worse: "One thing to be reckoned altogether to Southey's credit prosodically, in the devising of *Thalaba,* is that he saw, and deliberately set himself to avoid, the pit into which, as we have seen, his model Sayers fell before him, and into which, much longer after him, Mr. Matthew Arnold was constantly tumbling" (3:51).

One Romantic subcurrent that had continued from the time of "Ossian" was an interest not only in Celtic mythology, but also in the original language and meters in which the tales were recorded; this may account to some degree for Arnold's prosodic experiments. Nothing was well-understood on this subject, but the rough notion was that those ancient, authentically "British" materials, had been composed in some sort of loose, assonantal or unrhymed, accentual meter. That Arnold shared this fascination and these misconceptions is proved by a passage from "On the Study of Celtic Literature," which serves the additional valuable purpose of illustrating how the foggy concept of Pindarism had never dissipated completely, despite the strictures of Goldsmith, Johnson, and others in the previous century. The linking of "Ossian" and Pindar is remarkable evidence of how deeply Arnold was imbued with Romantic prejudices, despite his immersion in classical literature and despite his Victorian eminence as a most earnest critic and moralist.

> This something is *style,* and the Celts certainly have it in a wonderful measure. Style is the most striking quality of their poetry. Celtic poetry seems to make up to itself for being unable to master the world and give an adequate interpretation of it, by throwing all its force into style, by bending language at any rate to its will, and expressing the ideas it has with unsurpassable intensity, elevation, and effect. It has all through it a sort of intoxication of style,—a *Pindarism,* to use a word formed from the name of the poet, on whom, above all other poets, the power of style seems to have exercised an inspiring and intoxicating effect; and not in its great poets only, in Taliesin, or Llywarch Hen, or Ossian, does the celtic genius show this Pindarism, but in all its productions. (119–20)

Arnold appears to have been imposed upon simultaneously by a seventeenth-century misapprehension ("Pindarism") and an eighteenth-century fraud ("Ossian"), both of which had been exposed to contempt by Samuel Johnson. The need to believe in untutored poetic genius transcends the limitations of mere facts. It is not difficult to see how this belief authorized Arnold's own practice in his free-verse poems. Park Honan was so struck by the effect of primitive spontaneity that Arnold seemed to aim at in "The Forsaken Merman," that in *Matthew Arnold: A Life,* Honan says, "It is also a perfect illustration of Schiller's essay on the Naïve, so that it might complement almost any passage from that work" (93). Honan then quotes Schiller:

> Genius expresses its most sublime and its deepest thoughts with this simple grace; they are the divine oracles that issue from the lips of a child; while the scholastic spirit, always anxious to avoid error, tortures all its words, all its ideas, and makes them pass through the crucible of grammar and logic, hard and rigid, in order to keep from vagueness, and uses few words in order not to say too much, enervates and blunts thoughts in order not to wound the reader who is not on his guard. Genius gives to its expression, with a single happy stroke of the brush, a precise, firm, and yet perfectly free form. (Schiller 273–74)

That Arnold's free verse was the wave of the future was not immediately evident. Decades into the twentieth century, anthologies of Victorian literature simply omitted most such poems. The period from 1880 to 1900 saw mostly rhymed and metered verse, and the dominant direction seemed to be a continuation of Victorian experimentalism into forms borrowed from other literatures. For the first time "French forms" appeared in great numbers—the villanelles, sestinas, rondeaus, triolets, and ballades. Experiments in quantity revived, despite Tennyson's parodies of such efforts; Robert Bridges, for one, ought to have known that if Tennyson could not do it, it could not be done, but he tried it nevertheless. Yet simultaneously free verse continued to be composed. The prosodic bifurcation mirrored the central Victorian dilemma: Which way shall we go? Onward and upward, or back to the Middle Ages? Are we evangelists, or are we Catholic revivalists? Do we look to the troubadours for our poetic forms, or do we innovate in the spirit of progress, of modern science and technology? The enervation of the 1890s reflected the spiritual exhaustion of these unresolvable conflicts, and the best poetry of that time expresses a fastidious accidie, the so-called aestheticism or decadence.

Some of what appeared to be free verse in the later nineteenth century was actually composed according to theories of scansion proposed as

early as 1857, though not elaborated until 1878, by Coventry Patmore. In
some ways his "dipodic" theory can be seen as a precursor to the cadence
theories; the effect that it had on his own poetry, and a few others, was to
fracture the iambic norm. Or so it seemed to Patmore; many readers see
his "dipodics" as nothing more than tetrameters, roughened up a little in
the direction of the *Christabel* meter. His dipodic theory required that
every poetic line be divisible into units that were multiples of two. He
used, when it seemed to suit his needs, lines that we would call trimeters
and pentameters—that is, lines that cannot reasonably be said to consist
of even numbers of segments; his argument that they were really longer,
with implied additional feet, will not strike many as convincing. His
theory seems partly to have proceeded from some form of sexual
mania—the necessity for sexual pairing; or perhaps it was a kind of
Noah's Ark metrics: the animals marching two by two. His theorizing,
however, seemed to give him the confidence in some of his poems to
write with much freedom, although his practice does not really go be-
yond some of the irregular poems of the seventeenth century, and cer-
tainly not as far as Southey went. The essay by Basil Champneys that
introduces the collected *Poems by Coventry Patmore* of 1906 not only ex-
plains his metrics but also is a convenient summary of many things
already touched on here. I shall quote it at some length, since it provides a
valuable perspective on the history of free verse, written just at the mo-
ment when the new theories of vers libre and Imagism were germinating,
but before anyone was aware of their existence. Champneys's emphasis
is, as mine has been to this point, on the English and Italian antecedents,
rather than the French and American:

> The derivation of the meter of the Odes [as longer poems of Patmore's
> are often called] has been much discussed. Such precedents as have
> been found for it are but partial and at most suggestive. Considerable
> and irregular variation in length of line is as old as English poetry. In
> the "madrigals" and "epigrams" of Drummond of Hawthornden
> change in number of feet is found combined with varied distribution
> of rhyme. To these, in the preface to the third edition of the *Unknown
> Eros,* Patmore seems to acknowledge a debt. In "Lycidas" the occa-
> sional shortening of the line is productive of excellent effect. Cow-
> ley's Odes, so-called "Pindarique," may also have in some measure
> served as a precedent, notwithstanding Patmore's expressed con-
> tempt for them. Mr. Gosse holds that "the true analogy of his 'Odes'

is with the Italian lyric of the early Renaissance." . . . Spenser's "Epithalamium" seems to me to bear a closer resemblance to the Odes in actual flow and modulation than any of these. (xli)

According to Champneys, Patmore may also have used as a model certain irregular poems by Henry S. Sutton, who had in 1848 published a collection that contained "two poems in 'iambic' metre, of considerable length, in which the number of feet in the line and the incidence of rhyme is considerably varied, and in which the *cadence* [my italics] occasionally resembles that of the 'Odes'" (xlii). It is just here that a tenuous connection emerges between the tentative later-Victorian experiments in free verse and the robust contentiousness of free verse in the earlier twentieth century: Champneys's use of "cadence," a word that Ford Madox Ford, who was his contemporary, made much of and passed on to Ezra Pound, Amy Lowell, and W. C. Williams. Ford, like the name of the magazine he founded, was truly "Transatlantic"; having grown up among Pre-Raphaelites, and having heard Tennyson and Browning read their poems, he ended as a visitor to America, sought out by Robert Lowell in a Tennessee farmhouse owned by Allen Tate; as we shall see, his influence on prosody was out of all proportion to his abilities as a poet—because of his range of literary friendships and his integrity.

Champneys's reference to the now totally obscure Henry S. Sutton makes a connection with Emerson, who was one of Sutton's great admirers and who considered him equal to the Metaphysicals, especially Herbert. It was through Sutton that Patmore came to read and admire Emerson. J. C. Reid, in *The Mind and Art of Coventry Patmore,* argues at some length that Patmore's thinking about poetry was permeated with ideas from Emerson, and proves his point by quoting back and forth between the writings of the two (46–50). Patmore absorbed the ideas of the self-sufficiency of genius, of the poet's authority to generate his own structures, the "meter-making argument" of Emerson.

The best-known of Patmore's irregular poems is "To the Unknown Eros," from the opening of which I quote, to show the general effect of the prosody:

What rumour'd heavens and these
Which not a poet sings,
O, Unknown Eros? What this breeze
Of sudden wings

Speeding at far returns of time from interstellar space
To fan my very face,
And gone as fleet,
Through delicatest ether feathering soft their solitary beat,
With ne'er a light plume dropp'd, not any trace
To speak of whence they came, or whither they depart?

Patmore's biographer, J. C. Reid, writing in 1957, said admiringly of this poem: "The highest points of *The Unknown Eros* make Patmore a poet of the order of Donne, Crashaw, Hopkins, and Herbert." He then adds, "Yet the work contains that dross which is evidence of the intensity of his personal struggle" (303). The dross must have prevailed; in my university library's copy of the *Poems,* which was published in 1906 and which has been on the library shelves for at least thirty years, the pages following the lines quoted above are uncut. A hundred years is usually enough to allow the jury to reach a verdict.

One would like to hear Ezra Pound's reaction if it were pointed out to him that one of the better-known mid-Victorian poets, Thomas Edward Brown, had preceded him in writing free verse. Brown's diction was precisely that which the Imagists were anxious to trash, and the diction has nothing to do with the form, or the lack thereof. Indeed, "My Garden" is a free-form poem; this is the one that begins, "A garden is a lovesome thing, God wot!"

Published in 1870, George Meredith's "Dirge in the Woods" clearly anticipates the combination of metrical loosening and increasing precision of description favored by the Imagists:

DIRGE IN THE WOODS
A wind sways in the pines,
          And below
Not a breath of wild air;
Still as the mosses that glow
On the flooring and over the lines
Of the roots here and there.
The pine tree drops its dead;
They are quiet, as under the sea.
Overhead, overhead
Rushes life in a race,
As the clouds, the clouds chase;

> And we go
> And we drop like the fruits of the tree,
> Even we,
> Even so.

One could revise the poem to read:

> A wind sways the pines
>   And below
> Not a breath of wild air;
> Still as the mosses

> That glow on the flooring
> And over the lines of the roots;
> Here and there the pine tree
> Drops its dead. They are quiet
> As under the sea. Overhead, overhead,
> Clouds the clouds chase.

By eliminating the explicit moralizing and by internalizing the rhymes one ends with a piece close in form and manner to H.D.'s "Oread."

Most relevant to twentieth-century free verse are the experiments of W. H. Henley, for whom free verse was a way of stripping off the Tennysonian-Swinburnian rhetoric that prevented poetry from coming to terms with the hard facts of life. This is not true of all the poems in the series, *In Hospital,* some of which prefigure the technique of the "war poets" in adapting elegant measures and Romantic rhetoric for the purpose of emphasizing the horror of the experience. Henley had been a pupil of T. E. Brown, and in this 1875 volume may have borrowed the free forms from him and from Arnold. To them, he adds the liberty to do without rhyme, except for unusual emphasis (as in "Ache—-!", below). This poem, "Vigil," grows like the others out of his own experience of spending twenty months in a hospital following the amputation of a foot.

> VIGIL
> Live on one's back,
> In the long hours of repose
> Life is a practical nightmare—
> Hideous asleep or awake.

Shoulders and loins
Ache—-!
   Ache, and the mattress,
Runs into boulders and hummocks,
Glows like a kiln, while the bedclothes—
Tumbling, importunate, daft—
Ramble and roll, and the gas,
Screwed to its lowermost,
An inevitable atom of light,
Haunts, and a stertorous sleeper
Snores me to hate and despair.

All the old time
Surges malignant before me;
Old voices, old kisses, old songs
Blossom derisive about me;
While the new days
Pass me in endless procession:
A pageant of shadows
Silently, leeringly wending
On . . . and still on . . . and still on!

Far in the stillness a cat
Languishes loudly. A cinder
Falls, and the shadows
Lurch to the leap of the flame. The next man to me
Turns with a moan; and the snorer,
The drug like a rope at his throat,
Gasps, gurgles, snorts himself free, as the night-nurse,
Noiseless and strange,

Her bulls-eye half-lanterned in apron,
(Whispering me, "Are ye no sleepin' yet?")
Passes, list-slippered and peering,
Round . . . and is gone.

Sleep comes at last—
Sleep full of dreams and misgivings—
Broken with brutal and sordid

Voices and sounds that impose on me,
Ere I can wake to it,
The unnatural, intolerable day.

The sheer power of the writing makes a fastidious consideration of the metrics seem superfluous, even corrupt. But I notice that even as he abandons predictable form, Henley approximates the rhythms of Arnold's "Rugby Chapel"—or, to take an example of nearly a hundred years later—his practice resembles the tentative anapestic trimeter in which James Dickey's best poems have been written. It is more like returning periodically to memorable pattern instead of sticking to it throughout; for Henley in this poem, it is a dactylic trimeter, as in the lines, "Far in the stillness a cat," and "Sleep full of dreams and misgivings." Whatever it may be, it is surely *not* chopped-up pentameter, as Ford Madox Ford claimed.

In his poems of naturalistic description from the later 1890s, which anticipate Imagism or, even more, the urban desolation in T. S. Eliot's work, John Davidson could not quite relinquish meter and rhyme to the degree that Henley had—or rather, he let one go, or the other, but not both at once. His unrhymed lines that describe in painstaking detail the movements of an insect trapped in a railway carriage mark a new advance for the iambic pentameter, much like what Philip Larkin achieved with his matter-of-fact language sixty years later:

THE WASP
Once as I went by rail to Epping Street,
Both windows being open, a wasp flew in;
Through the compartment swung and almost out
Scarce seen, scarce heard; but dead against the pane
Entitled "Smoking," did the train's career
Arrest her passage.

"In the Isle of Dogs" rhymes, but irregularly; here is its third stanza:

From the pavements and the roofs
In shimmering volumes wound
The wrinkled heat;

Distant hammers, wheels and hoofs,
A turbulent pulse of sound,
Southward obscurely beat,
The only utterance of the afternoon,
Till on the silent street
An organ-man drew up and ground
The Old Hundredth tune.

Davidson may be the most underrated poet of the last century.

Additional minor examples from the 1890s can be noted, such as Richard Watson Dixon's "Ode on Advancing Age" and John Leicester Warren's choruses from his imitations of Greek plays. Francis Thompson's "The Hound of Heaven" was recognized as something unusual, and dignified by being called a "Pindaric." Most remarkable in the 1890s was the self-conscious cultivation of artifice for its own sake as, for example, when Oscar Wilde took Tennyson's *In Memoriam* stanza and employed it ironically for poems that were conspicuously "aesthetic" in their intent.

Swinburne tried so many experiments that it was inevitable that some of his writing should appear to be irregular, as in "Loch Torridan" where short lines, ranging down to monometers, rhyme with longer ones, ranging up to hexameters, in the first part of the poem. But Swinburne represents an attenuated and exhausted Tennysonianism—a metrical exhibitionism and mindless harmoniousness that every important poet of the earlier twentieth century reacted against.

Nor can Gerard Manley Hopkins be considered a vers-librist, though "The Wreck of the Deutschland" is arguably a latter-day English irregular ode—one of the last examples of the "Pindarique"—and though his experiments bear some relation to subsequent theories of cadence. Hopkins is another instance of Victorian experimentalism, stretching old forms and meters into improbable shapes, beating the pentameter until, like a sprung sofa, it is replete with interesting lumps and hollows.

Most nineteenth-century American instances of free verse—Whitman excepted, of course—are derivative of earlier British examples. Melville cultivated the irregular ode in "The March into Virginia" and "After the Pleasure Party," and numerous other poets employed this form, which was so long established as hardly to count as free verse. Emerson, in lines that are reminiscent of some seventeenth-century poems, though he may have been modeling his practice on that of Henry S.

Sutton, used phrase-reinforcing free verse—with some rhyme—in "Terminus" (1867):

It is time to be old,
To take in sail:—
The god of bounds,
Who sets to seas a shore,
Came to me in his fatal rounds,
And said: "No more!
No farther shoot
Thy broad ambitious branches, and thy root,
Fancy departs: no more invent,
Contract thy firmament
To compass of a tent.
There's not enough for this and that,
Make thy opinion which of two . . ."

Similar patterns appear in other poems, such as "Ode to Beauty" (1843), and in "Hamatreya," "Merlin," "Give All to Love," "Ode: Inscribed to W. H. Channing," and "Fable" (all printed in 1847). Emerson's use of shorter lines—most run from dimeters to tetrameters, and only a few are pentameters—distinguishes him from Wordsworth and Coleridge and makes him parallel Arnold. Wherever he got them, and his sources may include Goethe, these short-line free-form poems do fulfill his idea of poetry as a "meter-making argument" and of the poet as someone determinedly out of step, like his neighbor, Thoreau. Williams only continued what Emerson began.

An argument could be made that the numerous books of translations from Native American chants and songs constitute a kind of free verse. Also, when Thoreau contributed his translation of an ode by Pindar to the *Dial* he composed it in lines but made no effort to give them regular meter or rhyme. This willingness to abandon form in order to preserve the "authentic" qualities of the originals foreshadows the now widely accepted belief that the original genius of the individual poet should be accorded the same liberty.

Even more quirky than Emerson's are the short poems by Stephen Crane. The heavy-handed irony, obvious symbolism, and graceless flatness of diction in some of these snippets make it probable that they would be forgotten were it not for Crane's distinction as a novelist:

THE WAYFARER
The wayfarer,
Perceiving the pathway to truth,
Was struck with astonishment.
It was thickly grown with weeds.
"Ha," he said,
"I see that none has passed here in a long time."
Later he saw that each weed
Was a singular knife.
"Well," he mumbled at last,
"Doubtless there are other roads."

The sophomoric cynicism here would dignify a high-school yearbook, but that is about all it is worth as poetry. As an indication of an urge to break free from Longfellow at all costs, it is more interesting, even laudable.

The vulgarizing of poetic diction—which Yeats was to deplore and blame on "The Great War" and "Mr. T. S. Eliot," and which he attributed to "an overwhelming bitterness" (in one of the recordings of his voice)—had in fact been under way since at least as early as 1875. As we shall see when we take up Ford Madox Ford again, Whitman's American commonness was too much for many Englishmen, even those who felt strongly that something had to be done to eliminate what Pound called "Tennysonianness." To some extent the very favor that Whitman had found with Tennyson, Rossetti, and Swinburne may have hobbled his reputation in England after the turn of the century. But as is clear in the poems quoted above, the tendency toward a more colloquial literary language, an evangelistic-spirited distaste for "establishment" diction, often accompanied experiments with free verse. This was in some sense a renewal of Wordsworth's call for the discarding of eighteenth-century diction—just as ideas about "personal cadence" and organic form were a recurrence of the Romantic cult of personality and, especially, Coleridge's theories about poetry.

Timothy Steele's emphasis on the effect that the Pound/Eliot attack on older poeticisms had as an adjunct to free verse somewhat obscures the fact that this modification of Victorian vocabulary had begun much earlier. Helmut E. Gerber's concluding seminar lecture, first delivered as a formal paper in 1975, focused on just this issue:

One of the most radical developments in late nineteenth-century literature, in both prose and poetry, is the vast expansion of the literary vocabulary and the breakdown of traditional distinctions between poetic diction and prosaic diction or, for that matter, between the vocabulary of literature and the vocabulary of life. Dialect, vulgar language, argot of one kind or another had existed for centuries. Such language, however, was mainly reserved for comedy or for minor characters. But during the nineteenth century and especially after mid-century, such language more often became the language of central characters and even of serious poetry, drama, and fiction. (17)

Gerber then goes on to connect this with developments in free verse:

The distinction between poetic diction and prosaic diction, between the vocabulary of literature and the language men really speak nearly disappears. It is not a great span from the extended vocabulary of the 1880s and 1890s writers to the vocabulary of Sandburg and, later, Allen Ginsberg's "Howl." In the poetry and prose of the 1880s and 1890s there is a good deal of sweat and stink, smear and clank, as many vultures and crows as doves and nightingales, as much leek and garlic as plum and pomegranate. (19)

I would argue that there were two separate paths leading toward the employment of common speech—that Sandburg and Ginsberg derive directly from Whitman, whereas the British version took the form—at least in Eliot and Auden—of verbal slumming, an affectation of music-hall song and conversation. Davidson and Henley were, of course, more authentic. The important point is that an adjustment of diction in the direction of simplicity, directness, even vulgarity, parallels and accompanies prosodic liberties.

Ahead of us, at this point, lies the no-man's-land of twentieth-century metrics, but first we must again look backward, not just to Walt Whitman, but as far as the early seventeenth century. Here we will see examples of the variety of free verse that can be identified with the greatest certainty, and that has been frequently cultivated in this century, sometimes by those who are scarcely aware of just whom or what they are imitating.

regarding "Dexter"

Speech-like or colloquial or non-Poppean (?)

non-Poppean or non-Tennysonian language

includes: (1) non-formulaic phrasing, avoidance of "poeticisms"
(2) move away from elegant & vulgar language (courses
(attention trying to write is never-organized impulses)

(3) and phrasing / speech-like roughness (courses
pentameter pairs) certain types of enjambment
caesura, much varied place & length

↓ rhythm (& meter)

ie Tdalgaard: longings (diction)
↓ phrasing (caesurae/enjambment, (not verb/adj)
steep enjambment, (not verb/adj)
reduced "severity" "mellifluousness"
not descriptive (not "the Seasons" of Phosphor
not narrative (not telling Thalatha Smith)

in pursuit of various knots, but always
unstopped (or scattered)
varied length (or verse-span)
un-metered (non-stanzaic)

NEW: intense inward "space"
prelude (new to D.W.) construction
gladiator material?

Cowper's pindarics put that verse in new Pindaresque bottles
(not new wine in new bottles — Cowper better)
(not new wine in old bottles — language in
new bottles (several from)
which control is both neoclassical

How close to the correct really?
varied line lengths of
occasional rhyme in
varied stanzas?
values but not
period.

Chapter 7

Bards and Prophets

Dr. Mendes said "that rhyming was not a characteristic of
Hebrew poetry at all. Great poets discarded it; the early
Jewish poets knew it not."
—Walt Whitman, quoting De Sola Mendes
in "The Bible as Poetry"

Carl Sandburg's *Complete Poems* (1950) opens with "Notes for a Preface,"
in which he expressed with exemplary directness his prejudice against
rhymed and metered poetry:

> There is a formal poetry perfect only in form, "all dressed up and
> nowhere to go." The number of syllables, the designated and re-
> quired stresses of accent, the rhymes if wanted—they come off with
> the skill of a solved crossword puzzle. Yet its animation and connota-
> tion are less than that of "a dead mackerel in the moonshine," the
> latter even as an extinct form reporting that once it was a living fish
> aswim in bright waters. (xxiv)

On the next page he suggests a new beginning for poetry, one that had at
least the virtue of countering, forty years in advance, the crudely mecha-
nistic approach of some of those who espouse the New Formalist move-
ment of the 1980s and 1990s—

> A well-done world history of poetry would tell us of the begin-
> nings and the continuing tradition of blank verse, rhymed verse,
> ballads, ballades, sonnets, triolets, rondeaus, villanelles, the sestina,
> the pantoum, the hokku; also odes, elegies, idylls, lyrics, hymns,
> quatrains, couplets, ditties, limericks, and all the other forms. These

are fixed, frozen, immutable; in a Japanese hokku you are allowed seventeen syllables and if you make it in sixteen or eighteen you're out of luck. Such a history of poetry, however, might go a long way in research, chronicle, and discussion of a vital body of ancient and modern poems under the following (and more) heads:

1. Chants.
2. Psalms.
3. Gnomics.
4. Contemplations.
5. Proverbs.
6. Epitaphs.
7. Litanies.
8. Incidents of intensely concentrated action or utterance.

Of Sandburg's categories, at least five can be subsumed under a single heading: biblical-anaphoric free verse. This was the chief vehicle for his more impassioned utterances, and Sandburg found it difficult to conceive of other modes of organization that he could deem truly suitable for poetry. His "list of heads" assumes that there are only one or two ways of writing, and directs attention to the poem's occasion or intent rather than its form. His list also serves as an implied apology for the one way of writing in which he was most at home, the one that showed that he, more than any other poet up to that time, had thoroughly assimilated Walt Whitman, and through Whitman, the Bible. One wonders if it crossed his mind that two of the terms in his list are also the actual names of books of the Old Testament, and a third ("Litanies") designates a liturgical prayer that is modeled on biblical cadences. Many who practice that sort of free verse, which imitates some of the oldest written poetry, are genuinely innocent of mimetic intentions and imagine that they are speaking from immediate inspiration.

To say "the oldest poetry" is not quite accurate; what I really mean is a four-hundred-year-old attempt to render into English some of the oldest poetry. The committee of scholars who edited the King James Bible collected all the happiest turns of speech from earlier English translations, improving upon them if possible, and then compared the results for accuracy and felicity with all other available translations in ancient and modern languages. Until this century even the unchurched and lapsed believers, in England and especially in America where the Bible was often the only available literature, were at some point in their lives likely to have been imprinted with its language and rhythms. For many, biblical language seemed a natural extension of ordinary speech.

Although the following discussion relies on "Characteristics of Hebrew Poetry," in the *New Oxford Annotated Bible,* all quotations are from the King James Bible, including the Psalms, which are numbered differently from the Psalter in the *Book of Common Prayer.* The King James did not aim at reproducing exactly the metrics of the original Hebrew poetry, and could not have done so in any case, because the metrics were not understood. Even in the original Hebrew the meters of the poetic books of the Old Testament are not particularly consistent. When we say "poetical books" we mean many passages from the prophetic books, such as Isaiah, Jeremiah, and Ezekiel; most of the Book of Job; Proverbs and Lamentations; and preeminently the Psalms and the Song of Solomon. Even in the New Testament the original Greek was in some respects modeled upon Hebrew, though it was more the rhetoric and the tone that was reproduced. Curiously, the closest thing in English poetry to the original Hebrew may have been Anglo-Saxon alliterative meter—that is, both meters depended on a limited number of stresses together with an indeterminate number of unstressed syllables. The references to various kinds of harps in the Scriptures and in Anglo-Saxon poetry make it likely that a quasi-musical measure governed the recitation in both languages. Any records of Jewish instrumental music, as well as its use, disappeared following the destruction of the Temple in A.D. 70, but rhythmic chanting of Scripture, a tradition more or less continuous with the earliest practice of Jewish religion, survives to the present. Anglo-Saxon was quite regular, consisting of four-stress lines split in half by a heavy caesura, though occasionally the half-lines expand from two to three stresses. Hebrew is much more variable.

The method of delivery is called *cantillation* and employs fixed formulas, simple melodic lines that accompany the lines of text. Accentual notation called *ta'amin* indicates which formula is to be used; these markings in turn may have first occurred simply to indicate the proper emphasis, according to the article, "Jewish Music," in *The Harvard Dictionary of Music.*

The most common arrangement is a pair of three-stress half-lines. What follows is not offered as an accurate transcription of the original nor as a proper marking of the English stresses, but only as a rough English equivalent of what may have been the original rhythm in Psalm 78; this is not a scansion, but rather a diagram of a pervasive rhythmic iteration, such as might be fitted to a chant:

/   /   /
He destroyed their vines with hail,
       /   /   /
And their sycomore [*sic*] trees with frost

(48)

Even the English rhythm of these lines is uncertain. Nevertheless, by forcing the rhythm as I have done, the passage may be made to suggest something of the quality of the original poetry.

But the three-plus-three stress pattern is by no means the only one; lines can occur as two plus two, three plus two, and even four plus two. Often these are mixed within a single poem. The most important feature is the medial division, which encourages many forms of parallelism and antithesis, and, most importantly for its effect on poetry in English, lends itself to cumulative repetition. An obvious example of this is the passage from Ecclesiastes 3:

> To every thing there is a season, and a time to every purpose
> under the heaven:
> A time to be born, and a time to die; a time to plant, and a time to
> pluck up that which is planted;
> A time to kill, and a time to heal; a time to break down and a time
> to build up;
> A time to weep, and a time to laugh; a time to mourn and a time
> to dance.

The parallelism encouraged the recurrence of initial words and phrases, or anaphora, whether in the Hebrew or in locutions employed by the translators, as in Psalm 109:

> Let his days be few; and let another take his office.
> Let his children be fatherless, and his wife a widow.
> Let his children be continually vagabonds, and beg: let them seek
> their bread also out of their desolate places.
> Let the executioner catch all that he hath; and let the strangers
> spoil his labor.

Let there be none to extend mercy to him; neither let there be any
to favour his fatherless children.
Let his posterity be cut off; and in the generation following let
their name be blotted out.

(8–14)

Compare this with Whitman's "Respondez":

Let the worst men beget children out of the worst women!
Let the priest still play at immortality!
Let death be inaugurated!
Let nothing remain but the ashes of teachers, artists, moralists,
lawyers, and learn'd and polite persons!
Let him who is without my poems be assassinated!

(30–34)

Hebrew poetry communicated to its first English translators a rough accentualism, which they wielded with a greater freedom, converting it into irregular rhythmic prose. Often additional words were needed to expand meanings compressed into a single word in the original, and to supply implied connectives and articles; this caused the original meter to disappear in most verses of the translation.

The English versions preserved with greater accuracy the *rhetorical* patterns encouraged by the original meters, together with an approximation of the original line lengths. Whitman and others who have taken up this style have in their turn exercised even greater freedom, expanding or contracting their lines to fit the sense of what they had to say and to add both emphasis and variety. But their poems sound sufficiently similar to the Bible to lend their pronouncements an aura of prophecy, a messianic portentousness that was already familiar to their readers who had grown up listening to Scripture. However natural repetitive chanting, as a form, may be in any number of languages, the model for this type of free verse, as used by Whitman and others, is undeniably the English Bible, reinforced on occasion, as for Allen Ginsberg, by exposure to the original Hebrew. And yet not everyone agrees that this is true—not, astonishingly, Karl Shapiro, who spoke slightingly of this idea in his Pope-like enterprise, the long poem entitled *Essay on Rime*.

English vernacular versions of portions of the Old Testament were available as early as 1530, when William Tyndale published his translation of the Pentateuch. But poems in English modeled on the Bible are not evident, so far as I can tell, until about 1625. By "poems" I mean, somewhat arbitrarily, writings in which the lines stop short of the right-hand margin of the page unless they continue on a subsequent indented line. Prose imitations of the Bible came earlier; as the vogue for long-winded Protestant sermonizing took hold in England, it was natural that preachers would model their style on the English Scriptures. It should not be surprising that among the great prose writers who adorn the seventeenth century, those who were also poets were likely, in their prose, to sense the latent poetry of the Bible and reproduce it. One thinks immediately and inevitably of Donne, who, though his verse stayed within regular metrical bounds, wrote a prose that had more poetic form to it—even considered as free verse—than much of what we read today that is printed as if it were poetry. Here is Donne—

XIII. MEDITATION

We say that the world is made of sea and land, as though they were equal; but we know that there is more sea in the western than in the eastern hemisphere. We say that the firmament is full of stars, as though it were equally full; but we know that there are more stars under the northern than under the southern pole. We say that the elements of man are misery and happiness, as though he had equal proportions of both, and the days of man vicissitudinary, as though he had as many good days as ill, and that he lived under a perpetual equinoctial, night and day equal, good and ill fortune in the same measure.

Donne, of course, departs from his biblical template into all sorts of baroque extravagance, but the Hebraic pattern is ubiquitous in his prose. Take these sentences from sermon 49, in which biblical parallelisms, though rather swollen out of shape, may still be discerned:

A house is not clean, though all the dust be swept together, if it lie still in a corner within doors; a conscience is not clean by having recollected all her sins in the memory, for they may fester there and gangrene even to desperation till she have emptied them in the bottomless sea of blood of Christ Jesus and the mercy of his Father by this way of confession. But a house is not clean either, though the dust be thrown out, if there hang cobwebs about the walls in how dark corners soever. A conscience is not clean, though the sins be brought to our memory by this examination . . .

Thomas Traherne's *Centuries of Meditations* are another instance of prose that verges on free verse. In this example, from Meditation 18, he reproduces the reassuring cadences that sometimes occur in the Psalms; notice, however, that he uses pairs of complete short sentences in place of the Hebrew half-lines:

> The world is not this little cottage of heaven and earth. Though this be fair, it is too small a gift. When God made the world he made the heavens, and the angels, and the celestial powers. These also are parts of the world. So are all those infinite and eternal treasures that are to abide for ever, after the Day of Judgment. Neither are these some here, and some there, but all everywhere, and at once to be enjoyed.

We may see Traherne's cosmic vision as an extension of the piety expressed in more local terms in Psalm 121:

> I will lift up mine eyes unto the hills, from whence cometh my help.
> My help cometh even from the LORD, which made heaven and earth.
> He will not suffer thy foot to be moved: he that keepeth thee will not slumber.
> Behold, he that keepeth Israel shall neither slumber nor sleep.
> The LORD is thy keeper: the LORD is thy shade upon thy right hand.
> The sun shall not smite thee by day, nor the moon by night.
> The LORD shall preserve thee from all evil: he shall preserve thy soul.
> The LORD shall preserve thy going out and thy coming in from this time forth, and even for evermore.

Anaphora is not so prominent here as in the series of maledictions quoted above from Psalm 109, but the tendency toward parallel structure is obvious.

None of the passages quoted up to this point seem to me to qualify as free verse—though they resemble so closely the biblical-anaphoric free verse of the twentieth century that there are those who would award them that distinction retroactively. The poetic books of the Old Testament were somewhat rough and unpredictable in their rhythms, but the aim was a quasi-musical regularity. It was an effort to bring greater order into ordinary speech, and this is the opposite of free verse, which aims at playing *against* the possibility of a regular meter. Whitmanian free verse is certainly biblical, but the original biblical cadences are not Whitmanian free verse. English translations of these passages attempt to carry the spirit of the Hebrew into the modern language. It is therefore difficult to see the King James Bible itself as free verse though—as will be amply illustrated—it is certainly the earliest model in English for certain kinds of free verse. Because many rhyming versions of the Psalms had been attempted, however, none of which are satisfactory, it is reasonable to think of the King James Psalms and the Psalter of the *Book of Common Prayer* as a type of free verse. Yet the translators' real intention was to convey the *poetry* of the original, the Hebrew meters. Whatever it may be, it is beautiful poetry, and I would refuse to quarrel with anyone who wanted to call it free verse.

I have spoken of Donne and Traherne as "verging on free verse" in their prose. Here we do have two poets, well disciplined—if ebulliently expressive—in accentual-syllabic meters, who may have enjoyed some sense of additional freedom afforded by a freely accentual prose. Traherne, in fact, went one step further in his *Thanksgivings* (ca. 1670). A note on page 282 in the Coffin and Witherspoon anthology, *Seventeenth Century Prose and Poetry,* states:

> Bertram Dobell, Traherne's first editor, wrote as follows of this and similar poems by Traherne: "It is written . . . in a kind of unrhymed verse, which is curiously suggestive of the style of Whitman's *Leaves of Grass,* particularly in the frequent passages in which the author enumerates or catalogues, as the American poet does, every object he can think of which bears any relation to his theme. . . . Do we not see in both poets the same deep love of, and delight in, humanity, the same feeling of comradeship and brotherhood with all men, the same hunger for sympathy and reciprocal affection, the same pleasure in the common things of life and nature . . . ?"

Indebted as we are to Dobell for noting this similarity, I cannot help remembering "I celebrate and sing myself," and compare it with Traherne—

> Thou, Lord, hast made Thy servant a sociable creature, for which
>   I praise Thy name;
> A lover of company, a delighter in equals.

This sweet-tempered camaraderie of souls seems a far cry from the garrulous egotism that sometimes breaks out in Whitman. Also, the bulk of Traherne's poetry is in regular, though gracefully varied, metrical stanzas; the *Thanksgivings* comprise only a small portion of his writings and are little known and seldom read. All that the two poets have in common is that it did occur to both to profit from the biblical model.

Biblical-anaphoric free verse before the twentieth century was not a perfectly continuous development; instead, there were several independent recurrences, in which the poets went back to biblical patterns. A certain degree of continuity followed the publication of "Ossian" in 1760: Blake, Southey, Whitman, and others discovered these "Celtic" epics for themselves, and James Macpherson's utterance seemed to authorize a form of writing that was based on the Bible. In this century, influence of Whitman is pervasive, and yet one is never perfectly confident that every patch of anaphora is a birthmark that identifies a Child of Walt. Continued familiarity with Scripture, storefront preaching, quasi-biblical speechifying—all these remain available as models.

Returning to Traherne, we see a more extended example of his practice in the opening to *Thanksgivings for the Body:*

> Bless the Lord, O my soul: and all that is within me bless his holy
>   name.
> Bless the Lord, O my Soul: and forget not all his benefits.
> Who forgiveth all thine Iniquities: who healeth all thy Diseases:
> Who redeemeth thy life from destruction. Who crowneth thee
>   with loving kindness and tender mercies.

This sounds like nothing more than a paraphrase of one of the Psalms, or a conflation of several different psalms. But further on (43–59) we see him departing into a truly idiosyncratic free verse that may, because of its subject, again make us think momentarily of Whitman:

> Thou hast given me a Body.
> Wherein the glory of thy Power shineth,
>   Wonderfully composed above the Beasts,
> Within distinguished into many useful parts,
> Beautified without with many Ornaments.
>   Limbs rarely poised,
>   And made for Heaven:
>   Arteries filled
>   With celestial Spirits:
> Veins, wherein Blood floweth,
>   Refreshing all my flesh,
>   Like Rivers.
> Sinews fraught with the mystery
>   Of wonderful Strength,
>   Stability,
>   Feeling.
>   O blessed be thy glorious Name!

For Traherne, the rhythms of the Bible have provided a point of departure for even more radical experiments. "The drift of Traherne's technique is toward an 'open' form, representing a process of association, like reverie," writes Stanley Stewart in *The Expanded Voice: The Art of Thomas Traherne*. Stewart continues: "As we see in many of his other works, inconsistency is not only a structural feature but a distinguishing mark of the speaker's temperament" (209). Here is the recognition of another impulse behind free verse. In conjunction with the desire to run counter to established conventions, one often discovers uncontrolled association, or rather, association controlled by the writer, who may feel that he or she is following the dictates of the Holy Spirit or some less sanctified impulse.

Traherne had another model to work from, besides the Book of Psalms and his inner promptings. All devout, well-read English Christians of the later seventeenth century were familiar with the *Preces Privata,* or *Private Devotions,* of Lancelot Andrewes. Traherne incorporated passages from Andrewes in his own writings, as Stanley Stewart explains, making reference to the work of Carol Marks (86). The original *Preces* consisted of separate versions composed in Greek and Latin, and sometimes even in Hebrew. They were devotional exercises that demanded the intellectual discipline of thinking in the three languages anciently associated with Christianity. But beginning in 1630, five years after Andrewes's death, *Private Devotions* were regularly translated into English; more than eight versions had appeared by the end of the century. Here is a passage from the translation of F. E. Brightman (1903):

> Alleluia,
> for the Lord God omnipotent reigneth:
>> let us be glad and rejoice
>> and give honor to Him.
> Behold the tabernacle of God is with men
>> and He will dwell with them,
> and they shall be his people
>
> and God himself shall be with them,
> and He shall wipe away all tears
>> from their eyes,
> and there shall be no more death
>> nor crying
> neither shall there be any more pain,
>> for the former things
>> are passed away.

Nearly every second line in the original is a quotation or reformulation of a line from Scripture; it makes more sense to think of these as free-form notations to assist in the direction of one's spiritual life, and not as poetry. There are, however, passages in the poems of Allen Ginsberg that could be quoted here that would bear a close resemblance to this seventeenth-century devotional literature, and that spring from the same prosodic sources as the *Preces,* though less directly. Ginsberg, of course, sometimes gives us an obscene and blasphemous inversion of biblical phrasing as part of his critique of American complacency and hypocrisy.

Because of the grandeur of his prose, one might expect to find something useful to this discussion in the poetic efforts of Jeremy Taylor, which date from about 1650. Taylor did write a type of free verse, but one that, if it were worth reading at all, would be better considered as another instance of the "Pindarique." As Edmund Gosse wrote in *Jeremy Taylor* (1904),

The versification in the *Festival Hymns* [by Taylor] consists of short
lines, arbitrarily broken up by rhymes, and arranged on no rhythmi-
cal principle. No system could be less tuneful, and in comparison
with these hymns the worst odes of Cowley and even of Flatman are
musical; what is curious in so learned a writer, Taylor's rhymes are
often scarcely assonance. (115)

Moments occur in Taylor's prose, however, where he is as close as Donne
or Traherne are in theirs to biblical prosody. Here is a typical passage
from *Deus Justificatus,* included as part of *The House of Understanding,*
edited by Margaret Guest:

> For if God decrees us to be born sinners, then He makes us to be
> sinners; and then where is his goodness?
> If God does damn any for that, He damns us for what we could
> not help, and for what Himself did; and where is His justice?
> If God sentences us to that damnation which He cannot in justice
> inflict, where is His wisdom?
> If God for the sin of Adam brings upon us the necessity of
> sinning, where is our liberty? Where is our nature? What is become
> of all laws, and of all virtue and vice? How can men be distin-
> guished from beasts, or the virtuous from the vicious? (*The House
> of Understanding* 45)

The impulse to reproduce biblical cadences, then, was insistent
throughout the seventeenth century, sometimes issuing in prose and else-
where in works printed as poetry. This subcurrent of free-form devo-
tional poetry ceased to flow in the eighteenth century. No classical model
authorized its existence. Poetry after 1660 was increasingly public, secu-
lar, Frenchified, respectful of genres, didactic, political, and satirical. But,
exactly one century after the Restoration, poor Kit Smart lost his mind
for the second time and returned (in 1759) to St. Luke's Hospital. Here he
began to write his *Jubilate Agno,* which is easily recognizable as an imita-
tion, more often a parody, of the King James Bible. Because the delight-
ful "My Cat Jeoffry" is quoted frequently, let us look at another passage:

> For their spirits were broke and their manhood impaired by
>   foreign vices for exaction.
> For I prophecy that the English will recover their horns the first.

For I prophecy that all nations in the world will do the like in
   turn.
For I prophecy that all Englishmen will wear their beards again.
For a beard is a good step to a horn.

(Frag. C: "For" verses 127–31)

Let Nehum rejoice with the Artichoke.
Let Ginnethon rejoice with the Bottle Flower.
Let Zidkjah rejoice with Mulberry Blight. God be gracious to
   Gum my fellow Prisoner.

(Frag. C: "Let" verses 142–45)

Jubilate Agno does not figure in the literary history of the following
180 years because it was unpublished, and scarcely known, until 1939. In
the decades from about 1950 to the present it has established itself as a
locus classicus for visionary free-verse poetry and has restored the eigh-
teenth century to respectability for some readers. To put it less disingenu-
ously, the cult of madness popularized by William Burroughs, Allen
Ginsberg, Gregory Corso, and others found in Smart a patron saint and
poetic model for wildly funny, or—at times—morbidly disoriented, pro-
tests against and burlesques of the status quo. Smart, Blake, and Whit-
man have served, for many poets in the later twentieth century, as succes-
sive reincarnations of the genius of poetry, and as models to emulate,
because each of them gave the appearance of something lawless and
spontaneous, enthusiastic and subversive.

In the same year that Smart was writing *Jubilate Agno,* 1760, James
Macpherson published the first fragments of what was to become a liter-
ary happening of the eighteenth century, "Ossian." To the extent that
Macpherson or anyone else represented these writings as translations, the
whole thing was the fraud that Dr. Johnson took it to be, and for expos-
ing which he received and defied physical threats from Macpherson. Had
Macpherson only done as did William Yeats, whose *Celtic Twilight* (1893)
was honestly presented as a collection of rambling fragments of hearsay
mythology that he used as sources for his own poems, there would never
have been the "Ossianic controversy." (That Yeats followed, with greater
prudence, in Macpherson's footsteps would be evident if in no other way
from his "Oisin," which is another form of "Ossian.") As late as 1896,
William Sharp, remembered as "Fiona Macleod," was still, in words of
Romantic defiance, denouncing Johnson; but Sharp was forced to admit

"that Macpherson's 'Ossian' is not a genuine translation of authentic Dana Oisin mhic Fhionn, but, for all its great and enduring beauty, a clumsily-constructed, self-contradictory, and sometimes grotesquely impossible rendering of disconnected, fugitive, and for the most part, oral lore" (*From the Hills of Dream* xxiii). For nearly a century and a half, "Ossian" provided a useful variant of the myth of the noble savage: the wild Celt as author of an imaginary epic equal to *Gilgamesh* or Homer, brought forth in the remote reaches of northern Britain, expressing the genius of a forgotten race and proving that classical authority and example were quite unnecessary to surpassing literary achievement. Goethe recommended it enthusiastically and lent his copy to Herder while they were still friends. Thomas Jefferson considered "Ossian" to be the greatest poet that had ever existed, and William Hazlitt was a devout believer. All the American Transcendentalists accepted its authenticity.

Few people today make reference to "Ossian" and fewer yet have read it, even in parts. The occasional references give the impression that it is, in some way, poetry. That is by no means certain. Here is the opening of "Carthon," one of "Ossian's compositions," according to Macpherson's "Argument," which relates a jumble of battles, murders, desertions, and betrayals much like the various Irish sagas collected by nineteenth-century folklorists and later drawn on by Yeats and Lady Gregory.

> A Tale of the times of old! The deeds of days of other years!
> The murmur of thy streams, O Lora! brings back the memory of the past. The sound of thy woods, Garmallar, is lovely in mine ear. Dost thou not behold, Malvina, a rock with its head of heath? Three aged pines bend from its face; green is the narrow plain at its feet; there the flower of the mountain grows, and shakes its white head in the breeze. The thistle is there alone, shedding its aged beard. (172)

And a little further on—

> Sons of Morven, began the king, this is no time to fill the shell. The battle darkens near us; death hovers over the land. Some ghost, the fiend of Fingal, has forewarned us of the foe. The sons of the stranger come from the darkly-rolling sea. For, from the water came the sign of Morven's gloomy danger. Let each assume his heavy

spear, each gird on his father's sword. Let the dark helmet rise on every head; the mail pour its lightning from every side. The battle gathers like a storm; soon shall ye hear the roar of death.

Like Poe, Macpherson certainly succeeded in inventing a new literary mode. One thinks inevitably of the speeches of James Fenimore Cooper's Indians. The pseudoprimitive linguistic mannerisms of "Ossian" survive in older Hollywood versions of Native American speech, and even in the idiom of certain space aliens in recent films. Pearl Buck waxed Ossianic in recounting the saga of a Chinese peasant in *The Good Earth,* and numerous writers have instinctively slipped into the mode in hopes of capturing an epic portentousness. But where did Macpherson get his rhythms?

There are phrases in *The Poems of Ossian* that contain more than ten words, but one looks for a long time before finding one; the usual pattern is a sentence of about sixteen words that is split in half by a semicolon, or into two clauses separated by a comma; or else there may be two short sentences of about six to eight words. The parallelisms are sufficiently different from biblical language so that the text does not read continually like a parody of the Old Testament, but that, clearly, was the model. I have counted words rather than syllables or stresses because the sentences in "Ossian" do not seem to me particularly rhythmic, and yet it does seem clear that the model was the biblical verset. Macpherson did not know poems in Old English that could also have provided an example of strongly marked bipartite line division, and even if he had, those poems are too terse, taken half-line by half-line, to have provided a model for "Ossian." Despite Macpherson's efforts to make his work sound as much like the *Iliad* as possible, the King James Bible remained the true source of his style.

Northrop Frye saw "Ossian" as the paradigm for much of Blake's work:

Most of the "prophetic" sketches are printed in the form of that unreadable anomaly, the prose poem. Blank verse, as one edition has grimly shown, is still the underlying meter; but whereas in the lyrics Blake had the whole weight of a great tradition behind him, in these he had only Ossian and his own originality. They show that Ossian played an important part in liberating Blake's meter. (184)

Frye is wrong about Blake's metrics in several respects. Leaving aside the question of what "great tradition" informed the short lyrics, we may note the near-total absence of anything resembling pentameter in the prophetic books. Moreover, although "Ossian" may indeed have helped "in liberating Blake's meter," a line-by-line examination of the prophetic books turns up little that resembles "Ossian." Few of Blake's long lines enjoy a medial division; many proceed in one sweep of ten or twelve words and, if divided, are likely to fall into uneven segments. Here, chosen at random, is a passage from "Night the Seventh" of *Vala, or the Four Zoas*:

> Where thou & I in undivided Essence walk'd about
> Imbodied, thou my garden of delight & I the spirit in the garden;
> Mutual there we dwelt in one another's joy, revolving
> Days of eternity, with Tharmas mild & Luvah sweet melodious
> Upon our waters. This thou rememberest; listen, I will tell
> What thou forgettest. They in us & we in them alternate Liv'd,
> Drinking the joys of Universal Manhood. One dread Morn—
>
> (271–77)

I break off because one does not reach a period until the end of the tenth line further on. Elsewhere, when he lapses into short stretches of anaphora or when, in *The Marriage of Heaven and Hell*, he apes the *Book of Proverbs,* Blake borrows more obviously from the King James Bible than he does in the passage above. More pervasive than Hebrew prosody is the employment of biblical locutions and the general air of messianic certainty; taken phrase by phrase, "Ossian" is closer to the Bible than is Blake, who managed to suggest simultaneously something of the classical hexameter, something of the English Alexandrine or fourteener, and something of the Hebrew. Frequently Blake wrote in pure fourteeners. This freedom and inventiveness with the longer line is scarcely surprising; Blake is the greatest poet ever to work in this particular free-verse medium, and his achievement consists in part of working *against* the conventions that he was assimilating. Most important of all is his challenge to the iambic pentameter and especially to the heroic couplet; prosodically he is flaunting the same impatience and rebelliousness that flash out in his annotations to Joshua Reynolds, and in many other places in his writings. Also, need we say, we see in Blake a prime exemplar of the Protestant spirit pushed nearly to its limit—not only to the establishment of a Church consisting of one soul, but a Church founded upon scriptures composed by its sole member, and mostly in meters peculiar to that autotelic messiah.

Blake, of course, was hardly noticed outside the immediate circle of his friends and admirers until rediscovered and republished by the Pre-Raphaelites toward the middle of the nineteenth century, and there is little evidence that he meant anything to American poets until the twentieth century. The prophetic books, in particular, were not easily available until the 1920s and did not inspire many imitators until the 1950s. Swinburne, toward the end of his groundbreaking study of Blake, did mention the similarity with Whitman, to whose work he was at that time still strongly attached, but he did not make a direct connection, suggesting rather that there had been some transmigration of soul. In a letter to M. D. Conway in 1866 Swinburne, who had labored hard to do justice to Blake's prophetic books, said a little more on the family resemblance, perhaps overstating it:

> I have printed (with comments of my own) a good deal of these books. Written in the same semi-metrical verse (or prose) as the Leaves of Grass, they preach almost exactly the same gospel; and I think it might interest Walt Whitman and his admirers in America, where I suppose these books of Blake's (who regarded them as the real grave work of his life) are as little known as here—less known they cannot be. (209)

Although one can never tell what pseudobiblical utterances may lurk in the recesses of tomes published by now-forgotten poets of the Romantic period, almost nothing of the sort can be found in the work of the major poets. A single very minor instance appears in Walter Scott's *The Betrothed,* when the minstrel Renault Vidal strums on his "rote" and sings

> a lay, of which we can offer only a few fragments, literally translated from the ancient language in which they were chanted, premising that they are in that excursive symbolical style of poetry which Taliessin, Llewarch Hen, and other bards had derived perhaps from the time of the Druids.
>
> > I asked of my harp, "Who hath injured thy chords?"
> > And she replied, "The crooked finger, which I mocked in my tune."

A blade of silver may be bended; a blade of steel abideth.
Kindness fadeth away, but vengeance endureth.
. . . .
I asked the green oak of the assembly, wherefore its boughs
    were dry and seared like the horns of a stag,
And it showed me that a small worm had gnawed its roots.
The boy who remembered the scourge, undid the wicket of
    the castle at midnight.
Kindness fadeth away, but vengeance endureth.

(chap. 33)

Scott allows the minstrel five stanzas and tells us that the singer went on much beyond this, always returning to the refrain. The debt to the Bible, to responsive readings in the *Book of Common Prayer,* and to "Ossian" seems obvious. Scott, like Macpherson, seemed to require the authority of some ancient text that had been "translated" to write as loosely as this, although by modeling other poems, especially *The Lay of the Last Minstrel,* on ballad meter and on Coleridge's *Christabel,* he had already reverted to a genuine native accentualism that permitted far greater freedom than eighteenth-century syllabism.

The chief secular model for American nineteenth-century poets of a greatly loosened—even prosaic—metric remained "Ossian." But also appearing from American presses throughout the nineteenth century were translations of songs and chants from various Native American languages. Sometimes a translator would attempt to cage these woodnotes in iambic pentameter or even in rhyming stanzas, producing an effect much like sixteenth-century metrical psalteries. More often, to judge from John Hollander's selection of "American Indian Poetry" in *American Poetry: The Nineteenth Century,* the translators employed a free-verse approximation of the original. These seem remarkably free from biblical diction, even though the repetitiousness of some chants must have invited a comparison with the Psalms. While these translations do not seem to have served as models for original poems, they did provide another example of a poetry quite outside the accentual-syllabic tradition. The Romantic interest in their savage nobility parallels that which inspired similar translations, in other European languages as well as English, of "primitive" or "authentic" poetry, of which "Ossian" was supposed to be an example.

In the January 1844 issue of the *Dial* Thoreau published a set of three brief essays, "Homer. Ossian. and Chaucer."; it is clear that he entertained no doubts about the authenticity of the Celtic epic and assumed that no one else did either. "Ossian reminds us of the most refined and rudest eras, of Homer, Pindar, Isaiah, and the American Indians. In his poetry, as in Homer's, only the simplest and most enduring features of humanity are seen, such essential parts of a man as Stonehenge exhibits of a temple" (293). He has here succeeded in cataloging almost every supposed original of the Romantic sublime in poetry, and surely his reverence for these sources was communicated to Whitman who if he read any periodicals must have known The *Dial*. Although only one reference to "Ossian" appears in *Leaves of Grass,* Whitman in his early years considered him among the world's great literary monuments, writing in "A Backward Glance o'er Travel'd Roads":

> Later, at intervals, summers and falls, I used to go off, sometimes for a week at a stretch, down in the country, or to Long Island's seashores—there, in the presence of outdoor influences, I went over thoroughly the Old and New Testaments, and absorb'd (probably to better advantage to me than in any library or indoor room—it makes such a difference *where* you read,) Shakspere, Ossian, the best translated versions I could get of Homer, Eschylus, Sophocles, the old German Nibelungen, the ancient Hindoo poems, and one or two other masterpieces, Dante's among them.

On other occasions he qualified his enthusiasm:

> Had I read Ossian? Was very circumstantial in talking about the book. Macpherson was a sort of rascal—had scamp qualities. There was a great Ossianic debate. I have always had an Ossian about me, though I can't say I ever read it with any great fervor . . . Ossian is of the Biblical order—is best to one who would come freshly on it—to one who knew nothing of the Hebrew Bible. (Quoted in Masters 264)

Macpherson does not figure in today's survey courses in world literature, but the rhythms of "Ossian" may at one point have reassured Whitman that he had rediscovered the natural form of poetry, predating even "Shakspere." Hugh Blair, an early editor of "Ossian," said of its language, in an edition that appeared in 1849—

The measured prose which he has employed possesses considerable advantages above any sort of versification he could have chosen. While it pleases and fills the ear with a variety of harmonious cadences, being, at the same time, freer from constraint in the choice and arrangement of words, it allows the spirit of the original to be exhibited, with more justness, force, and simplicity.

Whitman once clipped a paragraph in which Margaret Fuller recorded an "Ossianic" moment, and noted in the margin, "Don't fall into the Ossianic, *by any chance*" but added further on, "Is it not Isaiah, Job, the Psalms, and so forth, transferred to the Scotch Highlands?" (*Complete Writings* 94–95). Abraham Cowley had found "Pindaric" qualities in the same books of the Bible; writers of free verse are ever on the lookout for the original wellsprings of inspiration. A cautious discussion in Floyd Stovall's *The Foreground of Leaves of Grass* (185–88) suggests several works that might have been available before the composition of *Leaves of Grass,* in which Hebrew poetry was described or analyzed, but concludes that the only one that may have meant anything to Whitman was George Gilfillan's *Bards of the Bible* (1851). That book included, among other things, a call for a new poet of nature and genius reminiscent of Emerson's. In the end, it seems best to take Whitman at his word, that he immersed himself in the Old and New Testaments, and see there his chief inspiration and model. There seems little need to provide supporting quotations from Whitman's work; the evidence is not only abundant, but almost inescapable. Huge sections are blocked out for Whitman in any anthology to which he may be admissible, and numerous passages in these recall the Bible.

As with Blake, however, Whitman was hardly content simply to reproduce the features of the Bible. Like Blake's, his lines are likely to sweep straight through to their extended conclusions, without any breaks at all, or else with breaks early or late. But his *line lengths* do not resemble Blake. In the Bible there is great variation in length from one verse to the next, and Whitman allows himself that same freedom; whereas in much of Blake the lines approximate twelve to sixteen syllables (though not, of course, in *The Marriage of Heaven and Hell*). Whitman employs more frequent and more protracted episodes of anaphora, that semirhetorical structure that mirrors his predilection for cataloging or enumeration.

Bliss Perry's pioneering *Walt Whitman* (1906) mentions two other possible sources for Whitman's prosody; even if Whitman did not have these in mind, they are further evidence that his impatience with accentual-syllabic metrics was shared by others. I quote from Perry because the original texts are long forgotten, out of print, and difficult to obtain. First, he gives an example from Martin Farquar Tupper's *Proverbial Philosophy:*

> Where are the nobles of Nineveh, and mitred rulers of Babylon?
> Where are the lords of Edom, and the royal pontiffs of Thebais?
> The golden Satrap, and the Tetrarch,—the Hun, and the Druid,
>   and the Celt?
> The merchant princes of Phoenicia, and the minds that fashioned
>   Elephanta?
> Alas, for the poet hath forgotten them; and lo! they are outcasts of
>   Memory;
> Alas, that they are withered leaves, sapless and fallen from the
>   chaplet of fame.

Tupper's lines are, of course, directly imitative of the Bible in a way that neither Blake nor Whitman were.

Even more amusingly, Perry quotes from a poem, *The Lily and the Bee,* that was composed by the novelist Samuel Warren in honor of the English Great Exhibition of 1851, and that was printed in the United States as well as in England. Perry thought that Whitman must have read it. The poem is extravagant in its celebration of material human achievement and is a paean to Britain, Empire, Queen, and Progress—and, not least, to the author himself. The actual form is anticipatory more of Carl Sandburg than of Whitman:

> A unit unperceived,
> I sink into the living stream again!—
> Nave, transept, aisles and Galleries,
> Pacing untired: insatiate!
> Touchstone of character! capacity! and knowledge!
> Spectacle, now lost in the Spectators: the spectators in the
>   spectacle!
> Rich: poor: gentle: simple: wise: foolish: young: old: learned:
>   ignorant: thoughtful: thoughtless: haughty: humble: frivolous:
>   profound:

Every grade of intellect: every shade of character!

. . . .

Now he is speaking with brother engineers—English, French,
    German, Russian—showing the Hydraulic Press, which raised
    to the height of a hundred feet huge tubes of iron two thousand
    tons in weight: now the French Turbine: the centrifugal pump:
    the steam-hammer—oh, mighty Steam!
—Here behold Power!
Exact: docile: delicate: tremendous in operation: dealing, easily,
    alike with filmy gossamer lace, silk, flax, hemp, cotton, granite,
    iron!

The final catalog sounds much like the conclusion of a poem of Marianne
Moore's, "The Monkeys," but mostly the poem is pure rant. Warren's
reaction to the overwhelming spectacle in the Crystal Palace anticipates
the more genteel excitement of Henry Adams fifty years later at the Paris
exhibition, which, as I have pointed out, coincided with a sense of ur-
gency among poets to try new metrical experiments; it is another re-
minder of the extent to which experimentation with free verse has be-
trayed a half-conscious desire to emulate the triumphs of experimental
science and applied technology. We may also think of Whitman's enthusi-
asm for the steam locomotive, in a poem that conveniently assembles
most of the features found throughout his work and that appears in a
great many anthologies—"To a Locomotive in Winter."

Closer to Whitman's actual practice than any examples quoted by
Bliss Perry is Christopher Pearse Cranch's "Correspondences," origi-
nally published in 1839. Cranch was, like Emerson and other Transcen-
dentalists, a Unitarian minister, but he drifted by degrees into a commit-
ment to poetry and art in place of his religion. When he went west to
preach he worked for a time with another minister, William Greenleaf
Eliot of St. Louis; Cranch's sister married Eliot, thereby bequeathing
some of the family's poetic genes to her grandson, Thomas Stearns.
When he moved to Louisville, Cranch made the acquaintance of and
visited with George Keats, the brother of the poet, and even obtained the
manuscript of a poem by John Keats, which he published in the *Western
Messenger,* a notable precursor to the *Dial.* The *Western Messenger* origi-
nated as an official Unitarian publication, but under the direction of J. F.
Clarke and Cranch, it evolved into a literary magazine, printing poems
by Emerson and writings by Margaret Fuller, among others.

Cranch, who is now seldom read, possessed a lively awareness of intellectual currents in the new country, with which he was simultaneously engaged and at times humorously detached; he drew the famous caricature of his master, Emerson, as an eyeball perched atop elongated legs, surveying the countryside. In a letter to his father a few years later (1840) Cranch summed up accurately the drift of American letters and philosophy:

> But somehow the name "Transcendentalist" has become a nickname here [he was then back in Boston] for all who have broken away from the material philosophy of Locke, and the old theology of man of the early Unitarians, and who yearn for something more satisfying to the soul. It has almost become a synonym for one who, in whatever way, preaches the spirit rather than the letter. (50)

His poem "Correspondences" merges the old Puritan conviction that God continually makes signs, the meaning of which is clear to His Elect, with a more diffuse Romantic pantheism—

> All things in nature are beautiful types to the soul that can read
> them;
> Nothing exists upon earth, but for unspeakable ends,
> Every object that speaks to the senses was meant for the spirit;
> Nature is but a scroll; God's handwriting thereon.
>
> (609)

The lines are all long and are mostly end-stopped, and there are one or two touches of anaphora; it would be only a small step to a full-blown verset structure. But Cranch might have been aiming at something else; many of the lines work as hexameters, though not consistently (as they do in "The Thundergust," which immediately follows "Correspondences" in *Poems*). All the rest of Cranch's poetry—he continued to write for more than fifty years—mirrors styles in fashion in England and America during the century, from Spenserian stanzas to ballads and Browning-like octameter tercets, making him an accurate gauge of conventional taste. There seems no evidence that Cranch or Whitman acknowledged one another's existence, though both sent copies of their first books of poetry, and Cranch dedicated his, to Emerson. Emerson reprinted "Correspondences" in the *Dial* along with an introductory essay in which

Cranch admits to having been reading Swedenborg immediately before composing it.

Cranch's friend and fellow editor of the *Western Messenger,* J. F. Clarke, had a poem, "First Crossing the Alleghenies," that also appeared in the *Dial* and that is similar in meter to "Correspondences," but little else that is printed as poetry in that journal points toward Whitman's manner. Instead, we see poems imitative of British meters and forms, a movement in the direction of "Tennysonianness" and the bards of Mt. Auburn Street. As early as 1840 American poetry was already afflicted with what Santayana subsequently labeled "the genteel tradition," a false and spiritless refinement that plagues us to this day, now in the guise of New Formalism. What Robert Lowell labeled as the "cooked" poetry of the 1950s was in some respects warmed-over nineteenth-century porridge.

But also in the 1840s what is now familiar to us as the countercurrent of "organic" or "projective" poetry had already begun its surge in the person of Whitman, though it would not fountain forth until 1855. While next to none of the poetry that appeared in the *Dial* anticipates Whitman, much of the prose certainly does. Scattered everywhere are passages that bear the imprint of biblical utterance or that sound like as secular versions of Puritan sermons. Two recurring categories of prose are especially important: "Orphic Sayings" and "Ethnical Scriptures," which seem homegrown American parallels to the *style biblique* of French prose poetry. Here is "Enthusiasm," the second in a series of "Orphic Sayings" by Bronson Alcott, the doctrine of which even more than the manner is fully compatible with Whitman:

> Believe, youth, that your heart is an oracle; trust her instinctive auguries, obey her divine leadings; nor listen too fondly to the uncertain echoes of your head. The heart is the prophet of your soul, and ever fulfills her prophecies; reason is her historian; but for the prophecy the history would not be. Great is the heart: cherish her; she is big with the future, she forebodes renovations. Let the flame of enthusiasm fire alway your bosom. Enthusiasm is the glory and the hope of the world. It is the life of sanctity and genius; it has wrought all miracles since the beginning of time. (85)

An example of "Ethnical Scriptures" is a contribution from Thoreau for January, 1844, which purports to be a seventeenth-century translation of

Hermes Trismegistus by a "Doctor Everrard." A typical paragraph exhibits many of the hallmarks of what became Whitman's biblical-anaphoraic style:

> For the knowledge of it is a divine silence, and the rest of all the senses. For neither can he that understands that, understand anything else; nor he that sees that, see anything else, nor hear any other thing, nor move the body. For, shining steadfastly on and round about the whole mind, it enlighteneth all the soul, and loosing it from the bodily senses and motions, it draweth it from the body, and changeth it wholly into the essence of God. For it is possible for the soul, O Son, to be deified while it yet lodgeth in the body of man, if it contemplates the beauty of the Good. (403)

Several other Transcendentalists made similar contributions, including those by William B. Greene and W. H. Channing. These tend to be organized into long sentences printed like biblical versets. In the *Dial* for January 1842, Greene published "Creation," in which every sentence begins, "God thought . . . ." Religious enthusiasm, excluded from organized worship by the gentility of Unitarian practice, found in such writings a new outlet.

Although there was more than a sufficient heritage of American evangelical fervor to account for the inspirational utterances printed in the *Dial,* there was, in addition, echoing across the Atlantic and drifting westward on the intellectual trade winds from England, the blast from Carlyle's miraculous tuba. Justin Kaplan, in his *Walt Whitman: A Life,* warns against making too much of this—but at the same time points out that Whitman reviewed six of Carlyle's books and that he was thoroughly familiar with his style and his characteristic attitudes. Add to that the more general admiration of all the transcendentalists, Margaret Fuller's serving as Carlyle's avatar in America, and Emerson's submission of successive issues of the *Dial* to Carlyle for approval, and one has a strong argument for the effect on Whitman of what Kaplan calls Carlyle's "heroic affirmations." There is also the impassioned rhetoric, the calculated unrestraint in the torrent of his prose. Yet it seems best to see Carlyle more as a distant source of reassurance for Whitman's own self-generated enthusiasm than as a direct operative in the formation of his style.

Yet one more metrical suggestion on which Whitman acted is suggested by the word "recitative" in the first line of "To a Locomotive in Winter." He was an opera enthusiast, and the connecting dialogue between arias does constitute a kind of free-verse link between more regular lyrics. Robert D. Faner, in *Walt Whitman and Opera,* argues that "opera was a major influence on the formation of Whitman's poetry, and . . . [I have] treated that influence almost exclusively" (vii). It might have strengthened Faner's case to have allowed at least something to the Bible and to "Ossian," but he did provide an exhaustive and convincing argument for the importance of opera. A most telling paragraph is one in which he quotes two of Whitman's friends:

> One Thomas A. Gere, who had worked on a boat in the East River in 1852 and remembered Whitman in those days, recalled in 1882 that "Walt's musical ability was a very entertaining quality: he was devotedly fond of opera, and many were the pleasant scraps and airs with which he would enliven us in a round, manly voice, when passengers were few." Whitman's friend, Dr. Bucke, also remembered the poet's singing. "He had a way of singing, generally in an undertone, wherever he was or whatever he was doing when alone. You would hear him the first thing in the morning while he was taking his bath and dressing (he would then perhaps sing out in full, ballads or martial songs), and a large part of the time that he sauntered out of doors during the day he sang, usually tones without words, or a formless recitative." Later Bucke added, "He is fond of singing to himself snatches of songs from the operas or oratorios, often a simple strain of recitative, a sort of musical murmur." (63)

Whitman's ability to blend into his own style features of the Bible, "Ossian," and opera—all of which make powerful appeals to the ear—helps to account for the hold that he obtained on his readers. Gay Wilson Allen repeatedly and thoroughly analyzed the texture and structure that resulted from this blend; see, for example, the discussion in *A Reader's Guide to Walt Whitman.* Allen distinguishes "strophes" and "verse-clusters," and identifies self-contained units, which he calls "envelopes," as well as passages of "enumeration." By employing conventional symbols for stressed and unstressed syllables, Allen is able to account for the effect of rhythm in various individual lines and passages. For my purposes, what this analysis shows is the way in which Whit-

man constantly skirts some sort of regular rhythm, anapestic or dac-
tylic, but never allows it to control the line in a perfectly predictable
way. Whatever he does, it keeps our attention in the same way as does
expressive Bible reading, the periods of a master orator, or the recitative
of an oratorio or opera. And a large part of the attraction is the freedom
from metronomic versifying, what David J. Rothman calls "a meaning-
ful negation of traditional prosodic phenomena" (474).

Some readers, from Emerson and Thoreau to the present, have felt
that Whitman would have done well to rework his outpourings more than
he did. As Pound said, he broke the new wood. But he left a lot of splinters
lying around. With an ear like his, attuned to the euphonies of oral deliv-
ery, he could have left many more passages that attain the beauty of the
opening lines from the "Sea-Drift" section of the 1881 *Leaves of Grass,* the
justly admired "Out of the Cradle Endlessly Rocking." Here, before he
allows it to trail off—somewhat further on—into self-indulgent rant and
maudlin retrospection, is a passage that combines relaxation with control
in a way that I have not seen elsewhere. The control is the repetition of the
initial rhythm as well as the initial words; one can even employ the oldest
scansions available—from Greek and Latin, either calling the first four
syllables a choriamb (/ ** /), or pointing out that the first five syllables
approximate the typical rhythm of the sapphic's last line (/ ** / /), which is
called Adonic. The first five syllables of each line pull us back to the
rhythm of the first line, as if we were given a series of fixed units, each
followed by a variable line segment:

    /   *   *   /   * [*] /   *   *   /   * [*]
    Out of the cradle   endlessly rocking

This rhythm could also be explained, using the implied offbeats (asterisks
enclosed in brackets), as accentual dactylic tetrameter, or even as a redis-
covery of the Old English four-beat line. But it seems to me to work as
much in terms of quantity as stress, and to be reminiscent of the typical
rhythm of sapphics. In any event, it serves to implant an expectation that
is satisfied at the beginning of each of the next six lines—which then vary
among themselves, producing an effect of great loveliness:

    Out of the cradle endlessly rocking,
    Out of the mocking-bird's throat, the musical shuttle,
    Out of the Nine-month midnight,

Over the sterile sands and the fields beyond, where the child
  leaving his bed wander'd alone, bareheaded, barefoot,
Down from the shower'd halo,
Up from the mystic play of shadows twining and twisting as if
  they were alive,
Out from the patches of briars and blackberries . . .

Had Whitman continued in this way—not necessarily using the same
introductory rhythm throughout, but employing some combination of
expectation and variation—he would have accomplished a true revolu-
tion in metrics in the older sense of *revolution,* an orderly movement into
a new cycle.

At first there was considerable resistance to Whitman's seductive
cadences—along with a more enthusiastic reception in some quarters,
especially among his women readers, than he is usually given credit for.
Gerard Manley Hopkins read Whitman and felt powerfully attracted to
him, but felt an equally powerful obligation to reject him. Someone told
Emily Dickinson that he was disreputable, and she did not read him. It is
difficult to discover much evidence of his being imitated prior to 1915 by
any of his fellow Americans, although William James quoted him with ap-
proval in one of the lectures that make up *Pragmatism* (1907). Justin Kaplan
makes clear in his biography of Whitman that he was much better known
in his own day than some may imagine. Indeed, there was copious journal-
istic coverage of Whitman's obscurity. Some of this celebrity was due to
the vogue he enjoyed with many of his leading British contemporaries—
including Tennyson, Swinburne, Rossetti, and even Rossetti's nemesis,
the Scottish critic Robert Buchanan. Later, of course, Wilde, Symonds,
and Edward Carpenter not only admired him but came to visit him person-
ally. But initially he seems to have been talked about rather than imitated.

Adah Isaacs Menken, an American actress, poet, and adventuress
who had at one point met Whitman, wrote her own version of the story
of Judith, a fierce dramatic monologue that, however, more resembles
Samuel Warren's Great Exhibition poem than it does Whitman; it was
included in a collection published in London in 1868.

Oh, what wild passionate kisses will I draw up from that
bleeding mouth!
  I will strangle this pallid throat of mine on the sweet blood!
  I will revel in my passion.

At midnight I will feast on it in the darkness.

For it was that which thrilled its crimson tides of reckless
passion through the blue veins of my life, and made them leap up
in the wild sweetness of Love and agony of
Revenge!

I am starving for this feast.

Oh forget not that I am Judith!

And I know where sleeps Holofernes.

Menken's poem provides an example of a type of free-form effusion that
is really more a parallel to Whitman than either a source or a descendant.
A burlesque of Whitman by Bayard Taylor, who had at one time been a
friendly companion, appeared in 1876: "Night the Eighth: Camerados,"
from *The Echo Club*. It makes fun of Whitman's following, or at least the
following he aspired to—

Drunkard, leper, Tammanyite, small-pox, and cholera patient,
    shoddy, and codfish millionaire,
And the beautiful young men, and the beautiful young women, all
    the same,
Crowding, hundreds of thousands, cosmical multitudes,
Buss me and hang on my hips and lean up to my shoulders,
Everywhere listening to my yawp and glad whenever they hear it;
Everywhere saying, say it, Walt, we believe it;
Everywhere, everywhere.

Ernest Fenellosa's poems, published in 1893, resemble Whitman. Fenel-
losa's *Ode on Reincarnation* employs a long-line, verset structure but lacks
the anaphora as well as the oracular intensity of Whitman. Poems by
other nineteenth-century American poets that are composed in sprawling
lines turn out to be rhyming imitations of Tennyson and Browning, for
the most part.

The French and Belgian Symbolists and *vers-libristes* of the later nine-
teenth century picked Whitman up as a model sooner than did most of his
compatriots. Émile Verhaeren blended Whitman's enthusiasm for the
commonplace with Victor Hugo's humanitarianism; but the Whitman-
esque metric could also be employed by those whose concerns were
remote from ordinary human experience. Take, for example, this passage
from Maurice Maeterlinck's "Regards":

O ces regards pauvres et las!
Et les vôtres et les miens!
Et ceux qui ne sont plus et ceux qui vont venir!
Et ceux qui n'arriveront jamais et qui existent cependant!
Il y en a qui semblent visiter des pauvres un dimanche;
Il y en a comme des malades sans maison;
Il y en a comme des agneaux dans une prairie couvertes de linges.
Et ces regards insolites!

[O these impoverished and exhausted glances!
Both yours and mine!
Both those which are no more and those which are yet to come!
Both those which will never occur and those which exist anyway!
Some there are that seem like Sunday visits with the poor;
Some there are like the sick and homeless;
Some there are like lambs in a meadow strewn with linen.
And these unaccustomed glances!]

After the turn of the century Whitman's presence in French poetry became even more pervasive; his example authorized the abandonment of rhyme in vers libre as well as the by then well-established freedom in syllable count. "Ode" by "A. O. Barnabooth," the imaginary author invented by Valèry Larbaud, even recalls Whitman's enthusiasm for the locomotive. Larbaud's enjambments, of course, disrupt the verset pattern of Whitman's end-stopped lines, but the Whitmanian presence is impossible to deny:

Prêtez-moi, o Orient-Express, Sud-Brenner-Bahn, prêtez-moi
Vos miraculeux bruits sourds et
Vos vibrantes voix de chanterelle;
Prêtez-moi la respiration légère et facile
Des locomotives hautes et minces, aux mouvements
Si aisés, les locomotives des rapides,
Précédant sans effort quatre wagons jaunes a lettres d'or
Dans les solitudes montagnardes de la Serbie,
Et, plus loin, à travers la Bulgarie pleine de roses.

[Lend me, O Orient Express, South Brenner Line, lend me
Your deafening miracle of sounds and

Your resonant high-pitched music;
Lend me the light and easy respiration
Of locomotives, high and thin, with movements
So free and easy, the express train locomotives,
Leading effortlessly four yellow carriages with gold lettering
Through the mountainous solitudes of Serbia,
And, further on, across Bulgaria burgeoning with roses.]

But in allowing Whitman, as they had done for Poe before him, to affect the course of French poetry, these writers were simultaneously building on foundations traced out by certain earlier poets in their own language. An example from Aloysius Bertrand's *Gaspard de la Nuit* will appear in chapter 9—and clearly, at least for purposes of the individual versets of his poems, Bertrand meant to suggest the phrasing of the biblical verse. The example of Whitman often serves to reinforce an impulse that has already arrived from some other direction; even in explicit rejection—such as that of Pound and Eliot—there may be an admission that his method is not itself inadmissible, only misapplied or mingled with other qualities that are not to be imitated. The French poets, however, were less guarded than Pound and Eliot, and Whitman was accepted early on as an explicit model and continued to be such on into the twentieth century in, for example, many poems by Paul Claudel, whose reactionary views and Thomistic theological outlook did not prevent his cultivating the American's evangelistic manner.

Poems and passages influenced by Whitman can be traced in other European languages, but I am primarily concerned with his presence in poetry written in English. The earliest example of British Whitmanian poetry is that of Edward Carpenter. In a preface to *Towards Democracy* (1883–1902) he wrote:

"Leaves of Grass" "filtered and fibred" my blood; but I do not think I ever tried to imitate it or its style. Against the inevitable drift out of the more classic forms of verse into a looser and freer rhythm I fairly fought, contesting the ground ("kicking against the pricks") inch by inch during a period of seven years in numerous abortive and mongrel creations—till in 1881 I was finally compelled into the form (if such it can be called) of "Towards Democracy." I did not adopt it *because* it was an approximation to the form of "Leaves of Grass." (xviii)

Carpenter continues, protesting rather too much that his work is parallel rather than derivative; it is true that his units are often longer than Whitman's, and often contain two or more sentences. But the connection is obvious, as in this passage from page 4 of *Towards Democracy*:

> I arise out of the dewy night and shake my wings.
> Tears and lamentations are no more. Life and death
> lie stretched below me. I breathe the sweet aether blowing
> of the breath of God.
> Deep as the universe is my life—and I know it;
> nothing can dislodge the knowledge of it; nothing
> can destroy, nothing can harm me.
> Joy, joy arises—I arise. The sun darts overpowering
> piercing rays of joy through me, the night radiates it from me.
> I take wings through the night and pass through all the
> wildernesses of the worlds and the old dark holds of tears
> and death—and return with laughter, laughter, laughter:
> Sailing through the starlit spaces on outspread wings,
> we two—O laughter! laughter! laughter!

Section 51 of *Towards Democracy* intersperses "Holy! holy! holy!" with other visionary outbursts; it once seemed impossible to me that Allen Ginsberg could have known this poem, but in tracing a homosexual line of descent from Whitman to himself—on camera in the *Voices and Visions* segment on Whitman—Ginsberg mentions Carpenter. So far as I can tell, no anthologist of the period 1880–1920 included any of Carpenter's work, though he continued to be known in British literary circles. After his death he appears to have been totally forgotten, earning an occasional scant reference in histories of the 1890s. Bliss Perry mentioned him in *Walt Whitman* (1906):

> His [Whitman's] imitators on the Continent, as in England and America, have not thus far been able to bend his bow. Edward Carpenter, who has a message of his own to deliver in Whitmanian verse, has handled the instrument not unskillfully. But most of the experiments in "free verse" make but melancholy reading. (285)

Perry did not—understandably—recognize "Miss Fiona Macleod" (William Sharp) as a follower of Whitman. Under that pseudonym Sharp composed in many modes; for a time in the 1890s it was thought that the real author of his work was Yeats. He was capable of opening "The Rose of Flame" with the line, "Oh, fair immaculate rose of the world, rose of my dream, my Rose!" But he had also read Whitman, and even more fatally, "Ossian," which work he eventually edited. Take the opening of "The Rune of the Passion of Women" (ca. 1895):

We who love are those who suffer,
We who suffer most are those who most do love.
O the heartbreak come of longing love,
O the heartbreak come of love deferred,
O the heartbreak come of love grown listless.

In *The Silence of Amor* he pushed the looseness of "Ossian" and Whitman even further, into an extraordinary series of prose poems.

In 1906, when Perry published *Walt Whitman,* those who were aware that Oscar Wilde had paid Whitman a visit may have felt that it might damage Whitman's reputation further to mention this fact. As we know, Wilde sent back a report in a letter, saying that he still bore the imprint of Whitman's kiss upon his lips. The imprint may likewise be seen in some of his writings; the preface to *The Picture of Dorian Gray* (1891) is a notable piece of biblical-anaphoric writing, though Wilde may well have intended it more to resemble some of the prose poems by French writers whom I will take up in chapter 10. But even more obviously biblical—the purpose being partly to scandalize his readers by the incongruity of style and subject—are Wilde's explicitly labeled prose poems:

THE MASTER

And when darkness came over the earth, Joseph of Arimathea, having lighted a torch of pinewood, passed down from the hill into the valley. For he had business in his own home.

And kneeling on the flint stones of the Valley of Desolation he saw a young man who was naked and weeping. His hair was the colour of honey, and his body was as a white flower; but he had wounded his body with thorns, and on his hair he had set ashes as a crown.

And he who had great possessions said to the young man who was naked: "I do not wonder that your sorrow is so great, for surely He was a just man."

And the young man answered: "It is not for Him that I am weeping, but for myself. I, too, have changed water into wine, and I have healed the leper and given sight to the blind. I have walked upon the waters, and from the dwellers in the tombs I have cast out devils. I have fed the hungry in the desert where there was no food, and I have raised the dead from their narrow houses; and at my bidding, and before a great multitude of people, a barren fig-tree withered away. All things that this man has done I have done also. And yet they have not crucified me."

Ernest Dowson's prose poems might also be cited, though he succeeded even better than Wilde in approximating the manner of Baudelaire and Mallarmé, and in avoiding the *style biblique* of those nineteenth-century French poets who based their manner first on the Bible and then, subsequently and only in part, on Whitman.

Variants of Whitmanian free verse have been cultivated continually in the United States since about 1915, when Edgar Lee Masters's *Spoon River Anthology* appeared. Long-lined, prosy, anaphoric poems, by Sherwood Anderson among others, spread across the pages of some of the earliest numbers of *Poetry* magazine. Such poems were even more common in the *Little Review* because that magazine published short pieces of prose—including prose poems—as well as poetry. Charles Ashleigh contributed a review of poems by Arturo Giovannitti to the *Dial* for September 1914, in which he noted, "Sometimes the formal verse forms are used and, at other times, the poet has recourse to the free rhythmic mode of Whitman." A passage of long, sprawling lines soon follows as illustration.

To point out the sudden burgeoning of Whitmanesque writing is not to argue that all poets employing this mode are Children of Walt, or even to assert that most of the features—such as those identified by Gay Wilson Allen—of Whitman's own prosody carry over into the work of those who will be mentioned in the rest of this chapter. It seems fair, however, to give Whitman most of the credit. Often his familiar prophetic or messianic tone accompanies the form.

A vexed question is the extent to which biblical-anaphoric poetry by African-American poets has taken Whitman as a model. Earlier writings by these poets clearly derived from preaching, which was in its turn based upon reading in the King James Bible. But among black poets, beginning about 1915, Whitman came to stand alongside Abraham Lincoln as a prosodic emancipator and sympathetic figure, who had cemented this identity by composing the most memorable tributes to Lincoln. This occurred despite the fact, not then well known, that Whitman did not like African-Americans personally, considered them an inferior race, and was in some respects a Southern sympathizer; he did not believe that the righteousness of the Union cause warranted the continuation of the Civil War. These unpleasant truths are thoroughly documented in Kaplan's biography (291–92).

But Langston Hughes characterized Whitman as a Lincoln of poetry and included poems by Whitman in an anthology of "negro poetry," as it was then called. Carl Sandburg and Edgar Lee Masters, in addition to employing Whitmanesque patterns in their poetry, wrote biographies of Lincoln; Vachel Lindsay, another great admirer of Lincoln, carried the spirit of Whitman, more than the form, into his poetry. Sandburg and Lindsay were important sponsors of African-American poetry; their prophetic manner and their enthusiasm for America as a forum in which all voices might be heard encouraged black self-expression. Whitman, then, has been perceived by several constituencies as carrying into the twentieth century the reestablished and extended democratic principles symbolized politically by Lincoln, and Whitman's particular type of free verse does imply a political outlook. In 1925 the Lincoln-Whitman parallel was commonplace; Louis Untermeyer, in the preface to his *Modern American Poetry* (1925) spoke of Whitman as "the Lincoln of our literature" and "our great poetic emancipator"; the content of that anthology is heavily populist.

Whitman tended to be adopted as a precursor by African-Americans who had already begun to think consciously of their own position in American literature—that is, poets who thought of themselves as poets, and who aspired to literary careers. As Arnold Rampersad explains, Langston Hughes was introduced to Whitman at the precise moment that Whitmanian influence finally began to make itself felt in American poetry:

> In large part, Hughes owed this leap in the quality of his work to his new English teacher, Ethel Weimer, a former student at Central [High School in Cleveland] and perhaps its most popular and progressive instructor. Unafraid of the new, she held up to him the example of poets such as Edgar Lee Masters, Edwin Arlington Robinson, Amy Lowell, Vachel Lindsay, Carl Sandburg, and, towering above them all, Walt Whitman, who had died only twenty-seven

years before. His admiration for Whitman would last the longest; Carl Sandburg, however, became his "guiding star." (28–29)

Hughes composed in many styles, his special innovation being the adaptation of blues and jazz rhythms to poetry, but on occasion he employed biblical-anaphoric free verse, most memorably in the much-anthologized "The Negro Speaks of Rivers."

Sterling Brown, by drawing the title for his poem from Sandburg and by leading off with a line of Sandburg's as an epigraph, insisted on his connection with the Whitmanian populists. "Strong Men" begins—

> *They dragged you from homeland,*
> *They chained you in coffles,*
> *They huddled you spoon-fashion in filthy hatches.*
> *They sold you to give a few gentlemen ease.*
> *They broke you like oxen,*
> *They scourged you,*
> *They branded you,*
> *They made your women breeders,*
> *They swelled your numbers with bastards. . . .*
> *They taught you religion that they disgraced.*

But the groundwork for an appreciation of Whitman's style among African-American poets was—and in some cases still may be—Bible reading and preaching. In the preface to *God's Trombones* (1927) James Weldon Johnson made a good case for bypassing Whitman altogether.

The old-time Negro preachers, though they actually used dialect in their ordinary intercourse, stepped out from its narrow confines when they preached. They were all saturated with the sublime phraseology of the Hebrew prophets and steeped in the idioms of King James English, so when they preached and warmed to their work they spoke another language, a language far removed from traditional Negro dialect. It was really a fusion of Negro idioms with Bible English; and in this there may have been, after all, some kinship with the innate grandiloquence of their old African tongues. (9)

What Johnson says seems essentially true, beyond what historical linguistics might be able to prove; it is very moving. Zora Neale Hurston provided an example of what he describes in her transcription of a sermon preached by C. C. Lovelace on May 3, 1929. After a prose beginning, the preacher slips into biblical-anaphoric utterance. These lines describe the moment of Jesus' death:

> And de sun
> Batted her fiery eyes and put on her judgment robe
> And laid down in de cradle of eternity
> And rocked herself into sleep and slumber.
> He died until the great belt in the wheel of time
> And de geological strata fell aloose
> And a thousand angels rushed to de canopy of heben
> With flamin swords in their hands
> And placed their feet upon blue ether's bosom and looked back at
>   de dazzlin throne
> And de arc angels had veiled their faces . . .

James Weldon Johnson took his own experience of the "old-time Negro preachers" as the inspiration for *God's Trombones*, explaining, "I claim no more for these poems than that I have written them after the manner of the primitive sermons." The following passage is from "Noah Built the Ark":

> And a little black spot begun to spread,
> Like a bottle of Ink spilling over the sky;
> And the thunder rolled like a rumbling drum;
> And the lightning jumped from pole to pole;
> And it rained down rain, rain, rain,
> Great God but didn't it rain!
> For forty days and forty nights
> Waters poured down and waters gushed up;
> And the dry land turned to sea.
> And the old ark-a she begun to ride;
> The old ark-a she begun to rock;
> Sinners came a-running down to the ark;
> Sinners came a-swimming all round the ark;
> Sinners pleaded and sinners prayed—
> Sinners wept and sinners wailed—
> But Noah'd done barred the door.

The transcription of the sermon that Faulkner made part of the "Dilsey" section on *The Sound and the Fury* might provide another example. Though written out as prose, some of it divides easily into lines of anaphora:

> "I sees hit, breddren! I sees hit! Sees de blastin, blindin sight! I sees Calvary, wid de sacred trees, sees de thief en de murderer en de least of dese; I hears de boasting en de bragging; Ef you be Jesus, lif up yo tree en walk! I hears de wailen of women en de sevenin lamentations; I hears de weepin en de cryin en de turnt-away face of God: dey done kilt Jesus; dey done kilt my Son!"

If we go back even further, the biblical and liturgical models in African-American free verse are even more prominent. Fenton Johnson's "Aunt Jane Allen" dates from about 1915:

> State Street is lonely today. Aunt Jane Allen has driven her chariot
>   to Heaven. I remember how she hobbled along, a little woman,
>   parched of skin, brown as a leather satchel and with eyes that
>   had scanned eighty years of life.
> Have those who bore her dust to the last resting place buried with
>   her the basket of aprons she went up and down State Street
>   trying to sell?
> Have those who bore her dust to the last resting place buried with
>   her the gentle word *Son* that she gave to each of the seed of
>   Ethiopia?

"The Song of the Smoke" by W. E. B. Du Bois employs short-line anaphora. Published in 1899, it sounds so remarkably like Carl Sandburg that one wonders if Sandburg learned from it:

> I am the smoke king,
> I am black.
> I am swinging in the sky.
> I am ringing worlds on high:
> I am the thought of the throbbing mills,
> I am the soul of the soul toil kills,
> I am the ripple of trading rills.

The use of rhyme, however, parallels what Henley and Davidson were doing in England at about the same time, making this one of the most extraordinary early examples of American free verse of any kind. That Du Bois's inspiration was largely biblical or liturgical, however, shows in "A Litany of Atlanta," which begins—

> O Silent God, Thou whose voice afar in mist and mystery hath
> left our ears an-hungered in these fearful days—
> *Hear us, good Lord!*
> Listen to us, Thy children: our faces dark with doubts are made
> a mockery in Thy sanctuary. With uplifted hands we front Thy
> heaven, O God, crying:
> *We beseech Thee to hear us, good Lord!*

Even long after Whitman's influence had made itself felt in African-American poetry, there are moments when the older biblical or preaching tradition seems stronger. Here is the conclusion of Margaret Walker's "For My People," the title poem of her Yale Younger Poets volume in 1942:

> Let a new earth rise. Let another world be born. Let a bloody
> peace be written in the sky. Let a second generation full of
> courage issue forth; let a people loving freedom come to
> growth. Let a beauty full of healing and a strength of final
> clenching be the pulsing in our spirits and our blood. Let the
> martial songs be written, let the dirges disappear. Let a race of
> men now rise and take control.

This, of course, is the "let" pattern anaphora, employed, as we have seen by Christopher Smart and Whitman, and taken straight from the Psalms. At any given point, therefore, and in any given poem, it remains difficult to be sure if, or to what extent, Whitman supervenes on the older patterns.

Even more difficult to untangle are the implications of biblical-anaphoric meter in the work of British poets. Whitman's vitalism, for example, appealed to D. H. Lawrence, but Lawrence's politics, such as they were, involved strands of Nietzschean hero-worship quite foreign to the spirit of American democracy. Patrick Kavanagh's allegiance to the "other Ireland," remote from Yeats's Romantic pageantry, may have led him to find in Whitman an authentic voice of the common laborer. More complex still is the appearance of passages of anaphora in T. S. Eliot's poetry. I will examine Eliot's work at length in the next chapter, and will simply remark at this point that his use of anything resembling Whitman involved a definite rejection of Whitman himself, but an openness to rhythms from Scripture and opera, and also to patterns in religious writings in other languages, including Sanskrit.

Merely to quote representative examples of Whitmanesque poetry in this century would require a thick anthology. To explain their exact relationship to Whitman would require an additional book. In order to identify this particular variety of free verse and to give some idea of its extent, I shall do no more than list poets and titles of poems, together with the page number on which the poem begins in *The Norton Anthology of Modern Poetry* (2d ed.). In some of these examples, only scattered portions are biblical-anaphoraic free verse.

Edgar Lee Masters, from *Spoon River Anthology* (206)
Gertrude Stein, "A Valentine for Sherwood Anderson" (238)
Carl Sandburg, "Chicago" (270)
D. H. Lawrence, "The Wild Common" (353)
Ezra Pound, "Hugh Selwyn Mauberly," part 4 (384)
Robinson Jeffers, "Hurt Hawks" (431)
Edith Sitwell, "The Poet Laments the Coming of Old Age" (453)
Langston Hughes, "The Negro Speaks of Rivers" (647)
Stevie Smith, "Admire Cranmer" (656)
Patrick Kavanaugh, from *The Great Hunger* (678)
Robert Penn Warren, from *Penological Study: Southern Exposure* (699)
Theodore Roethke, "The Far Field" (784)
William Everson, "The Poet Is Dead" (848)
Robert Hayden, "The Ballad of Sue Ellen Westerfield" (863)
Dudley Randall, "The Poet Is Not a Juke Box" (890)
Gwendolyn Brooks, "Young Africans" (984)
Kenneth Koch, "To Marina" (1132)
Allen Ginsberg, "America" (1216)
Galway Kinnell, "On the Oregon Coast" (1254)
W. S. Merwin, "Home for Thanksgiving" (1274)
James Wright, "Sappho" (1281)
Adrienne Rich, "Yom Kippur in 1984" (1332)
Richard Howard, "Wildflowers" (parts, 1345–59)
Bruce Dawe, "Drifters" (1382)

June Jordan, "Poem about My Rights" (1470)
Diane Wakowski, "Thanking My Mother for Piano Lessons" (1490)
John Tranter, "Mark" (1589)
Michael Ondaatje, "Burning Hills" (1601)
Norman Dubie, "At Midsummer" (1629)
James Fenton, "A German Requiem" (1657)
Gjertrud Schnackenberg, "Darwin in 1881" (1712)

One group of poets, because they made anaphora a hallmark of many of their poems, needs to be singled out. The Beat Generation, subsequently continued as the San Francisco Renaissance, saw themselves as assuming the mantle first worn by Emerson, Thoreau, and Whitman. Conspicuous in this garment's design was the Whitmanian line, sometimes employed with obviously imitative (if ironic) panache, as in Ginsberg's "Howl," and in other poems truncated and disguised. Lawrence Ferlinghetti is especially skillful at amalgamating his poetic constituents, moving easily from cummings-like typography, to Williams's "triadic" structure, and alternating or modifying both on occasion with a syncopated or jazzed-up Whitman. To say this is not to suggest that the poetry is imitative or derivative, but it is to say that Ferlinghetti brings to his prosody a conscious purpose that is lacking in too many of those who fall into this line of descent. Ferlinghetti is deliberately literary, wearing the robes of the poet rather than the messiah. Ogden Nash ridiculed formal stanzas by pushing rhyming to its absurd conclusion; Ferlinghetti, heading in the opposite direction, abbreviates the Whitman line for comic effect (though not, of course, to burlesque Whitman):

FROM "DOG"
The dog trots freely in the street
and the things he smells
smell something like himself
The dog trots freely in the street
past puddles and babies
cats and cigars
poolrooms and policemen
He doesn't hate cops
He merely has no use for them
and he goes past them
and past the dead cows hung up whole

in front of the San Francisco Meat Market
He would rather eat a tender cow
than a tough policeman
though either might do

Among the poems, and poets, removed from the second edition of
the *Norton Anthology of Modern Poetry* was "Marriage" and its author,
Gregory Corso. That revision, along with the excision of J. V. Cunning-
ham, rendered the collection more middle-of-the-road, but deprived read-
ers not only of the opportunity to enjoy in Cunningham the greatest
epigrammatist of the century, but also, in Corso, an example of what
Whitman might have been capable of if he had had a sense of humor.

FROM "MARRIAGE"
All streaming into cozy hotels
All going to do the same thing tonight
The indifferent clerk he knowing what was going to happen
The lobby zombies they knowing what
The whistling elevator man he knowing
The winking bellboy knowing
Everybody knowing! I'd be almost inclined not to do anything!
Stay up all night! Stare that hotel clerk in the eye!
running rampant into those almost climactic suites
yelling Radio Belly! Cat Shovel!
O I'd live in Niagara forever! in a dark cave beneath the Falls
I'd sit there the Mad Honeymooner

The possibilities of this mode of writing are far from exhausted. The
most sensitive analysis yet of Whitman's metric is that by W. D. Snod-
grass in his essay "Pulse and Impulse." Snodgrass, however, is taking
Whitman as an opportunity to move in the direction paralleled by T. S.
Eliot and William Carlos Williams, toward some new musical order: "It
seems to me that when such a music works it will be not merely a
restraint, a limit on the poem's energies, but will come to be identified
with that energy itself, an energy which can only be realized as it is
restrained and channeled" (512–13). Other poets, without announcing
their intentions, may already have been doing the same thing; one could
argue that the best poems of James Dickey break a Whitmanesque line
into approximately regular shorter segments. The example that Snod-

grass gives of his own practice, "Owls," is a poem of extraordinary beauty, illustrating what may yet turn out to be the most important legacy of Whitman, his bequeathing us the "wide use of freedom," to use a phrase originally invented by Alfred North Whitehead, but since the poem is testing the possibilities of a new order, rather than counter-pointing older meters, it does not belong in a discussion of free verse. The same might be said of Eliot's last poems, but not of his earlier work, to which I now turn.

Chapter 8

"No Verse Is Really Free"

By the time that Ezra Pound discovered him in 1914, T. S. Eliot had, in Pound's view, already modernized himself on his own. Eliot had been writing poetry for several years before Amy Lowell endowed and then took over the Imagist movement, and even before the Imagists' first fruits in poetry and theory had seen print. He was innocent of tutelage beyond his formal studies as a Harvard undergraduate and then as a graduate student in philosophy during the great days of that department. Only the accident of a canceled sailing, when submarine warfare broke out in 1914, prevented him from completing his degree, and possibly from taking some academic position in the United States. In any event, Eliot was well formed by the time that Pound got hold of him, though the nervous collapse that coincided with the writing of *The Waste Land* in 1921 gave Pound a chance to intervene in the writing of that poem. Eliot brought the manuscript with him to Paris that year and turned it over to Pound for editing.

But in helping to shape *The Waste Land,* Pound had to abandon his usual role of self-appointed teacher. Eliot had already appointed his own faculty, as we know, eclectically constituted of the French Symbolists, the Jacobean playwrights, and the Metaphysicals. Amy Lowell, too, gave close attention to the late-nineteenth-century Symbolist *vers-libristes,* and brought them to the attention of many of her contemporaries. But Eliot had already arrived at his own opinions without Lowell's help; Arthur Symons's book had some years earlier been his introduction to Symbolism and through that, to French vers libres. He was also independent of the Anglo-American speculation on prosody that Pound, T. E. Hulme, and F. S. Flint initiated in the Poet's Club in 1908–9, though he may have modified his views somewhat in light of Flint's writings. Eliot charted his own course and is, for that reason, the most important writer of free verse in English. His way was to assimilate all the earlier models, including the *vers impairs* of the earlier Symbolists, the biblical-anaphoraic models (though not from Whitman), the colloquial looseness of Henley, some hints from Milton, and a range of effects introduced by Pound.

Harvey Gross, in chapter 7 of *Sound and Form in Modern Poetry*, "T. S. Eliot and the Music of Poetry," provides as complete and sensitive an account of Eliot's metrics as one could hope for. Charles O. Hartman builds on this analysis (in his book, *Free Verse*), explaining more of the principles behind the metrics and expanding Gross's treatment, which had—I think rightly—placed heavy emphasis on musical models and analogies in Eliot's prosody (111–29). Hartman argues, "But Gross's description must also be expanded to include *all* of Eliot's rhythmic techniques: counterpoint and metrical approximation as well as syntactical manipulation" (129). This statement is in fact a summary of what Hartman has already demonstrated, at length, and convincingly. Taken together, Gross and Hartman furnish an assessment of Eliot's prosody so thorough that little of value can be added to it except by considering at greater length than they do precisely what Eliot owed to French poetry.

Gross and Hartman agree with Eliot in his early insistence that no verse is really free for the poet who wishes to do a good job. The label *free verse* was originally applied to Eliot's early work by some critics as a term of derogation, suggesting that it was without principle, rhythmic or otherwise; it is therefore proper to insist that not only did Eliot know what he was doing, but that he had taken a profitable new direction. Since 1910, however, *free verse* has lost any flavor of simple-minded opprobrium that it originally carried; to a very few it may still seem a chimera in the barnyard of domesticated poetic forms, but familiarity renders it less menacing. Applying the criterion of free verse as a type of poetry that presupposes established conventions as a possibility, but which steps outside those conventions, I therefore will treat Eliot, in his earlier work, as a writer of free verse; in this capacity, as in many others, Eliot was the legitimate successor to Matthew Arnold. Indeed, Eliot is the greatest master of free verse of all time, one who provides first-rate examples of most of its possibilities. At the same time, he was the only poet writing in English in this century who carried the formal structuring of poetry decisively to a new level. It might be argued that Hardy, Yeats, and Frost, who continued to work within ancient traditions, were greater poets, but Eliot was beyond question the greatest innovator, rivaled and assisted, of course, by Pound.

As long ago as 1948, many readers had arrived at a fundamentally sound view of Eliot's prosody, aided by Eliot's own perspicuous admissions. Samuel Chew described it this way: "In style the modern and the traditional were fused into a new synthesis: on the one hand, there is indebtedness to Ezra Pound and the Imagists and to certain French poets, particularly Tristan Corbière and Jules Laforgue; and on the other, there is the use of simple, inherited verse forms, especially the quatrain, and blank verse modeled upon that of Webster and Middleton" (Baugh 1585–86). In assessing the prosody of Eliot's earlier poems, those which belong to his disintegrative or iconoclastic phase, we need to take account of his historical connections with nineteenth-century free-verse writers, especially the French, and to examine precisely what were the analogies between French and English practice. The Indian writer Ved Mehta, in an autobiographical piece in the *New Yorker* (November 11, 1991, p. 84), recalled conversations with the brilliant British classicist Jasper Griffin when both were Oxford undergraduates; at one point Griffin said, "Eliot knew the classics pretty well, too. He was very much interested in Heraclitus and Virgil. There's not much Greek and Latin in his poems, though—there's more French." Griffin was contrasting Eliot with Milton, Tennyson, and Arnold. Eliot was sufficiently imbued with French that he could compose poems in the language that at least some French readers find quite successful. That alone should suggest the extent to which he had absorbed—not just read—the poets with whom he became familiar after reading Arthur Symons's *The Symbolist Movement in Literature* (1899).

[H]is own poetry, in so far as it was a kind of *vers libre,* was only so in the limited sense that certain of the French Symbolists' verse (he mentions Laforgue in particular) was "free" in relation to the French Alexandrine. (48–49)

And C. K. Stead continues in the next paragraph—

It is easy to *decide* to break out of the traditional form; but to do so effectively the ear must be re-educated—and it is likely that Eliot achieved this by submerging himself so thoroughly in the French language and in French poetry that he was able after a time to return to English liberated. (49)

It is therefore most important to examine the nature of the French *vers-libristes* who meant much to Eliot, and to account for the ways in which their practices could be accommodated to English metrics. I will begin by treating them on their own terms.

The evolution of vers libres in nineteenth-century France was a more continuous process than anything in English. In his preface to *Cromwell* (1830) Victor Hugo had called for a reform of the French poetic line, using vers libre as a term; he meant only a relaxing of the classical criteria for the placement of the caesura in the Alexandrine and the requirement that it be end-stopped, but at least the idea of tampering with fixed prosody was enunciated by the poet who was, as André Gide admitted, "le plus grand poète du dix-neuvième siècle, hélas." The practice of introducing semipredictable variations into French poetry went much further back.

L. E. Kastner, in *A History of French Versification,* traces instances of such poetry through the preceding three centuries:

> If lines provided with *rimes mêlés* [patterns of alternating masculine and feminine rhymes that do not observe classical rules] are at the same time of different lengths, they are known as *vers libres.* The earliest French *vers libres* occur in the works of Melin de Saint-Gelais (1487–1558), and were probably written in imitation of Italian madrigals and *pasquilli.* But it was not till the seventeenth century that such verses appeared in any number, in the guise of madrigals and epistles, which were much favoured by the poets of the Hôtel de Rambouillet. (68)

For my purposes, the connection of this sort of free verse with the madrigal—which, in chapter 4, I pointed to as the initial model for English free verse—is especially important in establishing the parallels between English and French practice. A well-marked trail connects Eliot's prosody with the choruses of Milton's *Samson Agonistes,* and these in turn owed much to the example of Italian irregular verse. In reading the *vers-libristes* Eliot encountered a cousin of the same prosodic line of descent, and married them in his own work.

Because it is likely that Kastner's book, published by the Clarendon Press at Oxford in 1903, was available to and read by Eliot, I quote another extensive paragraph from it:

Vers libres have been largely used during the last ten or fifteen years by the Symbolists, or rather a ramification of the same school, which is known as the *école vers-libriste*. In the free verses of the classicists, and later in those of Voltaire, Andrieux, and A. de Musset, the choice of meter is not absolutely left to the poet: he must not, for example, place very short lines after very long lines, or combine lines which differ by only one syllable more or less. No such considerations are taken into account by the *Vers-Libristes,* and it is for that reason chiefly that their free verses, though they may occasionally be harmonious prose, cease to be French verses. The classicists, and those who have tried their hand at such verses after them, felt that syllabism, and consequently number, was one of the fundamental conditions of French verse, and that, if it were lost sight of altogether, their *vers libres* would cease to be French verses at all. The *Vers-Libristes* have made their case still less defensible by weakening, and not infrequently totally effacing, the role of rime in these irregular verses. (69–70)

An important footnote at this point states that "Walt Whitman's *irregular meters* seem to have been the starting point for some of the *vers-libristes.*" I have already illustrated this with examples in the previous chapter; here I am concerned with the parallels between French syllabism, as practiced by the *vers-libristes,* and English accentual-syllabic meter, as partially retained by Eliot. Eliot's relations with Whitman, such as they were, are better accounted for by considering Whitman directly, though there is a way in which Eliot was affected by Whitman—through the Symbolists—of which he may have scarcely been aware; to the extent that he knew Whitman directly Eliot simply left him—as well as Longfellow—behind on the western side of the Atlantic, along with the unsatisfying genteel academicism of Cambridge, Massachusetts, and the commercial rawness of St. Louis.

A common way of analyzing Eliot's early work is to insist on the lingering presence of some familiar metric, usually iambic pentameter, behind and at times within the lines of the poem. Eliot himself authorized this approach in his early comments on what free verse ought to be. The best example of this is "The Love Song of J. Alfred Prufrock," which opens with lines that resolutely evade iambic pentameter, but that—after many previous lapses—settle, like the speaker, into conformity at the conclusion, "Till human voices wake us, and we drown." Commonplace ideas are often correct; that Eliot should have periodically reverted in other poems, with evident delight, to iambics of ironic regularity proves sufficiently well that this was the heartbeat of his poetry, whatever fibrillations he may have induced elsewhere. Lingering iambics are common to all poetry in English that I would call vers-libristic and are, with sporadic rhyme, one of its defining features.

Helen Gardner said essentially the same thing in her chapter entitled "Auditory Imagination" in *The Art of T. S. Eliot* (1950). Because of her own strong grounding in classical languages, Gardner thought it inadvisable to use *iambic pentameter,* fearing that this suggested a quantitative meter, and proposed "heroic line" instead (16–17n). In making this qualification she formulates in a particularly concise way a fundamental difference between quantitative and accentual-syllabic meters: "[W]hile in classical metre the quantitative pattern has actually to be preserved in each line, in English the regular alternation of unstressed and stressed syllables is only an ideal around which the actual line varies." I would take this one step further in describing what happens in "Prufrock," arguing that Eliot steps completely outside of the iambic pentameter (or, according to Gardner, heroic meter). Indeed that is another aspect of "Prufrock's" antiheroism, another way in which, for example, it works as an inverted version of Tennyson's "Ulysses." Gardner also states, "The underlying rhythm is unmistakable; it remains a duple rising rhythm, the staple rhythm of English verse, the basis of our heroic line" (17).

If what we have in "Prufrock" is "the staple rhythm of English verse," how do we account for Stead's perception that Eliot's metrics were radically defined by his immersion in French? Is there anything in French vers libres that corresponds to the iambic in English and which Eliot allowed to affect the nature of his poetic line? It turns out that there exists a clear analogue in the concept and the aural habit of the *vers pairs* in French. Most formal poetry in French has been composed in lines which contain twelve, ten, or eight syllables. These are *vers pairs,* meaning that they contain an *even* number of syllables. The ear of readers of French poetry, at least in earlier centuries, had become so accustomed hearing an even number (*pair*) of syllables that an irregular line (*vers impairs*) was immediately recognizable. In the same way, those who read enough English poetry learn to discriminate sensitively between a line that satisfies the requirements of iambic pentameter and one that does not. We are more flexible now, even those of us who are saturated with traditional iambics; but when Eliot began to write poetry the iambic was the general expectation. Whitman was scarcely read and was generally disliked by those who did read him; no one said much about Henley, and discussions of Matthew Arnold tended to deplore or ignore his free-verse poems. The ears of English-speaking readers of poetry had been conditioned to expect the regular recurrence of an established meter and line length—to recognize substitutions, of course, but nothing that made the line unscannable in terms of the fundamental rhythmic template. This expectation was analogous to the expectation in French of the *vers pairs*.

Some French poems, indeed well-known poems, had been composed in *vers impairs;* these include the Old French *Aucussin et Nicolette* in heptasyllabics, and some of La Fontaine's *Fables*. Lamartine and Hugo introduced the same, seven-syllable, line as a Romantic variant, and others—most notably Théophile Gautier—continued to employ it. Shorter *vers impairs* tend to be heard as halves of even-syllable lines or, conversely, as in Leconte de Lisle's poem "Les Elfes," the decasyllabic line tends to break into five-syllable halves. The heptasyllabic line is the stablest of the *vers impairs*. Its use, particularly as another expression of Romantic impatience with classical symmetry, drew attention to itself, in somewhat the same way as had Blake's catalectic tetrameters, which are also seven-syllable lines.

The interesting thing about the *vers impairs* in connection with French vers libres, however, is the way in which many compositions in vers libres in the later nineteenth century *failed* to exploit this new freedom, or did so only in part. The lines may be of irregular length; the rhymes may be placed unpredictably or not at all; but in many poems the line lengths are all predictably even in syllable count, that is, two, four, six, eight, ten, twelve, and occasionally fourteen or more syllables. Numerous poems by Émile Verhaeren and Henri de Régnier furnish examples of this; on the page the configuration of the poem and the disposition of the rhymes may seem quite spasmodic, but upon examination every line turns out to contain an even number of syllables. Even poems that introduce *vers impairs,* such as the later poems of Laforgue, are preponderantly even-syllabled. My argument is that this predilection for an evenness of syllabification corresponds to—even when it does not directly influence—a similar tendency of English-speaking writers of vers-libristic poetry to retain something of the iambic rhythm. This is especially important in T. S. Eliot's work, because he knew French and the French *vers-libristes* better than he

knew many English poets, immersing himself in the language to the point
that he composed not only letters and critical articles, but even—as I have
mentioned—poems that have met with the approbation of French readers
and that he retained in his *Collected Poems*.

The most important examples of Eliot's French models may be
found, as is well known, in the poetry of Jules Laforgue. I quote "Solo
de Lune" in its entirety because it includes many features common to
"Prufrock," such as repeated refrainlike lines and couplets, verbal leit-
motivs. I cannot begin to say with certainty how Laforgue heard each
line. Mostly I have applied classical rules in determining whether the
final *e,* or the last syllable of a third-person plural verb, should count as
a syllable, when not elided and when not found at the end of the line.
But in some instances the poet may not have been that formal. Since I
lack both the ear and the learning needed to make these discriminations,
there will certainly be those who will want to correct my specific ex-
amples below. L. E. Kastner's *History of French Versification* devotes a
thirty-four-page chapter to the mute, or feminine, *e,* subdividing the
topic into seventeen sections and providing more than a thousand ex-
amples of individual lines and words, and their variant pronunciations.
After making my own scansion, I came across Clive Scott's detailed
analysis of the same poem in *A Question of Syllables* and changed the
syllable count for some lines to accord with his, while retaining others
that differ from his. The real problem, however, is whether and to what
extent Laforgue decided to ignore the classical rules for syllable count-
ing altogether. The tone is personal, whimsical, and colloquial, so that
it may have been of no concern at all to him whether "La lune se lève"
should count as five syllables, using classical scansion, or whether the
mute *e* of "lune" should simply be ignored, since one hardly hears it in
actual speech. There are even some who argue that feminine endings
such as in "cahotée" or "fumées" should count as additional syllables
when they appear before a comma in the middle of a line, making those
words four and three syllables, respectively. All that the scansion can
really tell us is that there exists great variety in the line lengths, except
for one or two passages in which the poem regularizes itself for several
lines.

Fortunately for my purposes, however, it is quite clear that—
whether one applies the classical rules or whether one relaxes them
somewhat—about 70 of the 107 lines in this highly irregular poem con-

tain *even* numbers of syllables (six, eight, ten, etc.). Most frequent is the octosyllable, which occurs twenty-eight times, followed distantly by lines of six and nine syllables, with twelve examples of each of these; many nine-syllable lines are ambiguous, reducing to eight under certain rules or exceptions. It therefore appears that the norm around which the poem oscillates is the familiar and ancient octosyllable—much as "Prufrock" oscillates around the pentameter.

When we get past the first two stanzas, in which the poet seems striving consciously for irregularity, the odd-syllabled lines mostly occur in couplets, giving the effect of an evenly divided six- or ten-syllable line: "Que ma vie / Fait envie!" and "O Solo de lune, / Vous défiez ma plume." Few freestanding lines contain an odd number of syllables. The point of this somewhat labored discussion is to establish, as objectively as possible, that a tendency toward even-numbered syllabism persists even in so freewheeling a piece as this, much as the iambics persist in the background of "Prufrock." Eliot, in turn, remains the most conspicuous model in English for the kind of free verse that I call—with a certain redundancy—vers-libristic, although one can always look back to the practice of Drummond and Milton, which owed much to Italian poetry. In any event, the importance of Laforgue to Eliot is beyond dispute, and Eliot's mastery of the method of varying a poem against an implied metrical possibility owes much to his immersion in Laforgue. Clive Scott, seeming almost to echo Eliot's own account of free verse, describes it this way:

> Laforgue's lines encourage the reader to reach through to a prosodic model and then to withdraw from that model immediately it is identified. In other words, Laforgue's verse enacts a process of prosodic re-education; it is much less an "errance," than an itinerary from the metrical to the non-metrical in which the metrical retains an orientating capacity. Free verse is not so much "metre undone" as "learning to undo metre," not so much "rhythm made wayward" as "rhythm redistributed." (158)

Lines that—as best I can judge—are *impairs* are marked with an asterisk. A translation of the poem by Leigh Palmer may be found in the appendix.

SOLO DE LUNE [CA. 1885]

syllables

8	Je fume, étalé face au ciel,
11	★Sur l'impériale de la diligence,
11	★Ma carcasse est cahotée, mon âme danse
4	Comme un Ariel;
9	★Sans miel, sans fiel, mon belle âme danse
11	★O routes, coteaux, o fumées, o vallons,
9	★Ma belle âme, ah! récapitulons.
8	Nous nous aimions comme deux fous,
8	On s'est quitté sans en parler,
8	Un spleen me tenait exilé,
9	★Et ce spleen me venait de tout. Bon.
9	★Ses yeux disaient: "Comprenez-vous?
8	Pourquoi ne comprenez-vous pas?
11	★Mais nul n'a voulu faire le premier pas,
10	Voulant trop tomber *ensemble* à genoux.
4	(Comprenez-vous?)
6	Ou est-elle à cette heure?
6	Peut-être qu'elle pleure . . .
6	Ou est-elle à cette heure?
10	Oh! du moins, soigne-toi, je t'en conjure!
10	O fraicheur des bois le long de la route,
16	O châle de melancholie, tout âme est un peu aux écoutes
3	★Que ma vie
3	★Fait envie!
16	Cette impériale de diligence tient de la magie.
8	Accumulons l'irréparable!
8	Renchérissons sur nôtre sort!
12	Les étoiles sont plus nombreuses que le sable
12	Des mers où d'autres on vue se baigner son corps;
8	Tout n'en va pas moins à la Mort.
4	Y a pas de port.

8	Des ans vont passer là-dessus,
9	★On s'endurcira chacun pour soi,
10	Et bien souvent et déjà je m'y vois,
8	On se dira: "Si j'avais su . . ."
12	Mais mariés de même, ne se fût-on pas dit
8	"Si j'avais su, si j'avais su . . ."
6	Ah! rendez-vous maudit!
6	Ah! mon coeur sans issue! . . .
6	Je me suis mal conduit.
7	★Maniaques de bonheur,
9	★Donc, que ferons-nous? Moi de mon âme.
9	★Elle de sa faillible jeunesse?
8	O vieillisante pécheresse,
10	Oh! que de soirs je vais me rendre infâme
4	En ton honneur!
9	★Ses yeux clignaient: "Comprenez-vous?
8	"Pourquoi ne comprenez-vous pas?"
8	Mais nul n'a fait le premier pas
9	★Pour tomber ensemble à genoux. Ah! . . .
5	★La lune se lève,
5	★O route en grand rêve! . . .
13	★On a dépassé le filatures, les scieries,
9	★Plus que les bornes kilométriques,
14	De petits nuages d'un rose de confiserie,
12	Cependant qu'un fin croissant de lune se lève,
10	O route de rêve, ô nulle musique . . .
8	Dans ces bois de pins où depuis
7	★Le commencement du monde
5	★Il fait toujours nuit,
9	★Que de chambres propres et profondes!
8	Oh! pour un soir d'enlèvement!
8	Et je les peuple et je m'y vois,
8	Et c'est un beau couple d'amants,
8	Qui gesticulent hors la loi.

8	Et je passe et les abandonne,
8	Et me recouche face au ciel.
9	★La route tourne, je suis Ariel,
10	Nul ne m'attend, je ne vais chez personne.
11	★Je n'ai que l'amitié des chambres d'hôtel.
5	★La lune se lève,
5	★O route en grand rêve,
5	★O route sans terme,
5	★Voici le relais,
8	Où l'on allume les lanternes,
8	Où l'on boit un verre de lait,
7	★Et fouette postillon,
6	Dans le chant des grillons,
8	Sous les étoiles de juillet.
4	O clair de Lune,
14	Noce de feux de Bengale noyant mon infortune,
9	★Les ombres des peupliers sur la route . . .
6	Le gave qui s'écoute . . . ,
6	Qui s'écoute chanter . . .
12	Dans ces inondations du fleuve du Léthé . . .
5	★O Solo de Lune,
5	★Vous défiez ma plume.
8	Oh! cette nuit sur la route;
10	O Étoiles, vous êtes à faire peur,
6	Vous y êtes toutes! toutes!
8	O fugacité de cette heure . . .
5	★Oh! qu'il y eût moyen
12	De m'en garder l'âme pour l'automne qui vient . . .
7	★Voici qu'il fait très, très frais,
6	Oh! si à la même heure,
11	★Elle va de même le long des forêts,
6	Noyer son infortune
8	Dans les noces du clair de lune! . . .
7	★(Elle aime tant errer tard!)
8	Elle aura oublié son foulard,
12	Elle va prendre mal, vu la beauté de l'heure!

8   Oh! soigne-toi, je t'en conjure!

11   ★Oh! je ne veux plus entendre cette toux!

11   ★Ah! que ne suis-je tombé à tes genoux!

11   ★Ah! que n'as-tu défailli à mes genoux!

10   J'eusse été le modèle des époux!

16   Comme le frou-frou de ta robe est le modèle des frou-
frou.

Supporting the choice of this particular poem is a statement by Edward J. H. Greene in *T. S. Eliot et la France:*

Quant à la forme et la versification du poème d'Eliot, elles ont aussi leur origine dans les *Derniers Vers* de Laforgue. La forme est un développement de celle de "Légende" où de "Solo de Lune," monologues intérieurs où le poète cherche à donner un sens aux moments qu'il évoque. (31)

[As to the form and the versification of Eliot's poem, both find their origin in Laforgue's *Last Poems.* The form is a development of that of "Légende" or of "Solo de Lune," interior monologues in which the poet seeks to give meaning to the moments that he evokes.]

In 1928 Faber and Faber published Ezra Pound's *Selected Poems,* and in the introduction Eliot discussed his own debt to Laforgue— acknowledged repeatedly earlier and later—and continued with general observations on his own metrics. In taking issue with what a great poet says about his own practice, one should give the poet his say, in case one's own point of view should be incorrect; I therefore quote at length.

The form in which I began to write, 1908 or 1909, was directly drawn from the study of Laforgue together with the later Elizabethan drama; and I do not know anyone who started from exactly that point. The *vers libre* of Jules Laforgue, who, if not quite the greatest French poet after Baudelaire, was certainly the most important technical innovator, is free verse in much the way that the later verse of Shakespeare, Webster, Tourneur, is free verse: that is to say, it stretches, contracts, and distorts the traditional French measure as Later Elizabethan and Jacobean poetry stretches, contracts, and distorts the blank verse measure. But the term is applied to several types of verse which have developed in English without relation to Laforgue, Corbière, and Rimbaud, or to each other. To be more precise, there are, for instance, my own type of verse, that of Pound, and that of the disciples of Whitman. I will not say that subsequently there have not appeared traces of reciprocal influence of several types upon one another, but I am here speaking of origins. My own verse is, so far as I can judge, nearer to the original meaning of *vers libre* than is any of the other types. (viii)

To start with, I believe that Eliot was mistaken in saying that Jacobean blank verse is free verse in the same way that Laforgue's is. English dramatists, as I have earlier argued, certainly did stretch the pentameter to the point of disintegration, but it nevertheless remained the norm; *King Lear* and *The Duchess of Malfi* conclude with rhyming couplets. It will not do to lift passages from the middle of a play and compare them with complete poems written by a poet in another language nearly three hundred years later. Second, Laforgue does not stretch the Alexandrine; he totally abandons it. "Solo de Lune" as much as says, "Look! No Alexandrines! Nor anything else!" Eliot is, however, perfectly correct in identifying his practice as the nearest thing to French vers libre of the later nineteenth century. In that distinction I find much support for the identification of a category called vers-libristic in my own classifications of free verse.

Edward J. H. Greene explains Eliot's effort to find an equivalence between Laforgue and the Renaissance dramatists in a perfectly sensible way:

Remonter aux derniers Elisabéthains, étudier de près leur versification, était pour le jeune poète se retremper dans la meilleure tradition de l'expression dramatique anglaise, c'était en quelque sort se garantir contre le danger qu'il courait de pasticher Laforgue. (34)

[To go back to the last of the Elizabethans, to study their versification close up, was for the young poet to immerse himself in the best tradition of English dramatic expression; it was to some extent a way to preserve himself from the risks that he ran of producing a pastiche of Laforgue.]

It was for somewhat the same reason that Eliot squirmed when the label of free verse was pinned on his work; his insistence on the importance of a poet's assimilating tradition made him reluctant to admit that he had ventured beyond tradition. He wished to claim Shakespeare's authority as a fellow adventurer into the new field of free verse, arguing that he had only done the same as Shakespeare, and that neither was "really free."

It is difficult to judge if, in directing attention toward the French Symbolists and the Jacobean playwrights as his precursors, Eliot also meant to minimize anything that he might have learned from English poetry of the Victorian era. Coventry Patmore's reputation both as a poet and as a prosodic theorist was still intact, if fading, when Eliot was a student, and he surely must have known Patmore's "The Unknown Eros," the patterns of which are comparable to some of Eliot's verslibristic compositions. I have mentioned how quotidian routine, urban dreariness, and the antiheroic tone of Henley and Davidson coincide with their employment of free verse as a medium better suited to convey the tedium of actual existence. Eliot may have felt reassured by their example; his interest in Davidson is evident from his composition of an introductory essay to an edition of that poet's works. Very close to Eliot's skirting of regular meter and rhyme, in "Prufrock" and elsewhere, is "Dover Beach," in which the uncertainty of the form—at least in comparison with most of Tennyson and Browning, and much of Arnold himself—mirrors the disappearance of moral and religious landmarks on the "darkling plain." The terrain of *The Waste Land* is similar, only more confused than ever with alarms of struggle and flight. But Eliot wanted to separate himself from the immediate past and initially, by his early rejection of Milton, from anything later than 1660— anything that smacked of a dissociated sensibility.

In 1942 Eliot delivered a lecture, "The Music of Poetry," in which he dwelt on the use of musical models in poetry, thereby explaining his aims in the recently completed *Four Quartets*. He also reviewed, by implication, his earlier work by taking up again the question of free verse, seeming to reassert his former position but in fact modifying it quietly. Early in the lecture he even speaks of "free and formal" as distinct categories; when he turns to the question of form at greater length he is more circumspect:

As for "free verse," I expressed my view twenty-five years ago by saying that no verse is free for the man who wants to do a good job. No one has better cause to know than I, that a great deal of bad prose has been written under the name of free verse; though whether its authors wrote bad prose or bad verse, or bad verse in one style or in another, seems to me a matter of indifference. But only a bad poet could welcome free verse as a liberation from form. It was a revolt against dead form, and a preparation for new form or for the renewal of the old; it was an insistence upon the inner unity which is unique to every poem, against the outer unity which is typical. The poem comes before the form, in the sense that a form grows out of the attempt of somebody to say something; just as a system of prosody is only a formulation of the identities in the rhythms of a succession of poets influenced by each other. (*On Poetry and Poets* 17–33)

The question that one would like to put to Eliot is, "Does what you say mean that free verse has no value other than as preparation for some new or restored tradition?" To put it in seventeenth-century political terms, one might ask, "Is the justification of Cromwell that he made possible the Restoration?"

The last part of Eliot's paragraph seems perilously close to the doctrine of organic form, and the remark about the "inner unity" of the poem sounds much like the emphasis put by Protestant theology on the inner life of the spirit. He seems closer than usual in this passage to his American contemporaries. To introduce again an analogy between religion and prosody may be even more relevant to Eliot; the ecclesiastical and liturgical tone of his poetry helps to legitimize such a line of speculation. We might recall that the most catholic of Anglo-Catholics must still subscribe to the Thirty-nine Articles of Religion of the Anglican Church, one of which makes room for belief in divine election so as to accommodate those with Calvinist leanings. Eliot was aiming here, as in all things, at a stable centrism, a Church of England inclusiveness. But gazing across the Atlantic from his literary chair at Faber and Faber, he may have seen America from the point of view of a seventeenth-century Stuart loyalist as an asylum for a ragtag mob of dissenters, in poetry as in much else. Indeed what has occurred in American poetry bears a close analogy to the proliferation of competing sects in American religion. The consequence, which Eliot foresaw, is that we enjoy a freewheeling competition between rival poets for congregations and contributions; the local poet usually takes on some of the characteristics of the local preacher, and on a national scale we have our poetic Billy Grahams, our Father Divines, and our Moonies. But in speaking of "inner unity" and in saying that the "poem comes before the form," Eliot was extending himself in the direction of Williams and even of Charles Olson—without, of course, having these particular poets in mind—offering a haven for those who wished to put emphasis on private inspiration as well as tradition.

In his 1942 lecture Eliot clearly was calling for an improved and restored catholicity in the forms of poetry, with the implication that his own earlier poems were stages to be got through on the road to this prosodic consummation. But Eliot's work prior to 1930 remains intrinsically interesting, satisfying as poetry, the free verse of a poet who has a profound understanding of metrical conventions.

In 1917, however, even Ezra Pound was a little uncertain as to what Eliot was accomplishing by his prosody. In a review of *Prufrock and Other Observations* he struggled with the question of free verse:

> A conviction as to the rightness or wrongness of *vers libre* is no guarantee of a poet. I doubt if there is much use in trying to classify the various kinds of *vers libre,* but there is an anarchy which may be vastly overdone. . . .
> In a recent article Mr. Eliot contended, or seemed to contend, that good *vers libre* was little more than a skilful evasion of the better known English metres. His article was defective in that he omitted all consideration of metres depending on quantity, alliteration, etc.; in fact, he wrote as if metres were measured by accent. (268)

In faulting Eliot for neglecting other meters, Pound neglected to add that few English poets had ever composed successfully in quantitative meters, and that alliterative meter, though natural to English, was never used after 1450. But Pound, like Eliot, seems to have been extremely close to the point that I am arguing: that free verse is indeed "a skilful evasion of the better known English metres." To judge from what Pound says ("little more than a skilful evasion"), neither of them was aware of just how remarkable their own achievements were—or perhaps one should say that, as uprooted Americans striving to *attach* themselves to English and European culture, they were reluctant to be seen as in any way subverting those traditions. Pound does not succeed in resolving the question, here or anywhere else; he wants to reject stultifying conventions, but he loves the beauty of rhythmical proportions:

Alexandrine and other grammarians have made cubby-holes for various groupings of syllables; they have put names upon them, and have given various labels to "metres" consisting of combinations of these different groups. . . . The known categories would allow a fair liberty to the most conscientious traditionalist. The most fanatical vers-librist will escape them with difficulty. However, I do not think there is any crying need for verse with absolutely no rhythmical basis. (269)

Eliot's poetry, at any rate, was never "verse with absolutely no rhythmical basis." In the end his most important contribution to English prosody was to introduce musical analogies, in a more sophisticated way than ever before, as a basis for the organization of poetry. This is not to say that he lapsed into the fallacy, much belabored by Timothy Steele in *Missing Measures,* of trying to achieve an equivalence with music. As much as I admire the details of Harvey Gross's analysis of the specific qualities of Eliot's poetry, I cannot agree with Gross that "Eliot has quarreled with Pater's ethical notions, but Eliot's prosody—the function of the 'auditory imagination'—aspires toward the condition of music" (170). He went precisely the other direction, starting with a musical impulse that aspired to expression in language. Early on Eliot began to suggest musical analogies in his titles ("rhapsody," "prelude," even, with heavy irony, "love-song"); it is hard to see, however, how he could possibly have intended the *Four Quartets,* with all their historical, literary, and theological baggage, as poems that "aspired toward the condition of music." Instead, there is an explicit analogy with the late-classical sonata form, as a model or metaphor of form, but not as a condition to which poetry could aspire. Composition in painting has for centuries employed geometrical strategies for the purpose of organization, yet only a few naive Platonists would say that all painting aspires to the condition of geometry. This is not the place to analyze at length Eliot's use of musical patterns in his poetry or to trace the origins of his thinking along these lines—origins that included, among other things, that part of Pound's Imagist manifesto that spoke of composing in the rhythm of the musical phrase. Such composition is not free verse; it is aimed at new and more subtle organization, the *establishment* of conventions rather than the ironic exploitation of previous rhythmic modes. To claim that such musically organized language as Eliot's *Four Quartets* is free verse seems to me radically misguided. To take the most obvious examples, the short tetrameter "movements" (such as the "Garlic and sapphires in the mud" segment that Eliot borrowed from Mallarmé), it is very hard to see how anyone could contend—as some have—that this is free verse.

Complicating the treatment of Eliot further is the way in which he could be simultaneously iconoclastic and constructive. As he said in "The Music of Poetry," "Forms have to be broken and remade." At one extreme is *The Waste Land,* the prosody of which, like everything else in the poem, is a pile of fragments that he has shored against his ruin, fragmentation having been provided by his own wrecking ball. The genius of the poem—the final form of which, as we all know, owed as much to Pound as it did to Eliot—is to introduce abrupt and surprising shifts, incongruities of tempo as well as theme—similar in their way to the fierce inconsistencies of Stravinsky's *Rite of Spring* (1913). But even as he clipped and pasted European literature into a cubist collage, Eliot was reaching toward, though never attaining, some model of organization. Conversely, the orderly movements of *The Four Quartets* include many an instance of effects initially achieved in free verse: iambics freed to the point of disintegration, sometimes by the superimposing of Old English alliterative meter; direct and inverted anaphora; broken phrasing with extreme enjambment; and, of course, the substitution of natural syntactic phrasing for meter. But in *The Four Quartets* the dominant direction is reintegration through musical analogy, often reinforced by reversion to regular iambic meters, even tightly rhymed tetrameters as illustrated above. This is quite the opposite of what occurs in *The Waste Land,* where the regular meters, and especially the rhyming passages, are permitted only for the purpose of accomplishing their further destruction, even in the neoclassical burlesque of the "young man carbuncular." At the end of that poem the outlook for meter may not be any more hopeless than the outlook for anything else, but clearly a new dispensation is needed for metrics as well as for civilization.

Simply put, Eliot experimented with every variety of free verse that I have been able to identify, though he made sparing use of word-breaking or word-jamming techniques. He did not make the mistake of assuming that any one of these methods was anything more than a tool that could be applied to the renovation of English prosody. However ecclesiastical his manner may have been at times, he did not, in employing biblical-anaphoric free verse, assume the role of the prophet, let alone the messiah. When fracturing his lines in unlikely places he did not pretend to have discovered some new principle, some new foot, whose authority governed these displacements; instead, he was frankly arbitrary, even whimsical, twitting his earlier readers' expectations. Eliot makes no claims that his poems are the inevitable organic growth of a privileged artist; even in his demolitions he invites assent of the reader who is presumed to be familiar with—or at least to have had available to him—the treasures of Western culture. A useful approach to Eliot might be to consider how frequently his poetry is an *invitation* to shared experience ("Let us go then . . . ," "Come in under the shadow of this red rock," "If you came this way . . .").

Eliot's reverence for shared tradition extended even to his immediate predecessors against whom he appeared to be in such violent revolt. "Prufrock" and "Gerontion" belong to that favorite Victorian genre, the dramatic monologue. *The Waste Land* in one way serves as a conclusion to *The Idylls of the King,* a work in which even Tennyson recognized the corrupting effect of the grail quest, and to some of whose knights and ladies "The Fire Sermon" might have been preached with useful effect. Even *Old Possum's Book of Practical Cats* continues the inspired frivolity of Edward Lear and of Gilbert and Sullivan. It was this fundamental friendliness to earlier British literature and to European culture that William Carlos Williams detected in Eliot and despised; Williams saw that the iconoclast was in love with the icons.

What this means in terms of Eliot's prosody is that his free verse exhibits—to verge on a cliché—a clear awareness of precisely what it is free from. To judge from the extent of Pound's excisions from *The Waste Land* and from the nature of the lines excised, Eliot must have composed reams of verse of rhymed and metered verse that we will never see because he had the good sense, or the craftiness, to burn it up. To adduce nonexistent poetry as evidence may not be a good idea. One of Galileo's opponents argued that the moon was really without mountains because a smooth invisible substance covered it; Galileo responded that he was pleased with the idea and that there were immense mountains of that same substance. In similar fashion anyone prepared to counter my argument may invent still greater reams of incoherent free verse. Nevertheless, it seems reasonable to suppose that a poet who argues as persistently as did Eliot for the importance of immersing oneself in tradition, for assimilating tradition, put himself through late-Victorian drills in villanelles, rondeaus, and triolets, among other things. George Santayana speaks of a fad among Harvard aesthetes for "matching triolets." Eliot's early denials that he was engaged in free verse at all imply that he felt that he had so thoroughly mastered the conventions that his seeming departures were really evidence of control. That control could only have been achieved with much exercise.

Eliot's free verse, as I will now call it without further apology, began by diverging from what Helen Gardner wished to call the "heroic line," the iambic pentameter. Let us see exactly how this occurs in the opening of "Prufrock." W. D. Snodgrass claims that the opening lines can be sung to the tune of "Ain't Misbehavin'," but since I never did learn that melody well enough, I will employ traditional scansion. My marking of the accents will not accord with everyone's reading of the poem, but will do for purposes of discussion. The poem opens firmly with a catalectic trochaic tetrameter, a meter that, when continued for several lines, often conveys a sense of resolve or even of visionary certainty.

    /   *   /   *   /   *   /
    Let us go then, you and I

Metrical resolve vanishes with the second line, which retains some sense of a four-foot line but which includes three trisyllabic feet, if we use that nomenclature, two anapests followed by an amphimacer, concluding with an iamb, which has always been acceptable to the ear as a substitute foot in an anapestic line. In any event, there is a complete reversal of the rhythm of the first line.

    *   *   /   * *   /   /   *   /   *   /
    When the evening is spread out against the sky

Even if we choose to hear a stress on "When," which is a quite plausible variant of the proposed scansion, and interpret the line as a hexameter, it surely plays against the opening rhythm. With the third line we more or less retain the tetrameter, unless one chooses to stress "Like." If, however, we do keep a stress on "Like," thereby setting it up initially as a reestablished trochaic line, we must end with a strange foot (* * / *). The second stress in "etherized" is very light—though recognized in dictionary pronunciation of the word; "upon" is, by itself, a natural iamb that tends (as I hear it) to be speeded up here so as to lose its stress. At all events the meter has become even less certain—an uncertainty suggesting the irresolution that we will presently hear more about.

```
 *   *  /  *    / * /   *  *  *  / *
Like a patient etherized upon a table
```

Or, very possibly—

```
 /  *  /  *   /  *  /   *  /  *  / *
Like a patient etherized upon a table
```

—in which case we have the trochees back, but have lost the tetrameter of the opening. The rhythm dissolves totally in the next line, which can be converted into a tetrameter only by deemphasizing "Let" and "certain."

```
 /  *  /    *    /  *  /   * / *     /
Let us go, through certain half-deserted streets
```

What has actually occurred here is that Eliot has *almost* established an expectation of a trochaic hexameter as the fundamental meter, by approximating it in three successive lines. But if there were still any confidence left in the prosodic direction, it is shattered by—

```
 *   /  *  *  *  /
The muttering retreats
```

The previous line does, however, include two iambs, and rhymes with its immediate precursor, and suddenly we are much closer to the scansion of something like "Lycidas." The following two lines, with easily allowable substitutions, are a perfect heroic couplet. Each contains ten syllables.

```
 *  /  *   /   *  /   /   /   *  /
Of restless nights in one - night cheap hotels
```

```
 *   /  *   /  *  *   *  /  *    /
And sawdust restaurants with oyster shells:
```

So, after defeating our (early-twentieth-century) proclivities for the first five lines, Eliot abruptly reminds us of what he is *not* writing. And then the briefly established heroic meter dissolves, first inverted into trochaics, then into anapests:

```
 /    *   / *   *  *  / *   / *  *
```
Streets that follow like a tedious argument

```
 *   * /  *   * /
```
Of insidious intent

(Here I am using the convention of treating a "y-glide" synaeresis as a single syllable in "tedious" and "oblivious.") What might have been a resumption of the pentameter finally dissipates in a singsong couplet graced with a mosaic rhyme, something akin to Mother Goose.

```
 *  /   *   *  *  / * /   *   / *
```
To lead you to an overwhelming question . . .

```
 *  /  *  /   *   / *
```
Oh, do not ask, "What is it?"

```
 /  * /  *   /  *  / *
```
Let us go and make our visit.

The infamous couplet that follows, with its peripatetic ladies, does nothing to restore either dignity or heroic meter. Following that, a pair of fourteeners trail in with the yellow fog; the lines read so conversationally that one may miss the regularity, but one cannot miss the parallelism—continued alliteratively in the next three lines—that marks this paragraph as an instance of biblical-anaphoraic free verse. This time, the long lines shrink back toward the regular pentameter ("Curled once about the house and fell asleep").

It is easy to continue through "Prufrock," observing how the poem oscillates to either side of the heroic norm, from "Do I dare" to "Though I have seen my head (grown slightly bald) brought in upon a platter," the latter of which reaches nearly the proportion of Ogden Nash's rhyming lines. Some lines are hybrids, combining anaphora with internal or end rhyme. Missing, however, are any instances of phrase-breaking free verse; such enjambments as one finds, and there are not many, are scarcely noticeable.

Because "Prufrock" uses rhymes, because it does occasionally resolve into iambic pentameter, and because it ends with a regular line, some may see it as nothing but insufficiently loosened accentual-syllabic meter. In the other direction, those who think along the lines of Yvor

Winters will view the poem as imitative of the protagonist's irresolution, making it inadequate as an assessment of that irresolution. The meter of "Prufrock" is a perfect example of J. V. Cunningham's "parasitic verse," a term that could be useful so long as one remembers that certain parasitic relationships are beneficial to the host, and that forms of life such as mushrooms, which do not produce their own food, are saprophytic and convert rotting matter into edible substance.

Eliot's shorter poems work as textbook examples of most of the possibilities of free verse. "Rhapsody on a Windy Night" moves easily in and out of metrical norms, undercutting any regularity with sudden bursts of prosaic flatness and sardonically self-mocking rhymes. Short-line anaphora, such as we saw Ferlinghetti employing in "Dog," links many lines in the central part of the poem. In the end the poem collapses into hiccups and spasms, at one point shrinking to the single word, and the ultimate in end-stopped lines, "Mount." The macabre artificiality of the urban scene, which streetlights and the late-rising moon emphasize, dissipates as the central intelligence prepares to resume his dull diurnal routine. The tense approximations of the meter fracture into completely irregular fragments. "Morning at the Window," "The Boston Evening Transcript," "Aunt Helen," "Cousin Nancy," and "Mr. Apollinax" all employ phrase-reinforcing free verse; only "Aunt Helen" uses rhyme, and even there it is abandoned by the end of the poem. Close analysis could justify Eliot's sureness of ear in accommodating the line lengths for various ironic purposes, but it is easier simply to allow oneself to be entertained. Each of these poems presupposes a genteel Boston-academic milieu, one in which the metrics of Longfellow and Tennyson were held in high esteem. These "Cambridge ladies," to cite and quote the poem by cummings, "believe in Christ and Longfellow, both dead." At least part of the effect of these poems is to employ a prosody that is conspicuously at odds with the metrical creeds of the ladies. If anything can really succeed as a prose poem, Eliot's "Hysteria" must be allowed as poetry. That it is his sole entry in this division makes it triply to be cherished. Perhaps he felt that to register his credentials as a true disciple of the French Symbolists he needed to go on record with at least one prose poem. "Conversation Galante" and "La Figlia che Piange" revert to the metrical strategies of "Prufrock," shifting back and forth across the pentameter configuration, and placing rhymes at the convenience of the poet.

In *Poems* (1920) Eliot opened with "Gerontion," a "fragment" that

Pound had judged not necessary to *The Waste Land,* and the only poem of Eliot's that Yvor Winters read with any pleasure. Given the provenance of the poem, it may be wrong to read into it a more consistent prosodic plan than Eliot really conceived. "Gerontion" is, however, remarkable for giving the impression of a meditative monologue in blank verse, while resolutely avoiding a single line that can be unambiguously scanned as iambic pentameter until we reach the last fifteen lines or so. It is the greater regularity of the conclusion that leaves us with the impression of blank verse. In fact, this is the first poem (in the sequence of the *Collected Poems*) in which Eliot employs phrase-breaking free verse. The lines in the fifth paragraph of the poem, which begins with "After such knowledge, what forgiveness. Think now / History has many cunning passages, contrived corridors / And issues, deceives with whispering ambitions," are so strongly enjambed that one can scarcely find a place to break off. The next paragraph presses forward with equal urgency: "The tiger springs in the new year. Us he devours. Think at last / We have not reached conclusion when I / Stiffen in a rented house. Think at last." Even in the last long paragraph we find, "will the weevil / Delay?" The only stronger form of enjambment is to place a connective at the end of the line. "Gerontion," then, represents a definite further step away from heroic verse, the convention that it assumes as a normal possibility. "Prufrock" reminds us periodically, and at the end, of the meter that we are missing; "Gerontion" is more daring. And yet Eliot, in his ironic, almost perverse, way continued to honor the convention, not the least by representing himself as a descendant of Webster, Tourneur, and the later Shakespeare. He even misled Yvor Winters, who remarked, with typical testiness, "Mr. Eliot never got beyond Websterian verse, a bastard variety, though in *Gerontion,* he handled it with great skill—with far greater skill than Webster usually expends upon it" (*In Defense of Reason* 124).

As if to guarantee his competence in regular meters, Eliot followed "Gerontion" with a set of seven poems in rhyming tetrameters. I do not know Winters's opinion of these but am fairly confident that he would have dismissed them as doggerel. It may be a defect of character that makes me enjoy such quatrains as those in "A Cooking Egg." *Vive la bagatelle!* The wit here broadens into a humorous disengagement with serious literature and serious history that is the obverse of "Gerontion." It more resembles the rhymes of Blake's *An Island in the Moon* than anything else I can think of, though its immediate antecedents are Victorian comic verses. Prosodically these poems, which include "The Hippopotamus,"

"Whispers of Immortality," "Mr. Eliot's Sunday Morning Service," and "Sweeney among the Nightingales," all remind the reader that he or she is in the presence of a poetic technician who knows exactly what he is doing. They provide a foil for "Gerontion," and vice versa. Completing his second volume, Eliot included the French poems in which he directly rivaled Laforgue, and possibly others, including ironic verbal comedians such as Charles Cros.

The Waste Land accomplishes in a single poem all the prosodic excursions of Eliot's earlier work and adds many more of its own. An entire book would not suffice to account for the effects of the disruptions, juxtapositions, wrenchings of meter, sudden restorations of regularity, breaks, shifts, transitions, and modulations that Eliot and Pound accomplished in what became virtually a joint enterprise. And I am speaking only of prosody, not of the modifications made to the Tarot pack or the multiple implications of "Et O ces voix d'enfants, chantant dans la coupole!" The Waste Land is the most thoroughly surprising poem ever written, or at least the one in which surprise is not itself pushed to the point of mere tedious perverseness, as it is in some of Gertrude Stein's writings. The first draft of the poem went well past that point; Eliot may not have known when to stop, but at least Pound did, who in his editing of The Waste Land removed more than he left. Some readers wish that Pound had had similar assistance with The Cantos.

Eliot was so ingenious in concocting variants and hybrids of meters that one hesitates to apply simple categories to his work. Yet The Waste Land does serve as a happy hunting ground for species and subspecies of free verse. For example, part 5, "What the Thunder Said," leads off with a sequence of biblical-anaphoric verse, initially combined with heroic meter. The prophetic manner announces the failure of prophecy; there has—as yet—been no resurrection after the night in the Garden of Gethsemane and the crucifixion. I see Eliot here as turning resolutely to biblical phrasing for his model, bypassing Whitman.

As an instance of vers-libristic meter one might cite other paragraphs from "What the Thunder Said," in which one finds irregularly rhyming patterns and iambics of varying lengths. Paratactical constructions may suggest a kinship with anaphora, but the lines are mostly scannable in iambics.

So much of The Waste Land is made up of phrasal free verse, and the phrases come in such varieties, that it hardly seems useful to single out an example. Phrase-reinforcing prosody is the dominant mode. The characteristic movement of the poem is to shift continually between clumps of metered verse and monologues or snatches of conversation, carried on with or without the presence of another person. In this sense, the poem is about the failure of a civilized convention, and the retreat into amorphous utterance that mirrors a lapse into narcissism and solipsism. Some of these speeches are simply prose; several are transcripts of what Vivien Eliot said, or reported. Elsewhere Eliot disrupts the poem by breaking up the phrases, suggesting the pointlessness and vacuity of what one hears. Any reader who goes through the poem looking for such disruptions of metrical expectations will find numerous examples of all kinds of free verse.

At this point I begin to understand Ezra Pound's skepticism as to the usefulness of classifying free verse. Such categories work best in describing poems in which only one sort of free verse prevails. It is always less tiring to substitute method for intelligence, and to account for *The Waste Land* requires constant vigilance. Yet it serves a purpose if we can discover in the poem nearly all the violations of metrical expectations that any poet, working later in the century, has managed to employ, because in doing this we can simultaneously demonstrate that such prosperous iconoclasms achieve their best effects against a backdrop of well-established metrical expectations.

More tenuously than in "Prufrock," but just as surely, the prosodic landscape of *The Waste Land* is haunted by an array of metrical ghosts, the most persistent of which is iambic pentameter. Each section of the poem begins with a rough approximation of pentameter. Furthest from conformity is "The river's tent is broken: the last fingers of leaf"—a line that contains five feet only if we hear "fingers of leaf" as a choriamb (/ ** /). Throughout the poem we cross and recross the main stream of English meter, even dipping into it in the midst of so prosaic a section as the pub closing at the end of "A Game of Chess," in which—if we allow anapestic substitution—a few lines can be forced into pentameter. The prosodic center of the poem is the seduction scene in "The Fire Sermon," which originally was much longer and was divided into heroic quatrains. That center anchors the poem sufficiently to allow its formless conclusion; even at the conclusion an acceptable pentameter ("These fragments I have shored against my ruins") occurs only three lines before "Shantih Shantih Shantih."

In the course of *The Waste Land* Eliot uses several other patterns, from English and from other languages, which have been tried or even accepted as candidates for the heroic meter. These include English four-teeners, Swinburnian dactylic hexameter, Anglo-Saxon accentual meter, and the French Alexandrine. The function of these lines in *The Waste Land* is—because they carry a certain authority in terms of familiarity and stability—to modify the length of the pentameter. Pulling in another direction are iambic tetrameters and trimeters. Lest this sound too much like empty theorizing, or the enunciation of stultifying platitudes (i.e., "It's not the same because it is different"), I would like to examine in some detail the opening of the poem, scanning it as follows; most readers will disagree with some details of the scansion, but I think that the general effects are reasonably clear. The opening line—

          / * * * / * *   /   / *
          April is the cruelest month, breeding

—gives us ten syllables, which in a context of well-defined pentameter would fit in as a legitimate variant. But here it makes more sense to point out the dominantly falling rhythm—one associated by other poets with disappointment (as in Browning's "The Lost Leader" and Roethke's "Dolor").

          / * / * * /   /   / *
          Lilacs out of the dead land, mixing

This line continues the falling effect, adding to it the disappointment of any expectation of a heroic meter by reducing the line to nine syllables, a truncation that continues with—

          / * *   *   * /   / *
          Memory and desire, stirring

The inverted anaphora, with participles terminating each line, also weak-ens the active principle in each of the verbs—breeding, stirring, mixing—which in another context might convey energy and rejuvenation. The natural trochees, which suggest power or conviction in a poem like Blake's "Tyger" or Henley's "Invictus," are robbed of emphasis. Concluding this sentence, two spondees linked with a weak syllable close the lid on the sarcophagus:

    / /   *   / /
Dull roots with spring rain.

Metrical paradox governs the next two lines, in which the *morte saison* does get the trochaic treatment, keeping life going with artificial rhythmical stimulation.

    / * / * / / * *
Winter kept us warm, covering

But in the second of these we begin to sense again the falling-off that introduced the poem, as the trochees lengthen to an introductory dactyl.

    / * * / * / / *
Earth in forgetful snow, feeding

And a progression of three harmless iambs together with a repetition of the unemphatic concluding trochee confirm the diminution—

  * / * / * / / *
A little life with dried tubers.

At this point Eliot seems prepared to allow our metrical horizons to expand eastward, obscuring further any definite English basis—across France and into Bavaria, and he carries us in that direction with a long line that sounds vaguely like a French Alexandrine, or a Swinburnian hexameter. In any event its rhythm further disrupts the already halting and indefinite opening.

  / * * / * / * / * * / * * /
Summer surprised us, coming over the Starnbergersee

More nearly an Alexandrine is

  * *   / * / * / * * / * /
With a shower of rain; we stopped in the colonnade.

Let me repeat and summarize what has just occurred. The poem opens with a ten-syllable line that, were it immediately reinforced, could be heard as a pentameter. As it is, the syllable count rapidly shrinks to nine, eight, and then five, rebounding afterward to a succession of three eight-syllable lines. Here is the pull in the direction of tetrameter, though the meter is not regular enough to identify it with any particular foot. "Summer surprised us . . ." carries us into a fourteen-syllable line, but one that reads more like a dactylic hexameter; this is followed by a twelve-syllable line that hovers between pentameter and the French syllabic Alexandrine. All these wrenchings are analogues of the multicultural confusion introduced into the poem immediately after this.

The first confident pentameters occur with "What are the roots that clutch, what branches grow / Out of this stony rubbish? Son of man . . ." But the next two lines are hypermetric, and the third is a good fourteener, while syntactical structure is anaphoric. These oscillations continue over the next thirty lines, shrinking to the German dimeters from Wagner, and expanding to several Alexandrines, of which "Here is Belladonna, the Lady of the Rocks" is the most perfectly Gallic. Prior to that, a promising pentameter resumption has been bathetically punctured with flat prose: "Madame Sosostris, famous clairvoyante, / Had a bad cold." If one has any doubts about the presence of the Alexandrine in Eliot's prosody, one need only remember the last line of "The Burial of the Dead," which retains the French scansion of Baudelaire's original line, despite the insertion of the English word: "You! hypocrite lecteur!—mon semblable,—mon frère!"

Eliot may have believed that in all these distortions he was merely exercising a disciplined regular prosody to its limits. But, if I may paraphrase what one Southern general said on the question of whether slavery was an issue in the Civil War, "If it ain't free verse, I don't know what it is." Despite Eliot's disclaimers, it is not hard to separate his poems into those composed in well-established meters, those that presuppose older traditions as a background but that evade those traditions, and those that aim at a new order of musical organization. The second of these are his free-verse poems.

Eliot's progress after *The Waste Land* was not direct and uninterrupted, but rather a general slow advance, over several decades, with pauses and retrogressions. If one has to point to a poem that represents a turn from iconoclasm toward reintegration, or should one say, redemption, it would be "Ash Wednesday" (1930). Here the biblical phrasing seems an end in itself and not one more method of veering toward or away from iambic pentameter. Instead, after incorporating one of Shakespeare's better-known lines almost verbatim ("Desiring this man's gift [Shakespeare: "art"] and that man's scope") as the fourth line of his poem, Eliot leaves it definitively behind him. *Ecclesiastical* or *liturgical* would better fit "Ash Wednesday." It owes much to the *Book of Common Prayer,* and already he may be hearing the Christian mystics whose words echo in *The Four Quartets.*

The "Minor Poems" in Eliot's *Collected Poems* provide an additional showcase of free-verse methods. "Usk," for example, opens with a broken phrase, as extreme as anything William Carlos Williams did; only slightly less enjambed are lines in "Rannoch, by Glencoe." However spontaneous, however liberated, these poems may seem, it could never attain the necessary sense of inevitability without the inaudible presence of an ideal metric. The second leads off with two possible pentameters, both modified in the direction of Old English alliterative meter. Buried in the remaining lines are iambic sequences, not to speak of rhymes: "wrong," "strong," "long."

Ultimately Eliot set himself to putting into practice concepts of musical form, suggestions for which he may have found not only in the original Imagist manifestoes, but in some of Harriet Monroe's speculations in earlier issues of *Poetry* magazine, and elsewhere, even in the theories of Sidney Lanier. But this question belongs to an entirely separate line of investigation. Verse organized upon musical analogy is not free verse.

Chapter 9

Ideogrammatology

As we approach the end of the twentieth century, the truth is that for much published poetry its appearance on the page does matter—that in fact visual arrangement may be more important than any recurrent patterns that appeal to the ear. While to New Formalist critics this may seem to abandon form altogether it is at least evidence of a search for new methods of organization. New Formalists are correct in their dismay at seeing language treated as if it did not consist of sequential audible vibrations in the air—but at the same time, given the fact that most poems present themselves to readers via a printed page, the typographic dimension cannot be ignored.

To consider the effects of typography on free verse, or the use to which free-verse writers have put typography, is to take into account something that has often affected poetry since the invention of writing itself. The difference is that twentieth-century free-verse theory has become consciously involved with the history of writing systems—or at least with supposed histories of such systems—and with other speculations about the nature and function of signs and symbols. Ezra Pound, for example, at times seemed to feel that the Chinese ideogram was the ultimate model for the poem—a mode of signifying superior to the phonetic alphabets of the West. Pound's point of view is not shared by grammatologists who see that logographic method as an instance of writing arrested at a primitive stage of development. But whether or not Pound was misguided on that point, systems of writing have often affected the way in which poetry is composed, and to give attention to the symbols with which a poem is recorded is a useful way to proceed. The historical sketch that follows is intended to support two assertions: that the written record of a poem sometimes does change its nature, and that cycles of free-verse writing in the past coincide with episodes of experimentation in poetic typography.

It may be useful to distinguish five stages in the history of the poem as a written artifact. First, there were transcriptions of oral poetry by those who could write but who were not necessarily poets. These survive as "authentic" epics, chants, songs, and ballads that were originally composed or recited aloud in performances that were partly from memory and partly improvisation. The second stage was the "literary" epic or ballad, for which the poet had available writing materials that made possible leisurely composition and revision. The result was a more polished and compact form of expression and a more singular or personal style.

With the invention of printing came a third stage: the poet could exercise control over the precise shape of the poem on the page and know that the press would duplicate it with each impression. Printing also meant that each reader was more likely to have a copy of the poem, and could spend more time puzzling over the meaning and appreciating recondite references and ingenuities of thought. Convolutions of thought and imagery in seventeenth-century Metaphysical poems—especially Donne's—can scarcely be disentangled without repeated readings; a poet's awareness that poems might be available in printed copies encouraged greater complexity of expression. Other evidence of the printing press's effect on poetry exists: the fashion of emblem poems, dating from the same time, required the reproduction of their accompanying graphics as an aid to and object of the meditative process. By the end of the sixteenth century one could already see the interplay of text and graphics and a consciousness of the possibilities of typography.

Three centuries later, widespread use of the typewriter made possible additional experiments, allowing the poet to try out various idiosyncratic placements of letters and words in advance of publication. To some extent this fourth—typewriter—stage overlaps those that precede and follow it. Movable type, with multiple fonts, existed before the typewriter; that, together with woodcuts, engravings, stereotypes, and other graphic resources, led to experiments such as William Blake's engraved plates, Lewis Carroll's verbal/visual jokes, and, most important of all for some twentieth-century poetry, Stéphane Mallarmé's poem, "Un Coup de Dés." The typewriter gave poets a means to experiment even more freely with the appearance of the page and its now familiar keyboard continues as the fundamental input device for the fifth phase, the use of electronic/

xerographic media. CRT screens, with their multicolored layouts and ingenious graphics, have made possible complex varieties of what Joseph Addison called "false wit."

The progression just sketched might seem an argument in support of the views of, say, T. E. Hulme, who felt that poetry could dispense with its audible part and suffer little loss thereby. But in opposition to this semioticizing of poetry there have always been, simultaneously, practices that tend to restore it to the realm of the spoken word. Publication in the time of Horace and Virgil, when poets labored over their works with quill and papyrus, or stylus and wax tablet, consisted of reading one's poems aloud to a circle of friends. The written version of the poem was only a record of words intended for the speaking voice. The same was true in the Middle Ages, for the most part; illuminated manuscripts delighted the eye, of course, as did skillful calligraphy, but the text of most poetry retained its independence from such contexts. A favorite fantasy of the English Pre-Raphaelites was that of Chaucer reading his poems to courtly audiences, and the mellifluousness of the opening lines of *The Canterbury Tales,* as well as the easily followed narratives and songs that constitute his works, argue that they were suited for oral delivery. References to Chaucer by later poets always imply an acquaintance through a manuscript (or a printed copy), but that does not mean that the written version possessed any intrinsic typographical interest that is relevant to the poetry. In the nineteenth century, William Morris's Kelmscot Chaucer, with its woodcuts and gothic typeface, was a venture in book design that has the effect of paying homage to Chaucer and his times without pretending to modify the poems themselves. Every reader of Chaucer knows that the appeal is to the ear—that the written text aims at the illusion of a narrative voice. Typography in *The Canterbury Tales* is of no more relevance than it is in *Lord Jim.*

The most important literary works of the next age, Elizabethan and Jacobean plays, were designed for stage delivery, not for private reading. Many of them got to the printers only as pirated versions carried in the memories of actors who had not only learned their own parts thoroughly but who also managed to recall substantial sections of others. Printed versions of the plays served the same purpose as a musical score—or what is now achieved by the illegal taping of a performance, complete with inaccuracies and distortions. Many other literary monuments of the Renaissance make use of print for no other purpose than as a means of preservation. Milton, no stranger to the press, composed *Paradise Lost* in his head when he awoke early in the morning, retaining lengthy sections until his amanuensis arrived—at which point he would complain that he needed to be "milked." Surely that is the ultimate example of aural composition and the most remote from the seductions of typographic ingenuity.

It is easy to continue a survey of British and American literature, pointing out one instance after another in which the sole typographic function of the printed poem was to recognize the integrity of regular metrical lines or stanzas—lines or stanzas whose effects depended upon aural perception. Shelley, for example, used pen and paper to make revisions, but the entry of nonsense syllables ("na-na, na-na, na, na") in his manuscripts makes it clear that he was trying out lines aloud and that it was of little importance to him how they looked on the page. Ford Madox Ford complained endlessly about the emphasis placed on sound values and on oral performance by the Victorians; what Ford objected to was a preoccupation with the reciting voice and the attentive ear. Indeed, the hundreds of pages of small type crowded into double columns that one sees in late-nineteenth-century editions of Tennyson, Browning, and Swinburne suggest that the purpose was to provide as much text as possible; the presumption was that the poetry was to be read aloud for the diversion and edification of literate families, much as the Bible was read. Despite an occasional Pre-Raphaelite illustrative engraving, there is little to please the eye and much to offend it in many Victorian editions. The idea is to provide as much readable text as possible.

The reaction of the Imagists against those Victorian poets included paying more attention to the figure a poem makes on the page. Our contemporary American predilection for poetry readings has produced an opposite effect, favoring poems that are easy to follow when read aloud, and that contribute to an entertaining performance. Part of the appeal of the New Formalism is the pleasure that some audiences take in listening for a recognizable pattern, and in hearing the poet recite from memory; to other listeners the same performance seems a revival of mediocre nineteenth-century metrical verse. Tape recorders may turn out to be a promising extension of the public poetry reading, or a preparation for it, but as far as I know they have not been much employed for composition or revision. Tape recorders do serve somewhat the same function as those anonymous transcribers of the *Iliad* and *Beowulf,* capturing the performances of poets reading their own work.

In allowing for the tides and countercurrents that continually modify the contours of poetry, one must reckon with the opposing claims of the eye and the ear, the page and the oral performance. Sometimes the two may be combined. W. D. Snodgrass has experimented with poetry readings that are accompanied by color slides, and May Swenson sometimes used overhead projections of her iconographs. Those who make films of poetry readings sometimes cut to visual representations and graphics of various sorts; this happens throughout the *Voices and Visions* series.

It is difficult to guess what effect the writing down of poetry may have had on the earliest poets in various cultures. The introduction of a usable Roman alphabet—as opposed to the awkward system of runes— to the Germans living in England between about A.D. 600 and 1000 permitted the recording of oral poetry in Old English. It also encouraged rhyming stanzas and acrostics, the latter of which could only appeal to the eye. Looking further back, to the beginning of the Christian era and to ancient Rome, one may see that writing served as an aid to composition as well as a method of recording it. By most accounts, Virgil's method in composing the *Aeneid* consisted of writing out, early each day, a dozen lines or so; during the rest of the day he reduced these to one or two lines. But although he worked on a sheet or a tablet, the result was intended for the listening ear; even a half-trained student of Latin can appreciate many of the auditory phenomena of the *Aeneid,* especially the onomatopoeia. Horace's odes give the effect of polite conversation, not of objects on a page intended for contemplation by the solitary eye. Arrangements in modern editions, which give visual shape to Horace's formal stanzas—the alcaics, sapphics, and asclepiads—represent the labors of grammarians and prosodists; the original texts were copied out in continuous runs of lowercase letters on papyrus scrolls. Absence of punctuation, or even spaces between words, left much to the skills of the reader. In similar ways, poets employing accentual-syllabic meters in English have usually expected the reader to discover the scansion without explicit guides in the text. In ancient times laws of quantitative versification were so consistent as to leave few doubts about the integrity of each line in a Latin poem, no matter how it was written out.

Yet there were experiments with typography even in antiquity. Joseph Addison, as we have seen, was among the earliest who perceived the hazards of self-appointed "genius" in literature, especially as it showed itself in the production of the "abominable" Pindaric. Another variety of "false wit" that he discovered among English authors of the previous century was the shaped poem: "This fashion of false wit was revived by

several poets of the last age, and, in particular, may be met among
Mr. Herbert's poems" (*Works* 302). During the discussion he quotes from
John Dryden, who, some years earlier (1679), had identified several spe-
cies of poetry as deserving of disdain for what he saw as a specious
cleverness. Toward the end of *Mac Flecknoe,* Dryden's speaker offers the
crown prince of dullness some advice:

> Thy genius calls thee not to purchase fame
> In keen iambics, but mild anagram.
> Leave writing plays, and choose for thy command
> Some peaceful province in acrostic land.
> There may thou wings display and altars raise,
> And torture one poor word ten thousand ways.

(203–8)

Dryden, of course, had in mind the efforts of Herbert, Herrick, and
others. His own polished couplets illustrate the neoclassical reformation
of style, already well under way, which rejected Metaphysical extrava-
gances of all sorts. Addison's comments, however, look much further
back, to instances of shaped poetry from Hellenistic antiquity. The discov-
ery of these in the Renaissance had suggested that possibility to a number
of English poets. A handful of shaped poems, known as *technopaignia,*
survived, including one resembling an altar, by Dosiadas, and another
that can be arranged as a pair of wings, by Simias (circa 300 B.C.). One
may as well be encyclopedic and mention the other three: an egg and an
axe, also by Simias, and something entitled "Syrinx," which appears to
be a set of panpipes, by Theocritus. The egg is especially controversial;
arranging the lines according to the sense requires that it look like a
pyramid, with very short lines progressively extending to very long
ones. To make it into an egg you either have to print the first two lines
some distance apart and work inward, or else print them together and
work outward in an ovoid spiral (Buffière 141 n). Printers lose patience
with the poem; in one edition it looks like the cowling for a jet engine
(Powell 118), and in another, like a failed popover or partially deflated
soccer ball (Clack 57). The step from the sublime to the ridiculous is even
shorter in poems that rely on typography for their effects than in other
writings.

Addison traced the history of this eccentricity, which the revival of the reading of Greek in the sixteenth century had made available to English poets:

> The first species of false wit which I have met with is very venerable for its antiquity, and has produced several pieces which have lived very near as long as the Iliad itself. I mean, those short poems printed among the minor Greek poets, which resemble the figure of an egg, a pair of wings, an axe, a shepherd's pipe, and an altar.
>
> As for the first, it is a little oval poem, and may not improperly be called a scholar's egg. I would endeavor to hatch it, or, in more intelligible language, to translate it into English, did I not find the interpretation of it very difficult; for the author seems to have been more intent upon the figure of his poem than upon the sense of it. (*Works* 299–300)

Addison continues for several paragraphs, teasing the subject with light sarcasms; his concern in this essay and the four that succeed it is to identify and excoriate various forms of eccentricity. Well in advance of Samuel Johnson's strictures on Shakespeare's punning, for example, Addison expressed his contempt for mere wordplay, arguing that true wit is wit in any language—meaning, I suppose, that he would approve the humor in Donne's epigram "Antiquary" because the idea could be amusing even in translation: "If in his study Hammon hath such care / To hang all old strange things, let his wife beware." But when Donne writes ("A Lame Beggar") in a fashion that depends on a double meaning, the wit is false: "I am unable, yonder beggar cries, / To stand or move; if he say true, he lies." To discredit the shaped poem requires that Addison find other grounds; an egg is shaped like an egg in any language. His argument is that the sense of the poem cannot be usefully accommodated to the shape—a point of view shared by prosodists in this century, including Paul Fussell. Some twentieth-century translators of the poem, however, find much ingenuity in Simias's egg—a nightingale-egg as it happens; one hopes that someone brought it to the attention of May Swenson, iconographer and bird-watcher in one.

Typography played little part in English poetry before 1590. Most of the arrangements—whether in manuscript or in print—are intended to recognize the integrity of the spoken line of poetry and to reflect the organization into stanzas. A concern with achieving orderliness of expression dominated poetry in England for most of the century, as it did other arts: garden plans in England from that period were geometrical and symmetrical and many forms of dancing placed emphasis on stateliness and regularity. The entire country was just emerging from the Middle Ages and, a few hundred years before that, from barbarism; the heads of decapitated criminals and political victims were still displayed on London Bridge, but at least the appearance of a poem on the page could aspire toward a condition of civilized orderliness. One only needs to leaf through an anthology of sixteenth-century poetry to receive an impression of something analogous to carefully tended and geometrically arranged herb gardens and mazes.

A few poems from earlier decades of the sixteenth century do employ slightly unusual typographical patterns, but the page format of most is subordinate to the sense and rhythm of the words. Sometimes a pair of indented lines at the end of a stanza will signify a commentary on, or summary of, a "conceit" or image developed in the preceding lines. A change in the pattern may draw attention to the fact that the rhythm has changed. But, in the 1590s, at exactly the same time that the poetic madrigal appeared as a free-form competitor of the sonnet, there also appeared prefigurations of the shaped and emblem poems that became popular in the seventeenth century. In 1589 George Puttenham's book, *The Art of English Poetry,* appeared. C. S. Lewis says that, among other things—

> He also liked what he called "ocular proportion," by which he meant poems that present some geometrical figure to the eye; a beauty, he had heard, very common in China, Tartary, and Persia. His examples suggest rather the courtly poetry of Lilliput in the age of Gulliver. (Lewis 432)

To enjoy Puttenham's constructions—in the forms of diamonds, rubies, obelisks, and pillars—one may turn to Milton Klonsky's book, *Speaking Pictures.* Here one also finds numerous examples of other fads of the time. These include rebuses (poems that use pictures in place of words: an eye and a carpenter's saw, for example, means "I saw"); "Love Knots," which are woodcuts or engravings in which the sugared language weaves itself across and around the page like a piece of macrame; and emblem poems, some of which explicate complicated engravings and others simple woodcuts. Most of these date from some years later, 1600 to 1660.

But as early as 1593 there had appeared in the collection *The Phoenix Nest* an acrostic-like poem from which I quote the first two stanzas:

Her face,	Her tongue,	Her wit,
So fair,	So sweet,	So sharp,
First bent,	Then drew,	Then hit,
Mine eye,	Mine ear,	My heart.
Mine eye,	Mine ear,	My heart,
To like,	To learn,	To love,
Her face,	Her tongue,	Her wit,
Doth lead,	Doth teach,	Doth move.

The idea is that one may read the poem either horizontally or vertically, and in other ways as well, though only the horizontal lines rhyme.

Barely into the seventeenth century, the collections titled *England's Helicon* (1600) and *A Poetical Rhapsody* (1603) already included works in which the typography displays a greater exuberance; the second of these even features an altar-shaped poem by an anonymous writer. Baroque extravagance soon began to show itself in the far-fetched metaphors of Metaphysical poetry, in the appetite for unusual or even grotesque-sounding words, and in emotional displays in verse in which the sacred and the profane, the vulgar and the exalted, combine. This manneristic exhibitionism carries over into typography; a glance at the pages of any anthology of the seventeenth century shows poems whose shape on the page, though seldom aiming at actual iconographic imitation, betrays something essential about the period. Take, for example, Donne's "Song," printed in 1633—

> Go and catch a falling star,
>   Get with child a mandrake root,
> Tell me where all past years are,
>   Or who cleft the Devil's foot,
> Teach me to hear mermaids singing,
> Or to keep off envy's stinging,
>   And swear
>   No where
> Lives a woman true, and fair.

The playfully cynical exasperation of the lover shows itself here not only in the rhetoric and imagery, but also in the wilfully odd contours of the lines. Examples of asymmetrical verse from later in the century have been quoted in chapters 4 and 5: Milton's "On Time" and poems by Mildmay Fane and Abraham Cowley. By the time we get to Cowley's "Pindariques" in the mid–seventeenth century, we are seeing a poetry that advertises its irregularity through the typography, displaying "fire" and unpredictability, puffing up with Pindaric afflatus and then abruptly contracting. Irregular though still symmetrical—with the lines centered on the page—is Richard Lovelace's "A Black Patch on Lucasta's Face"; here the surprise is that such a polished Cavalier and Son of Ben could allow himself this degree of extravagance.

Most remarkable, of course, are Herbert's and Herrick's shaped poems; but Herbert's excursion into this mode is only an extension of the inventiveness that we see in his weaving phrases together in "A Garland," or, even more subtly and effectively, repeating the word "dust" as a rhyme and in the middle of line throughout "Church Monuments." His sole experiment in vers libres, "The Collar," has been examined earlier, but many of his poems indulge in idiosyncratic stanzas meant to be noticeable on the page as well as to the ear. Episodes of typographic ingenuity, then, usually coincide not only with cycles of free verse, but also with other experimental combinations of poetry and graphic art. The emblem poem, as I have mentioned, was a popular fashion in the middle of the seventeenth century.

It hardly needs to be said that Dryden was a major force in establishing Augustan neoclassicism. But one can also point to the typography of his poems that exploited the "Pindarique" fashion popularized by Abraham Cowley, to "Alexander's Feast" and his other poems on music, as well as "The Secular Masque," as works whose visual appearance signal to the reader that something is going on that will test the limits of prosodic propriety. As England settled into the eighteenth century, however, printers' conventions subsided into a stable framework. The sober format of a page filled with heroic couplets aimed at the rendering of regular lines of poetry that were meant to be heard, not seen. As with many generalizations, there are exceptions; minor poets, and minor poems by major poets, exhibit much variety and at times employ idiosyncratic typographies. But as Addison's contempt for all forms of "false wit" clearly shows, the dominant doctrine was formal and conservative. Indentations might announce the presence of a hymn composed in common measure and experiments in quantity could be instantly identified from their typographic resemblance to an ode by Horace, but most serious poetry simply filled page after page with couplets.

A continuation of this survey into, and through, the nineteenth century makes the same point repeatedly: at every stage typography parallels other developments in prosody. Sometimes this may be merely accidental; it would be hard, for example, to print Robert Burns's songs and poems, from the late eighteenth century, in any other way than that in which they appear. To contend that the way they look on the page suggests something fresh and spontaneous would be overingenious. But a few years later, Coleridge, apparently feeling that the ballad stanza did not lend "The Rime of the Ancient Mariner" enough of an air of the medieval, added marginal glosses to give the appearance of an old manuscript. Many of the *Lyrical Ballads,* indeed, look calculatedly spontaneous or newly antiqued with their short stanzas, the visual simplicity of which sorts well with their artificially simple language. When Byron, Keats, and Shelley revived the Spenserian stanza—or continued its revival— there may have been some awareness that the outline of stanza would declare itself on the page as conspicuously different from heroic couplets. That Byron also embellished the early parts of *Childe Harold's Pilgrimage* with lumbering archaisms shows a gothicizing spirit at work reminiscent of Spenser's late-sixteenth-century medievalism; Keats's "The Eve of St. Agnes" is a Gothic-revival poem through and through. (Both are in Spenserian stanzas.)

Comments that I have made on the Victorians, especially on Tennyson and Browning, as prosodic tinkerers hold true for their typography. Sometimes this is just a consequence of an unusual meter; one cannot venture into trochaic octameter (as in "Locksley Hall") without filling the line almost to the margin or beyond. It may be too much to argue, as David Scott does in *Pictorialist Poetics* (80), that Rossetti's Italian sonnets resemble, with their octaves and sestets, the main canvas plus the predella of their accompanying paintings; but the poets and painters of the century were always on the lookout for ways of reflecting or cross-fertilizing the arts.

This sketch of the function of typography is meant to emphasize that what seems to be a uniquely twentieth-century fascination has its antecedents, much as do free verse and the reforms of diction associated with free verse. Typographical ingenuities are often found along with experiments in prosody, whereas episodes of regularization and reaction usually involve rejection of such eccentricities. In the 1990s, typography serves as a signal on the page in advance of one's reading the poem, letting us know whether we are in for stretches of anaphora, snatches of broken phrases, jazzy fragments, or unpredictable huffings and puffings; whether we may expect what James Dickey called the "sober constipation" of ultra-formalist poems; or whether we will get something in between—something judiciously restricted to two-line stanzas, for example, but irregular enough to avoid seeming stuffy.

There have been many steps along the road toward the politicizing of the forms of poetry and most of them have occurred since 1910. But impulses in that direction made themselves felt earlier, and sometimes these impulses showed themselves in typography. Whitman, who had made his living as a printer, must have been aware of the revolutionary configuration that his lines would make on the page, and others who had earlier employed biblical-anaphoraic meter may likewise have had some sense of the unusual appearance that their poems would assume. William Blake deserves a chapter all to himself because of the unique way in which he mixed typographies, graphics, and lines of all sorts. But to account for the special place that all these concerns occupy in American poetry of this century, we find ourselves again turning to France; because of the continued political dislocations subsequent to the French Revolution and the end of the Napoleonic era, artistic experiments flourished the way that weeds often do on the site of a recent demolition.

In 1842 appeared Aloysius Bertrand's *Gaspard de la Nuit,* which had been written ten or fifteen years earlier. The pieces included in this volume are often cited as among the earliest prose poems, but their organization into versets identifies them as a Gallic parallel to Whitman, though the necrophilic imagery makes us think of Poe:

LA CHAMBRE GOTHIQUE
> *Nox et solitudo plenae sunt diabolo.*
> Les Pères de l'Église.

La nuit, ma chambre est pleine de diables.

—"Oh! la terre,—murmurai-je à la nuit,—est un calice embaumé dont le pistil et les étamines sont la lune et les étoiles!"

Et, les yeux lourds de sommeil, je fermai la fenêtre qu'incrusta la croix du calvaire, noire dans la jaune auréole des vitraux.

Encore—si ce n'était, à minuit,—l'heure blasonnée de dragons et de diables!—que le gnome qui se soûle de l'huile de ma lampe!

Si ce n'était que la nourrice qui berce avec un chant monotone, dans la cuirasse de mon père, un petit enfant mort-né.

Si ce n'était que la squelette du lansquenet emprisonné dans la boiserie, et heurtant du front, du coude et du genou!

Si ce n'était que mon aïeul qui descend en pied de son cadre vermoulu, et trempe son gantelet dans l'eau bénite du bénitier!

Mais c'est Scarbo qui me mord au cou, et qui, pour cautériser ma blessure sanglante, y plonge son doigt de fer rougi à la fournaise!

[THE GOTHIC ROOM
Night and solitude are full of demons.
The Church Fathers.

At night my room is full of devils.

"Oh! The earth," I murmured to the night, "is a perfumed calyx of which the pistil and the stamens are the moon and the stars!"

And, eyes heavy with sleep, I closed the window inlaid with the cross of Calvary, black within the yellow halo of stained glass.

Again—if it were only, at midnight, —at the hour emblazoned with dragons and demons! were only a gnome that soused himself with the oil of my lamp!

If it were only the nurse who was cradling with a monotonous song, in my father's breast-plate, a little stillborn child.

If it were only the skeleton of the infantryman shut up inside the wainscot, banging his forehead, his elbows and knees!

If it were only my grandfather stepping out of his worm-eaten picture frame, dipping his glove into the holy water of the font!

But it is Scarbo, who tears at my throat with his teeth, and who, to cauterize the bloody wound, plunges into it his forefinger of red-hot steel!]

Bertrand's practice, dating as it does from the earlier nineteenth century, further complicates the problem of determining Whitman's influence on French poetry of the period 1890–1910. While it is clear that many of those later poets knew of and read Whitman, it is also true that an independent tradition of biblical-anaphoraic writing existed in French, and developed parallel to what Whitman was doing. American poets who drew on the French Symbolists and *vers-libristes,* scarcely realizing it, opened themselves indirectly to a biblical-anaphoraic method that went directly into most American poetry from Whitman. Larbaud, Régnier, Maeterlinck, and others who composed in versets and who employed anaphora, in some sense handed back to Eliot, Pound, and the Imagists a form that was more acceptable to them than if it had come directly from Whitman.

In any event, Bertrand's individual lines clearly owe much to biblical cadences. Entire poems in *Gaspard de la Nuit,* however, are so self-contained and carefully executed that one can see why Whitman's name does not come up in discussions of Bertrand—leaving aside the impossibility of actual influence in one direction or the other. As David Scott points out in *Pictorial Poetics,* Bertrand's poems seem intended to take advantage of the framing space offered by a single page. Clearly—like Blake before him—Bertrand had in mind the visual aspects of his poems:

> A further interesting dimension to this problem is provided by the fact that Bertrand himself had intended *Gaspard de la Nuit* to be illustrated . . . This ambiguous relationship between source image, text and illustration, in which the poem is the pivot between two different transpositional activities, is significant in the more general context of the nineteenth-century prose poem. (129)

Beginning with Baudelaire, who was much affected by his reading of Bertrand, it becomes increasingly difficult to disentangle mutual and reciprocal influences and exchanges between French and American poets. Poe, of course, seemed a towering figure to Baudelaire, Mallarmé, and most other French poets; to this day the French exhibit a weakness for anything coming out of America that resembles Poe. But by 1890 the balance of trade had tipped in the other direction, and the French were resuming their status as net exporters to the English-speaking world of poetic doctrine and practice. Yet they continued to read Whitman and Poe, finding more to absorb and emulate in these poets than in anything by the British.

The problem at this point, however, is to explain just what the connection was between French Symbolism and typography. In some respects this is very easy to do. As with epochs of experimentation and irregularity in the past, the poems printed in great numbers in France after 1880 advertised their rebelliousness by their appearance on the page. They might be versets, prose poetry, *vers pairs* of different lengths, or *impairs* that retained rhyme. The direction was toward increasing outrageousness, culminating in unrhymed *impairs,* calligrams, and, ultimately, the Dadaist publication *Littérature,* in which all the pages were blank.

A single poem can be given most of the credit for validating the entire movement in the direction of typographically organized poetry. This was Mallarmé's "Un Coup de Dés jamais n'abolira le Hasard." An entire literature exists that takes this poem as its subject. Explications and counter-explications abound. Because the action of the poem involves simultaneously a shipwreck and a vision of the heavens, among which account is interspersed the title of the poem in very large capital letters, it is taken as Mallarmé's statement of the cosmic terms that dramatize the ultimate conditions of existence. The title itself is compact with paradox and invites meditation: to accede to chance, it says, will never abolish chance. Tychism affirms tychism—but can it affirm anything else? Others see it as an admission of the human inability, finally, to deal with the arbitrary side of the universe—or, put another way, a humble admission of ultimate impotence. Always fascinated with the concept of absence, of non-existence, Mallarmé in this poem allowed the blank page as much presence as the type that occupies it; Paul Valéry, the first to listen to the poem read, and the first to see its configuration, had the impression of looking at a thought occupying space.

"Un Coup de Dés" appeared with dramatic appropriateness just at the end of the nineteenth century, and it is reasonable to describe it as the most remarkable act of prosodic iconoclasm of all time. At one stroke it legitimized all the divagations of *vers libres*—which, in 1891, Mallarmé had expected to disappear—by surpassing them. I cannot comment on its residual musicality, to which those with finer ears testify. But the violence that the typography—with its numerous fonts and its double-page layout—did to conventional expectations makes cummings seem a timid practical jokester in comparison. Coming from the master who had assumed the mantle of Baudelaire, and among whose many pupils one numbers Paul Valéry, the effect is overwhelming. In his earlier work Mallarmé can be plausibly seen as a continuation of the great line of classical French poetry, as can Baudelaire, at least in his handling of the meter, so that the departure in "Un Coup de Dés" is very startling; had Haydn—at the peak of the classical sonata form in the eighteenth century—abruptly composed something in the manner of Bartók, he would have surpassed Mallarmé, but it would have taken something like that.

Not everyone agrees that the poem is a success. Marcel Raymond, in *From Baudelaire to Surrealism,* spoke of "Mallarmé's obscure, but pathetic, admission of failure is contained in the poem entitled *Un coup de dé* [sic] *jamais n'abolira le Hasard.* One may call it a Promethean failure" (19). But most see it as a daring final adventure of the master-navigator for an entire generation of French poets. Wallace Fowlie wrote admiringly of it, and described its form in this way: "The very typography and disposition of the large pages translated the work. Each page bore its own particularized graphic physiognomy" (219).

Indeed, the poem was so unprecedented and the demands of the typography so stringent that when it was published in 1897, the printed version did not conform to the requirements of the manuscript. Not until sixteen years after Mallarmé's death did the *Nouvelle Revue Française* publish the work much as he had designed it, and the effect on English-speaking poets was at first minimal. By that time (1914) the Imagist movement had fallen into Lowell's hands, and Pound and Flint had dissociated themselves from her. Imagist poems continued to appear, of course, but Imagism itself was defunct. Since that movement had been the major channel for conveying French influences into Anglo-American poetry—and also because of wartime disruptions—"Un Coup de Dés" remained largely unknown to poets writing in English or their public. In any case, there is little evidence of interest in the poem among English-speaking readers. Mallarmé's more conventional work had been difficult enough to follow. Eliot, who borrowed the "Garlic and sapphires in the mud" segment of "Burnt Norton" in *The Four Quartets,* as well as the phrase "To purify the dialect of the tribe," from Mallarmé, was the only poet of importance who could read Mallarmé with sufficient ease to assimilate anything from him.

The direct effect of "Un Coup de Dés" on poetry in English, then, is virtually nil. No English translation was published until 1956. Writing to Renée Taupin in 1918, Ezra Pound sketched a very loose connection to Mallarmé, but it was to the Mallarmé who presided over the cénacle of the 1880s and 1890s:

J'ai "lancé" les Imagistes (anthologie *Des Imagistes*); mais on doit me dissocier de la décadence des Imagistes, qui commence avec leurs anthologies postérieures (même le première de ces anthologies).

Mais "voui": l'idée de l'image doit "quelque chose" aux symbolistes français via T. E. Hulme, via Yeats < Symons < Mallarmé. Comme le pain doit quelque chose au vanneur de blé, etc. (*Critical Anthology* 98)

[I "got the Imagists moving" (the anthology *Des Imagistes*); but you have to dissociate me from the decadence of the Imagists, which begins with their subsequent anthologies (even the first of these anthologies).

Yes indeed [?]: the concept of the image owes "something or other" to the French Symbolists via T. E. Hulme, via Yeats < Symons < Mallarmé. As bread owes something to the person who winnows the wheat, etc.]

One turns to cummings, hoping that among the avant-garde hints he had acted upon one might find the typographical extravagance of "Un Coup de Dés," but a concordance to his entire work reveals no mention of Mallarmé, and those who dissect cummings's style do not mention him. William Carlos Williams's triadic structure, especially in its first manifestation in *Paterson* as "The descent beckons . . ." is so reminiscent of the appearance of Mallarmé's poem that one feels he must have at least seen it strewn across the pages of some publication or another. Yet in no discussion of Williams, including Stephen Cushman's exhaustive analysis of his typography, is there any reference to Mallarmé. It is common to mention Mallarmé in discussions of Wallace Stevens, because of the loose similarities in the ways that each pursued in his poems a more refined form of existence, and the manner in which each assumed the air of the magician. Like Eliot, Stevens had read Mallarmé and knew certain of his poems well. But Stevens's brand of whimsicality bears little resemblance to the cosmic dislocations of "Un Coup de Dés"; when Stevens takes liberties with typography his theme is likely to be playful, even frivolous. His most serious statements are in blank verse. There may be someone who can correct me on this, but it is difficult to point to a single poem in English—prior to 1940—that owes anything to this final monument of Symbolism, unless it should be a passage or two of *The Waste Land*. In the second half of the century I can point only to Robert Duncan.

Why, then, mention it at all?

The answer is that, inaccessible and unexplored by most American or English poets, that poem gradually assumed prominence as a distant and seldom-climbed peak in the Himalayas of modern poetry, and as such it helped to authorize the extension of iconoclasm from the metrics into the very typography of poetry written in all the European languages. Mallarmé had, in a final gesture, outdone the other *vers-libristes* with their progressive extensions of *vers pair* to *impairs,* their abandonment over several decades of most of the classical rules of scansion, and, finally, their ceasing to employ rhyme at all. Therefore, though one cannot make the same kind of comparison as is possible between an actual poem by Laforgue and one by Eliot, one must admit "Un Coup de Dés" as an important document, even for poets writing in English who have never read it, especially because of the example of its typography. It was, even before its original publication, a major landmark for the French avant-garde, and it helped to assure that Mallarmé remained a name to conjure with.

Various experiments in the mixing of genres and the combining of art forms characterize the romantic quest for intensified sensation throughout the nineteenth century—a quest that fulfilled itself most extravagantly in Wagnerian opera. It is possible to see in the work of the Imagists a continuation of the search for synaesthesia, though at least initially it was in a purified and classicized form. I am contending that the Imagists were fundamentally Romantics even though in their earlier efforts most believed themselves to be aiming at hard, dry, cleanly delineated poems. Their effort at reaction was rather different from the French Parnassians, whose exoticism and medievalism marked them, too, as Romantics despite their use of extremely regular meters and despite the solidity of their descriptions. The Imagists' achievement had much more in common with the Symbolists.

Because romanticism is part of human nature it is impossible to escape it. To understand how thoroughly romantic the formal doctrines of Imagism were, and how continuous with other nineteenth-century developments, it is necessary to glance even further back. On the very eve of the Romantic era, neoclassical affirmation of genre theory had found a reinforcing parallel in the insistence, in Lessing's *Laocoön,* on the separation of poetry from painting (or sculpture). Published in 1766, that work had sensibly pointed out fundamental differences, such as that poetry exists as a linear progression of words through time, whereas painting exploits spatial relationships. The argument extended the concept of genres or types into fields other than literature; on an even sounder logical basis, Lessing argued for the complete separation of the arts according to media. A century and a half later some of his basic contentions were reiterated—though with a less attractive conservative and moralizing tone—by Irving Babbitt whose *New Laokoon* set out to undo the aesthetic confusions engendered in the meantime by Rousseau, Baudelaire, Wagner, Rimbaud, and others. Just as with the Parnassians in France, the Imagists, too, seemed to espouse a revived classicism; but as we shall see, anti-Romantic as he believed himself to be, Imagism's chief philosopher, T. E. Hulme, argued for the spatialization of poetry and for the rejection of the poem as an oral performance with a temporal dimension. In that respect Hulme was radically anti-neoclassical; his arguments had the effect of reintroducing confusions between separate media. Hulme himself also had the temperament of a Romantic—impulsive, rebellious, and iconoclastic. And he was not alone in embracing these blurrings of artistic frontiers of which his immediate precursors, the Pre-Raphaelites, were so fond. When we think of Pound's close involvement with sculptors, painters, and musicians, when we remember Amy Lowell's efforts to capture in poems the essence of Stravinsky's music, and when we are reminded of the pivotal importance to William Carlos Williams of the paintings in the Armory Show, we realize to what extent these moderns took for granted one of the persistent consequences of the Romantic outlook, the effort to combine the effects of more than one of the arts in a single work, or to appropriate effects from one medium to another. Even today there are many who assume that a successful "multi-media happening" is intrinsically better than a single-media event, and who welcome any sort of graphic enrichment to the spoken—or printed—word. The Imagists, while aiming at the purification of Victorian practices, especially Victorian poetic diction and technical virtuosity in prosody, accepted French variants of late-nineteenth-century Romanticism. Rejecting Tennyson's gaudy neo-medievalism, Browning's Renaissance-worshiping evangelistic fervor, and Arnold's imperfect sublimation of his own fundamentally Romantic temperament—not to speak of the sentimentalities of Longfellow—they succumbed to other seductions. The Pre-Raphaelite fixation on the poem as painting, or painting as literary context, which Lowell, Williams, and many others accepted without question, helped prepare for more refined types of aesthetic confusion imported from France. As I have already mentioned, Harvard's Fogg Museum had actively acquired works by Rossetti and his compeers. For

Americans in the year 1900 the great contemporary painters were the Pre-Raphaelites: Rossetti and Millais, Holman Hunt and Edward Burne-Jones, William Morris and Aubrey Beardsley. Literary art and iconic poetry by those Englishmen made heavy use of symbolism. For Pound, Eliot, and Lowell (and in some ways for cummings, Williams, and Stevens) the French Symbolists represented a more refined version of an aesthetic that they had already become accustomed to in the work of the Pre-Raphaelites. And in embracing the French Symbolists they were reviving other varieties of Romanticism. Even as they tried to escape played-out Keatsian diction and the threadbare tapestries of the gothic revival they were absorbing (at second or third hand) Baudelaire's "Correspondances," Laforgue's Pierrot-like ironies, the poetic Prometheanism of Rimbaud, and the Hermetic heroism of Mallarmé—the triumphant alienation and victorious solitude of all these and many others. At the same time, these admirers of Faustian solipsism, the Imagists, aimed at program, a reformation, a movement.

The inconsistencies of Imagist doctrine may, in the short run, have been one of its strengths, adding to its aura of revolution and innovation. An eddy in the ongoing current of Romanticism, Imagism seemed, momentarily, to reverse the general flow, spiraling back upon itself, yet it was borne along by the same energies against which it appeared to be reacting. Escaping the pomposities of Victorian rhetoric, aiming at first at a classical chasteness in language, the Imagists felt the need to extend the range of the poem in another direction, toward the visual.

The impulse simultaneously to simplify and to enrich expressed itself in other self-contradicting announcements. In his original definition of Imagism, Pound called for composition according to the musical phrase instead of the metronome. On the face of it this seems a rejection of Tennysonian sonorities—and yet in another way it suggests the enriching of the poem by appropriating effects from music. H.D. was much affected by the clarity and definiteness that she found in ancient Greek poetry, as was Richard Aldington in his early years. Glenn Hughes described it this way: "The two young Hellenists set out together to recapture the beauties of an ancient world, and to create in modern English a poetry which in spirit and form would convey the Greek ideal" (109–10). Yet the poems that resulted from this impulse were, at least in their prosody, the opposite of classical symmetry and restraint. In their emphasis on the visual—on word-painting—the poems were an outright rejection of the neoclassical principles of the *Laocoön*. Poetry was to ignore and forget its beginnings as a temporal succession of sounds arranged in a recurrent frame of regular undulations. Instead, there was to be an attempt to arrest forward movement, to substitute for that a spatial development or, at most, a circularity. But this, too, proved unsatisfactory. It was precisely this halting of energetic forward movement that Pound sought to remedy when he abandoned Imagism for Vorticism.

Out of these contradictory motives there emerged a few definite changes of direction that identify what we now call "High Modernism." The Imagists' emphasis on clearly realized visual experience, and their interest in promoting free verse that inevitably *looked* different on the page, mark a distinct beginning of a concern with typography. I have mentioned Whitman, but his long, end-stopped lines simply continued until they reached their limits on the page; their nature required them to appear different from Longfellow's stanzas, but it does not much matter whether each verset takes up one, two, or three lines on the page. Whitman's typography was a challenge to prevailing ideas about poetry, but this was mostly an accidental consequence of their oral expansiveness. With the Imagists the visual statement made by the poem becomes more calculated.

Yet it is important not to overstate the importance of typography. The first printed version of H.D.'s "Oread" preserved capitalization of the first word in each line, a practice that suggests that the unity of each lineal phrase remained important, and that the intention was to make an appeal to the visual imagination through the sense of the words—and not to display them as any sort of graphic construct. The calligraphic extremes of Apollinaire, in French poetry, are remote from Imagism. And yet in some sense the text of H.D.'s poems *is* visual, in that the printed word is intended to produce a direct visual impression, without the intervention of audible speech. Or so it seems at first because of the absence of meter; as I shall show in a future study, H.D. took what had been ornamental excrescences—alliteration, internal rhyme, assonance—in Victorian poetry and made them essential.

Parallel to H.D.'s visual crispness was Pound's fascination with, via the manuscripts entrusted to him by the widow of Ernest Fenellosa, the unmediated communication of the ideogram. Willard Bohn argues that "Critics have often observed that our century has placed great value on seeing and sight," and continues:

As much as anything, the rise of modern visual poetry reflects a new awareness of the printed page. For various reasons recent criticism has stressed the physical dimension of the text, seeing its words as autonomous entities. According to Jacques Derrida the written word is an object in its own right, its different meanings detached and deferred indefinitely. Wolfgang Iser and others consider modern literature to be a series of self-conscious exercises designed to engage us in the process of reading. (2–3)

Bohn contends that early in this century poetry was becoming increasingly visual, and that even French poets of the period 1900–1920 rejected the Symbolists' interest in music in favor of increased emphasis on links between poetry and painting. He mentions the Imagists, along with the Ultraists and the Surrealists, and asserts: "Arresting similes and vivid metaphors became the order of the day as poets vied with each other in their quest for the ultimate image" (3).

Even if the Imagists had limited use for the musical preoccupations of the Symbolists, there is no question of the intense interest that those American and English poets took in their immediate Gallic precursors. We have seen how Amy Lowell put together a volume of commentary, poems, and translations designed to make these writers known to an English-speaking public. Two years earlier, in 1913, Pound had published a series of review essays in *The New Age,* "The Approach to Paris," which were meant to do much the same thing. At one point Pound considered the question of whether poetry could benefit by assimilating effects or methods from another medium:

> Because I praise these rhythm-units of M. De Gourmont and because they happen to be homogeneous, or very nearly so [they are in fact remarkably like Whitman or some of "Fiona Macleod"], I do not wish to appear hostile to rhythm-structures composed of units which differ among themselves. I do not hold a brief either for symmetrical or for asymmetrical structure; these things are a matter of music; they are perhaps as complicated as any problems of musical construction . . . The problem of how far principles of pictorial design can be applied by a sort of parallel, in verse, is a problem like any other. (Quoted by Pondrom 177)

Here we see Pound, in advance of the official debut of Imagism, recogniz-
ing the possibility of a new source of fertilization from another family of
art forms—graphic, pictorial, sculptural—and yet refusing it special
prominence. We see, too, Pound's openness to the possibility of the "mu-
sic" of poetry. He could even appreciate Swinburne, and tried to justify
that appreciation by finding evidences of nascent Imagism in Swinburne.

Since most of what I have to say in this chapter dwells on the visual
dimensions of free verse, it is well to mention repeatedly the tenacity
with which Eliot and Pound asserted claims of musical values in poetry.
At the same time, no matter what extremes the French Symbolists may
have gone to in this matter, it must be emphasized that Pound and Eliot
did not subscribe to the Paterian formula that required that all art aspire to
the condition of music, though Pound could quote Pater when it suited
his purposes. In "*Vers Libre* and Arnold Dolmetsch" (1917), Pound said
"Poets who are not interested in music are, or become, bad poets . . .
Poets who will not study music are defective." He concluded—

> It is too late to prevent *vers libre*. But, conceivably, one might im-
> prove it, and one might stop at least a little of the idiotic and narrow
> discussion based on an ignorance of music. Bigoted attack, born of
> this ignorance of the tradition of music, was what we had to live
> through. (*Critical Anthology* 83)

The most important document for establishing and understanding
the connections of Imagism with French Symbolism is the fifty-page
essay, "Contemporary French Poetry," that F. S. Flint published in *The
Poetry Review* in 1912. His answer to the question "What is symbolism?"
not only provides an enduringly succinct evaluation of that phenomenon,
but also makes clear what the Imagist movement would see in those
poets. Symbolism was, said Flint—

> First of all, a contempt for the wordy flamboyance of the romanti-
> cists; secondly, a reaction against the impassive descriptiveness of the
> parnassians; thirdly, a disgust of the "slice of life" of the naturalists.
> Ultimately, it was an attempt to evoke the subconscious element of
> life, to set vibrating the infinity within us, by the exquisite juxtaposi-
> tion of images. (Pondrom 86)

Flint identified Symbolism with the philosophy of Bergson, with whom
T. E. Hulme had studied and about whose work he wrote several essays.
Flint calls this "the philosophy of intuitiveness"; he quotes from Baude-
laire's "Correspondances," making him a harbinger of the new move-
ment, and names Mallarmé its "first prophet." By mentioning forty or
more French poets of the previous two decades, and by printing both
original texts and translations by many of these, Flint compiled a veritable
handbook of contemporary French poetic practice. This one essay served
as a breviary for Imagist devotions, and may have suggested to T. S. Eliot
additional experiments in free verse. And among his other concerns, Flint
did draw attention to the typographical aspect of these poems.

Several years earlier, however, Flint had made clear his interest in
reciprocal relations between poem, text, and illustrations. In an essay
entitled "Recent Verse," which appeared in *The New Age* for July 11,
1908, he took note of recent translations from the Japanese—

> As I turned over the pages of these Japanese Sword and Blossom
> Songs my fingers trembled with delight. Surely nothing more ten-
> derly beautiful has been produced of late years than this delicate
> conspiracy of Japanese artist with Japanese poet! The Blossom
> Songs, taken from the famous Kokinshiu Anthology of A.D. 906,
> and the Sword Songs of later date, are completed and explained by
> the exquisite illustrations on each page. (Pondrom 50)

Most significantly, he connects what he finds there with Symbolist po-
etry, mentioning Mallarmé and Maeterlinck. As Flint explained, when he
looked back at the period in the essay "The History of Imagism" (1915),
"We were very much influenced by modern French symbolist poetry."
Flint's purpose in this short piece was to set the record straight as re-
garded Pound, whom he considered as something of a latecomer and
then as something of a deserter:

> In that year [1909], Pound had become interested in modern French
> poetry; he had broken away from his old manner; and he invented
> the term "Imagisme" to designate the aesthetic of "Les Imagistes."
> In March 1913, an "interview" over my signature, of an "imagiste"
> appeared in the American review *Poetry,* followed by "A Few Dont's
> [*sic*] by an Imagiste" by Ezra Pound. The four cardinal principles of
> "Imagisme" were set forth as:

(1) Direct treatment of the "thing," whether subjective or objective.

(2) To use absolutely no word that did not contribute to the presentation.

(3) As regarding rhythm: to compose in sequence of the musical phrase, not in sequence of a metronome.

(The "doctrine of the Image" —not for publication.) (71)

The list quoted by Flint has got into print in so many places, with only slightly varying wording, that one can almost believe that it was repeated like a catechism. In the essay he continues, naming everyone involved in the original movement, who, he says, "were published in America and England as 'Des Imagistes: an Anthology,' which though it did not set the Thames, seems to have set America, on fire" (71). Here he raises the important issue, already touched on above, of the extent to which American poets were more receptive to, and more influenced by, Imagism than were British poets.

The American craving for immediacy of spiritual experience, at one time satisfied by a Calvinist sense of election, found in Imagism and in other European avant-garde movements a refinement of what is, in its essence, a religious enthusiasm. This is a continuing phenomenon: since the Second World War French intellectuals have been taken up eagerly by the American academy as well as by expatriate intellectuals. The Jansenist strain in Derrida—which set his conscience free to practice a species of literary vivisection—is only among the most recent to exercise a powerful appeal to these Puritanical spiritual hungers. Imagist doctrine— propounded by Ford, Hulme, Flint, Pound, and Lowell—absorbed many qualities of French avant-garde poetry; in America, *Poetry* magazine and the *Little Review* proved powerful organs for propagating the new faith and for promulgating the principles of Imagism. Pound, of course, was never satisfied with what these magazines achieved, feeling that Harriet Monroe was consorting with vulgar company in printing the populist poets (Sandburg, Lindsay, Masters, et al.).

But in placing special emphasis on the Gallic proclivities of many American poets, we must not forget that certain British poets, in addition to Flint and Aldington, were keenly aware of what was going on across the Channel. Wilde and Dowson had turned to Paris as a source for styles and attitudes that could hold their own against high Victorianism, and some years later Edith Sitwell drew in her own way on the *vers-libristes*.

Also, in considering the French, one must be careful to admit that the question of interests and influences is enormously complex—that just to start with, some of the figures I have mentioned were really Belgian, though they wrote in French. Paris was the wharf upon which cultural cargoes from any number of countries were unloaded—German, Russian, and Spanish merchandise figured as importantly as anything from America. But the particular way in which "high modern" poets—mostly of American origin—assimilated the Symbolists and the free-verse writers of France is remarkable—another evidence of the cultural insecurity that led to the expatriation of writers and artists from the States in such numbers between 1880 and 1930. And, at the same time, I found it astonishing to see Whitman obviously present in the French poetry of the 1890s and obviously absent from American poetry, until the populist poets began to get into print in about 1915.

Another Englishman who took a new direction, partly from French examples, was T. E. Hulme, who, though he wrote little in his short life, managed to get hold of the tiller and steer poetic developments upwind on an entirely new course. Ezra Pound saw to it that the new movement continued in that direction. He kept his friend's memory and his ideas alive after Hulme's death, of which almost no one else took note, early in the First World War. Flint, too, saw the importance of Hulme's ideas and identified him as the "ringleader" of the Poets Club of 1908, where those ideas were discussed that were ultimately codified as Imagism. Recently I came across a book review that congratulated an author for not "spouting great gouts of Hulme." But I find that Hulme's comments, especially in "A Lecture on Modern Poetry," which he began to deliver in 1908 or 1909, express more forcefully than anything else just exactly the new direction poetry was to take. Furthermore, we see clearly how attention was going to turn from the speaking voice to the page.

Hulme was as full of contempt for the later Victorians as was Ford Madox Ford. "They resemble the latter stages in the decay of religion when the spirit has gone and there is a meaningless reverence for formalities and ritual. The carcase is dead and all the flies are upon it" (*Further Speculations* 69). He is sick to death of sentimentality: "Imitative poetry springs up like weeds, and women whimper and whine of you and I alas, and roses, roses all the way." He feels that poetry must be on the brink of a revival that will parallel the Renaissance. But one need not look to the French Parnassians for help: "[T]heir pupils were lost in a state of sterile feebleness" (*Further Speculations* 70). Instead—

This check to the Parnassian school marked the death of a particular form of French poetry which coincided with the birth and marvelous fertility of a new form. With the definite arrival of this new form of French verse in 1880 came the appearance of a band of poets perhaps unequalled at any time in the history of French poetry.

The new technique was first definitely stated by Kahn. It consisted in a denial of a regular number of syllables as the basis of versification. The length of the line is long and short, oscillating with the images used by the poet. . . . The kind of verse I advocate is not the same as *vers-libre,* I merely use the French as an example of the extraordinary effect that an emancipation of verse can have on poetic activity. (*Further Speculations* 70)

With swift hatchet strokes, Hulme hacks out the outlines of the new poetry. It is possible to see here the rough contours of all manner of doctrines. Consider Eliot's "objective correlative" (a terminology partly drawn from Santayana, who spoke of "the correlative object") and then examine what Hulme says: "Say the poet is moved by a certain landscape, he selects from that certain images that, put into juxtaposition in separate lines, serve to suggest and evoke the state he feels" (73). The contribution to Imagism is even more obvious: "I quite admit that poetry intended to be recited must be written in regular metre, but I contend that this method of recording impressions by visual images in distinct lines does not require the old metric system."

Hulme heaps insult after insult upon Victorian prosody, suggesting that the effect is metrical inebriation so that we accept anything as poetry; or (a little inconsistently) that it is "cramping, jangling, meaningless, and out of place" like a barrel organ being played in the midst of a symphony. It becomes clear that his purpose is to insist that we cease to hear words, and instead simply imagine the objects signified by the words, that "there are, roughly speaking, two methods of composition, a direct and a conventional language. The direct language is poetry, it is direct because it deals in images."

Sometimes in reading a poem, one is conscious of gaps where the inspiration failed him, and he only used the metre of rhetoric. What happened was this: the image failed him, and he fell back on a dead image, that is prose, but kept an effect by using metre. That is my

> objection to metre, that it enables people to write verse with no
> poetic inspiration, and whose mind is not stored with new images.
> (74–75)

We begin to see what I have called the "spatialization" of poetry in
Hulme's thinking: "The new verse resembles sculpture rather than mu-
sic; it appeals to the eye rather than to the ear" (75). Here he seems closer
to the Parnassians than to the Symbolists.

One may disagree with Hulme, but at least one sees exactly what he
is driving at. The new poetry is to consist of the direct communication of
images from the printed page to the imagination of the solitary reader;
the images arrive on the page by a reverse process, from the imagination
of the poet. Edward Storer described it as "a form of expression, like the
Japanese, in which an image is the resonant heart of an exquisite mo-
ment" (quoted by Flint: *History of Imagism* 70).

Time and again Hulme employs the word "impressionist," or "im-
pressionism," though when he speaks of poetry he seems to identify this
with Symbolism. The word finally settled on by the movement that he
helped to set going, *Imagism,* partakes of both impressionism and Symbol-
ism; Imagist practice borrowed forms from the Symbolist poets, but
placed value on candid rendering of visual impressions that one associates
more with impressionist painters. In any event, the Imagists used typog-
raphy as a way to announce the news that innovations had occurred.

We cannot blame—or credit—Hulme for intentionally promoting
the sort of visual, or "concrete," poetry of Apollinaire's *Calligrammes* or
for the typographical whimsies of cummings. He clearly had in mind the
functioning of the word on the page as a signal or symbol of some visual
experience and not as—in itself—a significant shape. But by denying
words existence as sounds—sounds persisting in and continuing through
time—and by insisting that the visual experience be arrested and spa-
tialized, he opened the way to efforts to manipulate the page itself as a
concrete icon. He did not set up graven images himself, but his and
similar ideas, misunderstood and misapplied, have encouraged contempo-
rary tendencies, the most pernicious of which may be that the poet's
special gift is to arrange words so that their physical relationships to one
another on the page acquire ineffable significance.

But the initial effect was just what the Imagists had hoped for. By
encouraging one another to forget the tedious hexameters, heptameters,

and octameters—and even the pentameter—they freed themselves to rediscover a freshness and intensity that had been missing from poetry for several decades.

I can think of no better example of a poem made possible by Hulme's (and Ford's) ideas than Pound's "The Return." Pound, as we have already noted, understood and loved the rhythms of many languages and many periods too well to abandon them completely in favor of mute iconographs. But the clearing away of any expectation of rhyme or stanza, and the freedom to redistribute the elements of the poem to take advantage of typography, surely permitted the delicately improvised effects of this poem:

THE RETURN

See, they return; ah, see the tentative
        Movements, and the slow feet,
        The trouble in the pace and the uncertain
        Wavering!

See, they return, one and by one,
With fear, as half-awakened;
As if the snow should hesitate
And murmur in the wind,
        and half turn back;
These were the "Wing'd-with Awe,"
        Inviolable.
Gods of the wingèd shoe!
With them the silver hounds,
        sniffing the trace of air!

 Haie! Haie!

        These were the swift to harry;
These the keen-scented;
These were the souls of blood.

Slow on the leash,
        pallid the leash-men!

Pound employs anaphora here with a sensitivity seldom achieved by Whitman ("See . . . See . . . ," and "These were . . . These were . . .

These . . . These were . . ."). As we have seen, the French *vers-libristes* had taken up that manner. But more striking is the employment of spatial punctuation that alternately interrupts and urges forward the argument of the poem.

"The Return" is simultaneously an account of how, for Pound, the real power of the ancient myths, cleansed of rococo prettiness and Romantic false coloring, had revived and taken shape in his imagination, and a conjuring up of those same figures for the reader. He evokes moments from ancient poetry when the human and superhuman intermingle, when transformations occur, when the Erinyes suddenly become literal powers, or when the souls in Hades grow momentarily incarnadine and firm with the fresh blood of sacrifice. He could scarcely have produced these effects in a regular meter—and yet the ghost of the regular meter plays among these lines just as the diaphanous hints of a supernatural presence flutter among the images. The first line is an iambic pentameter, interrupted with a full stop and then yanked past its termination by the adjective-noun combination. The next line—

> /   *   *   *   / /
> Movements, and the slow feet

—arrests the forward progress with two long syllables, preparing for the calculatedly indefinite effect of "tentative / Movements."

> *   / *   *   *   /   *   *   *   / *
> The trouble in the pace and the uncertain

gives us a line in which amphibrachs (* / *)—in English, the most indefinite of any nameable trisyllabic foot—are further blurred by intervening unstressed syllables. The line, like the half-embodied wraiths whose procession it imitates, stumbles into yet another purposeful ambiguity: "Wavering." This word has a definite stress on the first syllable, but the third syllable, though given more emphasis than the second, is hardly equal to either.

To pay attention to these effects is to be convinced that Pound never came close to abandoning rhythm as an essential part of poetry, no matter what Ford and Hulme may have told him, no matter what emphasis Imagist doctrine placed on direct communication from the page, and no matter what irascible disruptions of convention might be found in the *vers-libristes* and elsewhere. His ear was too good. At the same time, there is no denying that this poem powerfully supplements rhythmic effects with typographical cues. One would not want the words placed otherwise than they are. "Inviolable" would seem a trifle more vulnerable if it appeared alone at the left margin, rather than isolated directly beneath "Wing'd-with Awe."

> With them the silver hounds,
> sniffing the trace of air!

would be too patently a revival of the classical hexameter, too obviously a declaration of the poem's intention to bring something from the classics back to life, were it printed as a single line. Thirty years earlier, Swinburne's strategy had been to fill pages with hexameters to evoke ancient times. Pound's breaking of the line in just this way suggests the tentativeness of the whole undertaking. Other lines hint at choriambs, Adonics, and sapphics that interweave with possibilities of pentameter:

> Haie! Haie!
> These were the swift to harry

Intercalations from the other arts into a discussion of prosody are always risky, but Pound's dipping into those meters recalls the classical lineaments, as well as the figures themselves, in one of Picasso's earlier periods. The typography makes it possible, among other things, to isolate rhythmic cross-references and draw attention to them. I am not certain of the meaning of the last two lines of this poem:

> /   *   *   /
> Slow on the leash,
> /   *   *   /   /
> pallid the leash-men!

The implication may be that the vision is now fading, or that the awakening never was complete; it could also be a sardonic comment on the relegation of the classics to the care of scholars and curators of various kinds. The lines give the effect of evanescent outlines, of half-remembered details from Greek figured ceramics or sculpture. Whatever the images may be, however, the typography isolates and intensifies two rhythmic effects borrowed from ancient quantitative metrics: a perfect choriamb followed by a perfect Adonic. The quantitative values were evident to Yeats, who, as editor of *The Oxford Book of Modern Verse* (1936), singled out this poem for quotation and said of it, "[O]ne gets an impression, especially when he is writing in *vers libre,* that he has not got all the wine into the bowl, that he is a brilliant improvisator translating at sight from an unknown Greek masterpiece" (xxvi). Yeats's intention was to suggest that on the whole Pound had been a bad influence, and that his writings were spasmodic and formless, yet he could not help admiring this piece; twenty years earlier he had found the poem admirable. In the 1930s, however, Yeats was ready to put his former secretary and advisor in his place, recognizing the typographical intention of Pound's scheme, but questioning its value:

> He hopes to give the impression that all is living, that there are no edges, no convexities, nothing to check the flow; but can such a poem [the *Cantos*] have a mathematical structure? Can impressions that art in part visual, in part metrical, be related like the notes of a symphony; has the author been carried beyond reason by a theoretical conception? His belief in his own conception is so great that since the appearance of the first Canto I have tried to suspend judgement. (xxiv–xxv)

This must have been the comment that inspired Pound's explosion, when he referred to "that god-damned paragraph of Yeats's" and accused Yeats of having caused readers to look for the wrong things in the *Cantos.*

Whether or not Yeats's evaluation of *The Cantos* may have been correct, Pound's typography in "The Return" is by no means impulsive, whimsical, or arbitrary; it is functional. It fulfills the aspirations of those who make claims for the possibilities of organic or expressive form; at the same time, it is accessible to anyone who will examine its form carefully. The sentence immediately preceding this one had already been written when I encountered these statements in a speech by Yeats, delivered under the auspices of *Poetry* magazine, and also printed in the *Little Review* for April 1914:

> We rebelled against rhetoric, and now there is a group of younger poets who dare to call us rhetorical. When I returned to London from Ireland, I had a young man go over all my work with me to

eliminate the abstract. This was an American poet, Ezra Pound. Much of his work is experimental; his work will come slowly, he will make many an experiment before he comes into his own. I should like to read to you two poems of permanent value, *The Ballad of the Goodly Fere* and *The Return*. This last is, I think, the most beautiful poem that has been written in the free form, one of the few in which I find real organic rhythm. A great many poets use *vers libre* because they think it is easier to write than rhymed verse, but it is much more difficult. (Quoted in "Poetry's Banquet" 27)

Most poems that, on the page, resemble "The Return" prove to be aimless hashings-up of uninteresting lines. One can sympathize with those who blame Pound and Eliot for setting fashions that glut our current poetic marketplace with shoddy goods, but no poet can be responsible for inept imitators. We are no worse off than readers of the later eighteenth century, who were treated to lame attempts at Pope's epigrammatic concision.

Pound, in "A Retrospect" (printed in *Pavannes and Divisions* in 1918), spelled out explicitly what his metrical intentions had been in these earlier poems:

I think that the desire for *vers libre* is due to the sense of quantity reasserting itself after years of starvation. But I doubt if we can take over, for English, the rules of quantity laid down for Greek and Latin, mostly by Latin grammarians.

I think one should write *vers libre* only when one "must," that is to say, only when the "thing" builds up a rhythm more beautiful than that of set metres, or more real, more a part of the emotion of the "thing," more germane, intimate, interpretive than the measure of regular accentual verse; a rhythm which discontents one with set iambic or set anapaestic.

Eliot has said the thing very well when he said, "No *vers* is *libre* for the man who wants to do a good job."

As a matter of detail, there is *vers libre* with accent heavily marked as a drum-beat (as par example my *Dance Figure*), and on the other hand I think I have gone as far as can profitably be gone in the other direction (and perhaps too far). I mean I do not think one can use to any advantage rhythms much more tenuous and imperceptible than some I have used. I think progress lies rather in an attempt to approximate

classical quantitative meters (NOT to copy them) than in a careless-
ness regarding such things. (*Critical Anthology* 86–87)

What he neglects to mention here is how, at the same time, he had begun
to apply ideogrammic method in conjunction with these other experi-
ments. Later on he was to insist that this was his main achievement. In
Carta di Visita in 1942 he claimed, "If I have made any contribution to
criticism I have done so by introducing the ideogrammic system" (195).
Earlier, in a letter to Kitasono Katue, a Japanese poet and editor with
whom Pound was in touch in 1937, he had written:

> Ideogram is essential to the exposition of certain kinds of thought.
> Greek philosophy was mostly a mere splitting, an impoverishment
> of understanding, though it ultimately led to development of particu-
> lar sciences. Socrates a distinguished gas-bag in comparison with
> Confucius and Mencius.
>
> At any rate, I *need* ideogram. I mean I need it in and for my own
> job, but I also need sound and phonetics. (*Critical Anthology* 194)

This obsession with the ideogram had not seized him so completely in
1915, but we know that from the earliest meetings of the Poets' Club and
of the Imagists, motifs and forms from Chinese and Japanese had been
eagerly discussed. The maniacal phase of Pound's thinking, which dates
from roughly 1935 onward and which included his suggesting over Ital-
ian state radio that Jews practiced cannibalism, may be found continuing
in the writings of Jacques Derrida. "On this subject [phoneticization of
language], what does the most massive, most recent, and least contest-
able information teach us? First, that for structural or essential reasons, a
purely phonetic writing is impossible and has never finished reducing the
nonphonetic" (88). The connection with Pound may seem tenuous until
we read, "This is the meaning of the work of Fenellosa whose influence
upon Ezra Pound and his poetics is well known: this irreducibly graphic
poetics was, with that of Mallarmé, the first break in the most entrenched
Western tradition" (92). It is highly significant that Derrida should reflect
so clearly the importance of, and even mention in the same sentence,
both Mallarmé and Pound; there could hardly be a better proof that
ideogrammic assumptions have become fully operative in contemporary
poetry. At the same time, as I have shown, Derrida is deceived in suppos-

ing that this is a giant leap forward unique to this century. Impulses toward iconic presentation in poetry are as old as writing itself in all the Western languages. The passage just quoted is merely another form of naive Romantic primitivism, hardly surprising in light of the omnipresence of Rousseau in Derrida's writing. But as a witness to the existence of assumptions so deeply felt as to remain, at this moment, largely unarticulated, Derrida's statement is invaluable.

While it is easy to assert the importance of typography in free verse, and easy enough to illustrate it by flipping through the pages of *The Norton Anthology of Modern Poetry*, it is not easy to trace precisely lines of descent or influence. One cannot point them out with the same assurance that one can identify biblical-anaphoric free verse, where the Whitmanian genealogy usually declares itself. It is not difficult to note the recurrence of images whose clarity owe much to H.D., Lowell, and Pound, but it is hard to point out the descendants of these poets in the matter of typography. What was handed on was a general assumption that typography, along with much else, was now a matter of choice rather than convention. Or at least this is the assumption of those American poets since 1950 who have accepted the "open form" preachments of the Black Mountain school. A person of no literacy in English whatever could open *The New American Poetry*, compare its pages with those of *New Poets of England and America*, and reach intelligent conclusions about the poetry purely on the basis of their contrasting typographies. Almost everything in the former sprawls across the pages unpredictably and irregularly, while the latter contains numerous identifiably similar patterns—whole poems in identical forms as well as stanzas within poems. In this War of the Anthologies these typographies were the uniforms—resembling either the ragtag outfits of Fidel Castro's early followers, or, in the second instance, a well-drilled detachment of Palace Guards. In more recent years we have something in between, like the French soldiers of the 1950s whose shirts and pants were the same but whose shoes were all different.

The formal poetry of the 1950s and 1960s—at this point I am speaking almost exclusively of American poets—has its own curious family history. These poets filled the pages of *New Poets of England and America* and the more conservative quarterlies; as representatives of formal, even academic, poetry they provided a goad and a foil for open-form poets. A fascination with difficult forms from Romance languages—the villanelle, sestina, or rondeau—continued as a distant inheritance of the 1880s, which had appealed to Pound in his earlier years. But the interest in form for its own sake had at least three additional causes. First, T. S. Eliot had predicted that this would be the new direction, and his authority was such as to make prediction a reality, at least briefly. Second, the subtleties discovered by the New Critics in old poems led to the belief that good new poems must be carefully crafted so as to include paradoxes and ambiguities whose compactness showed best in a constricting form. Finally, there was the example and prestige of Auden, technological engineer par excellence and aficionado of every kind of metrical strategy.

A threefold pattern of influence can also be identified behind the Black Mountain/Beat Generation poets as well—those included in *The New American Poetry*. Here it suffices to mention three names: Pound, cummings, and Williams.

Of Pound enough has been said. Despite his increasingly manic efforts to lend pictographic impact to the later *Cantos* by including actual ideograms and musical scores, he retained an appreciation for the effects of rhythm, for the music intrinsic to language and available to poetry. But *The Cantos* had been the most important of several contemporary documents—*Paterson* was another—that constituted the texts central to poetic studies at Black Mountain, and they continue to be imitated on occasion, even by rather middle-of-the-road poets such as Richard Howard. It is easy to find instances of poems that superficially resemble "The Return," but that lack entirely its sensitivity. A careful survey could identify much more of Pound's legacy, which, despite his support for Mussolini, extended into the ranks of the Beat Generation and, at the same time, affected the way that poets who followed the New Critics composed some of their work. A sensitive and accomplished formalist such as Daniel Hoffman, for example, could depart into a Poundian free verse.

Williams is the oddest case. As is well known, he was obsessed with discovering some new principle of rhythmic regularity; every time he raised the issue of poetic form, what he had to say hinged ultimately on this problem. It was his habit, using the typewriter, restlessly to arrange and rearrange the words of a poem until he felt he had it right, but apparently he believed that he was dealing with sound rather than with ideogrammic effects on the page. Consider this poem—which is, admittedly, an extreme example:

THE ATTIC WHICH IS DESIRE
the unused tent
of

bare beams
beyond which

directly wait
the night

and day—
Here

from the street
by
   ★ ★ ★
   ★ S ★
   ★ O ★
   ★ D ★
   ★ A ★
   ★ ★ ★

ringed with
running lights

the darkened
pane

exactly
down the center

is
transfixed

Almost everything about this poem is visual. "Pane" flattens out like the surface and opening it describes; "exactly" in isolation centralizes the viewpoint, while "down the center" takes us vertically down from that precise point. The way that we hear the "x" sounds in "exactly" and "transfixed" even has a visual effect, marking the spots to which our attention is directed. For the rest, one may invoke with irony Alexander

Pope's euphonious line, "The nameless graces that no methods teach," to account for Williams's success here. But he did not realize how thoroughly he had achieved the ideals proposed by T. E. Hulme for a visual poetry. Williams, who rejected the whole idea of vers libre and who refused to ally himself permanently with any school or doctrine, turns out to have been the most perfect Imagist of them all, achieving this by the vigor with which he rejected his own earliest proclivities for writing like Keats. But, to restate an earlier argument, he could never have remained so resolutely free of iambic rhythms had he not possessed them so thoroughly as to be able always to avoid them. His achievement was to recover for poetry the original representative force of the language that had revived in Keats ("While barred clouds bloom the soft-dying day / And touch the stubble fields with rosy hue") but that had, as Hulme and Ford insisted, been blurred into diaphanous mood-music by the end of the previous century. In doing this he contrives a pace and cadence that constantly thwart the regular poetic line.

Williams's organizational prosody—as opposed to his rhythmic iconoclasm—is mostly typographical. There are exceptions, such as "The Dance," and the opening of "The Yachts," where audible rhythm is prominent—though the pictorial effects are even more important in the latter. It is hard to decide if, in *Paterson,* the typographical tactics are under control or not; my impression is that Williams's reach there did exceed his grasp. But in many a short poem the placement of words and lines maximizes the visual—sometimes static, sometimes kinetic—force of the words. He has more to say than that, of course, at times even drawing back from the literally imaginable when it is necessary, even using vague personification in "Spring and All," in the midst of the precise detailing of that late-winter landscape in which nature stirs in its sleep. But the placement of words on the page—happily not often as literally as the "SODA" shown above—so as to communicate visual impressions directly to the reader without much intervention of sound is the essential thing. Even his triadic line, the culmination of a lifelong quest for an audible metric, turns out to have been—as Stephen Cushman argues—a typographic strategy: something that lends the page dignity. The contrarious rhythms of his poetry are far more complex than the typography and ultimately more important, and they resist the apparent simplicity of the step-down line.

Carole Ann Taylor is fundamentally correct in her assessment of what the visual arrangement accomplishes; to the extent that this is a recognition of the limitations of the method, these remarks apply with even greater force to Olson's *Maximus:*

> *The Cantos* and *Paterson* are most obviously alike in that they are both open-ended, ongoing works to which their authors added until their deaths; both poets weave documents, letters, conversations, and numerous personae into the fabric of their poems in progress. In both works, the variety of visual effects, many of them used with some consistency throughout *The Cantos* and *Paterson,* provides a sense of formal identity that importantly depends on the look of the pages. Different from other poetry I have discussed, the very look of the pages suggests that the poetic subject is the poet in the world. (289)

I would put it less kindly, feeling that both Pound and Williams overreached their genuine talents in these works, and remarking that by this criterion our attics, garages, and basements constitute art forms—that is, the "poet in the world" as a subject removes the barriers between ordinary existence with all its random events, vacillations, and indecisions and a work of art as a selected and intensified field of attention. Such an approach works very well for purposes of satire, as when the Dadaists included accidental features in their "happenings," in order to ridicule the stiffness of official culture, or when Swift dragged Augustan poetic conventions through the gutter in "A Description of a City Shower," where all the random effluents of market stalls, sewers, and gutters converge between the walls of the heroic couplet and discharge themselves in a final Alexandrine. The best analogy would be to say that in *Paterson* and *The Cantos* we see the interior of the studio. It is art in process, not art as a finished series of works; we may recall that for years *Finnegans Wake* bore the provisional title "Work in Progress," and we may think of Jackson Pollock's action painting and John Cage's musical experiments. The great unfinished work has long been a Romantic convention: Coleridge's *Christabel,* in only two of five projected parts, goes into every anthology from that period and remains among his most interesting poems; and Wordsworth's *Prelude* was a more or less open-ended account of "the poet in the world." Even neoclassical critics found their sensibilities stirred when they saw in Shakespeare the asymmetrical and incomplete grandeur of a Gothic cathedral. But if the liability of much eighteenth-century poetry was inconsequential neatness, the present-day pitfall is aimless divagation and interminable rant. The concept of the unfinished poem as the norm has been disastrous; even if the consequences are not physically or morally harmful, most are terribly dull. It is no wonder such poetry is for the most part the concern of academic coteries. The barbarians may not be at the gates but the crashing bores have certainly arrived in force; only those bred to patience through the tedium of graduate work can put up with them.

The work of e. e. cummings, whether more or less successful, does at least aim at unity and completion, and his typography usually is at least as constructive as it is iconoclastic. His numerous strategies I shall not attempt to classify. As everyone points out, cummings was in some ways rather conservative, always ready to slip back into the forms, and even some of the language, of his Pre-Raphaelite-imitating adolescence. In some poems typography is a thin disguise for traditional metrics. Even in idiosyncratic poems that are difficult of immediate access ("anyone lived in a pretty how town," for example), the meter often has a fundamentally regular beat and the inventiveness is syntactic and semantic, not typographical. But there do remain the numerous poems that turn on typographical humor, on iconographic puns and jokes, and my problem is to place cummings with regard to his immediate forebears on this matter.

To start with, he certainly admired the quirky side of Imagism. To this day people retell the incident when cummings, in order to discomfit President Lowell of Harvard at the commencement exercises of 1915, read something outrageous recently published by his sister Amy. More important may have been some exposure to Italian futurism, which he might have learned of from Alexander S. Kaun's essay, "Futurism and Pseudo-Futurism," which appeared in the *Little Review* for June 1914.

> To set art free of the atavistic fetters of the old culture and civilization, to imbue it with the nervous sensitiveness of our age, have been the negative and positive aims of Futurism. It is absurd to abide by the forms of Phidias and Aeschylus in the days of radium and aeroplanes. The influence of the old masterpieces is accountable for the fact that of late humanity ceased to produce great works of art. (12)

Kaun quotes from a poem in French by the movement's founder, Marinetti, the title of which is translated as "The Banjos of Despair." Of this, Kaun says: "The hysteric and savage banjos that meow like cats maddened by the odor of the storm; the sea which, swelling its back of a hippopotamus, applauds their songs with its sonorous twick-twacks and snorts—I understand the poet, I believe him" (13). Kaun then reproduces a poem in Italian that attempts a typographical imitation of a Bulgarian monoplane dropping bombs on a Turkish village. Kaun remarks that "present-day Futurism is abundant with quaint, grotesque features approaching caricature." This description fits cummings rather well.

The experiences of cummings during the First World War, serving in the ambulance corps and then finding himself imprisoned for suspected espionage by the French, put him in the frame of mind of many a young Frenchman when the war ended and left him receptive to the comic nihilism of the Dadaists. But even from the America of the 1920s there was much to absorb, from the humanitarian vulnerability of Charlie Chaplin's tramp to Krazy Kat and *archy and mehitabel*. The spirit at work in his poetry is more akin to Paul Klee (who, as it happens, also wrote poems that in some ways resemble cummings) than to Braque or Picasso (cummings's own paintings, of course, look like none of these). The best way to describe the poetry may be to invoke a general avant-garde proclivity on the part of cummings that makes him a natural continuation of Imagism, vorticism, futurism, fauvism, cubism, dissonance—an insouciant but humane nuttiness. There is a general air of irreverence, of taking liberties with assumptions and expectations, and at the same time a delight in the pace of modern existence, that make his typographical fancies appropriate. As I have already mentioned, he bequeathed to Charles Olson the idea of the typewriter as a technical aid to the poet in placing words in strategic locations and for managing the spaces between. But what in cummings is the lighthearted indirection of a great spirit becomes grimly programmatic in the hands of subsequent poets, and at times degenerates into mere silliness. Cummings preempted certain aspects of typography almost as effectively as—to make a far-fetched comparison—Milton took over blank verse; one can imitate him in a lame way, but almost no one can use his methods for any original purpose. Lawrence Ferlinghetti remains the most successful, partly by borrowing simultaneously from Pound and Williams, and partly by going back directly to that postwar zaniness that is the only decent response to wartime doublespeak. So, for the most part, there sits cummings in splendid isolation, a ne plus ultra of typographical wit; and of course there are many who feel that cummings himself went a little too far. The same frame of mind that, in the eighteenth century, could not allow Shakespeare his puns cannot today countenance typographic cleverness. For my part, I admit that whenever I encounter the lowercase personal pronoun "i," the jamming together of words, an excess of ampersands, and the abbreviation "cd" for "could" in a piece of writing by anyone other than cummings, I immediately stop reading. As with great epigrammatists, each century seems capable of producing only one or two poets who can manage typographical fancies, and those must be good poets in other respects as well.

I have already anticipated most of what I have to say about Charles Olson as a typographic compositor, implying what great store he set by the typewriter, and how the placement of the words on his pages demands unconditional assent from the reader. Speaking of the advantages of the typewriter, Olson wrote—

> For the first time the poet has the stave and the bar a musician has had. For the first time he can, without the convention of rime and meter, record the listening he has done to his own speech and by that one act indicate how he would want any reader, silently or otherwise, to voice his work.

> It is time we picked the fruits of the experiments of Cummings, Pound, Williams, each of whom has, after his way, already used the machine as a scoring to his composing, as a script to its vocalization. It is now only a matter of the recognition of the conventions of composition by field for us to bring into being an open verse as formal as the closed, with all its traditional advantages. (22)

Since means of recording the spoken voice had existed long before Olson wrote this, one has to account for the scriptolatry that permeates this utterance. Evidently the published *written* word was to him the only adequate proof of the greatness of a poet. Also, he is obsessed with the idea of compelling the reader to reproduce the performance; again, this is the sort of power that Chaucer and Shakespeare enjoy. Olson's dynamania made itself obvious on many occasions; once, after holding the stage for three hours before an audience of seven hundred, he grasped the lectern and bellowed, "I *love* power!"

Even Kenneth Rexroth, from whom one might have expected a sympathetic assessment, said: "The long passages of *Maximus* are denser and less interesting than the most self-indulgent *Cantos*" (170). None of this is really evil, of course, except to the extent that it may convince sensible fellow-citizens that poetry was just what, to echo cummings, Plato told us.

The threefold impact of Pound, cummings, and Williams has been evident in most of the poetry published in the United States since 1950 and always advertises its presence with idiosyncratic typographies. The earliest and best examples are to be found in Ferlinghetti's Pocket Poet series; Kenneth Patchen's *Poems of Humor and Protest* epitomize many of the styles and possibilities while, as I have remarked, Ferlinghetti's own work assimilates and recombines his three precursors, adding something from French poets such as Jacques Prévert. Some readers may remember the foldout of the poem "Bomb" by Gregory Corso, with its lines arranged so as to make the mushroom shape, which appeared in *The Happy Birthday of Death*. These and many other poems by Beats and San Francisco poets employ typography somewhat as cummings did, as part of an outlook that can be humane and funny—very far from the stuffy avant-garde elitism and self-promotion, the Daliesque snobbishness and literary modism, of others who have latched onto such methods.

Chapter 10

The Prose Poem

Typographical prosody of whatever sort has at least the virtue of recognizing that the poet's aim is to do something special with the words, that arrangement of some variety is important. In its most self-indulgent, derivative, or random forms it still pays tribute—even if unintentionally—to the idea of the poet as one who takes what ordinary speech has generated, and who rearranges these workaday items for the amusement, delight, consolation, or even edification of the reader. As most people will admit, incompetence in well-established forms and meters is easier to spot than in most varieties of free verse, just as badly played Mozart is easier to judge than badly done John Cage. Real achievement in free verse is more difficult to identify and to appreciate; the absence of self-declared form makes it easier to lay claim to nonexistent excellences, easier to tailor the emperor's clothes. But at least the arrangement in lines, or in some pattern, acknowledges the importance of pattern.

If lack of ability safely disguises itself for a time in bad free verse, the ultimate refuge of bankrupt talent is the prose poem. To say this is no more to condemn the prose poem per se than Samuel Johnson—a fiercely loyal Englishman—meant to condemn patriotism when he called it "the last refuge of a scoundrel." But as a weak or corrupt politician may hope to salvage a slippery reputation by invoking the memory of a Jefferson or a Lincoln, the latter-day prose poet often trusts to the reputation of Baudelaire or Rimbaud to do what talent has failed to do. This is a hard saying, but it grows out of repeated experiences of attempting to read with pleasure and sympathy writings that are announced as prose poems. The great majority of such pieces published in the last fifty years are pretentious and presumptuous bits of writing that fail to make use either of the discursive generosity of prose or the compressed energies of good

poetry. The editorial pages of county newspapers make more interesting
reading. This is not true of prose poetry by the French Symbolists and
their immediate followers in English.

To attempt a definition, or even a careful qualification, of the nature
of the prose poem is to venture into an arena of endless distinctions
between prose and poetry, free verse and meter, rhythmic prose and lax
versification—the terrain explored for years with enthusiastic inconclu-
siveness by Amy Lowell and her friend, Professor Patterson; conscien-
tiously surveyed by John Livingston Lowes; and plotted and pieced by
numerous others. W. B. Yeats, by taking a passage from Pater's *Renais-
sance* and printing it as a free-verse poem—the opening entry for *The
Oxford Book of Modern Verse* (1936), offered that confused region of dis-
course the status of a no-man's-land. Yet in taking a piece of professed
prose, and printing it as poetry, he was also supporting Livingston
Lowes's gently adumbrated conclusion that this was what all free verse
amounted to. Yeats chose to believe that Pater was the main source of free
verse, claiming that the "new generation" of poets had given him "its
entire uncritical admiration," and going on to explain—

> That is why I begin this book with the famous passage from his
> essay on Leonardo da Vinci. Only by printing it in *vers libre* can one
> show its revolutionary importance. Pater was accustomed to give
> each sentence a separate page of manuscript, isolating and analising
> its rhythm; Henley wrote certain "hospital poems," not included in
> this book, in *vers libre,* thinking of his dramatic, everyday material,
> in that an innovator, but did not permit a poem to arise out of its
> own rhythm as do Turner and Pound at their best and, as I contend,
> Pater did. (viii)

Because Walter James Turner is known to few readers today, we might
consider a specimen of his work, which Yeats placed alongside Pound in
his estimation and to which he gave more pages in the 1936 anthology
than he allowed T. S. Eliot:

THE WORD MADE FLESH?
How often does a man need to see a woman?
Once!
Once is enough, but a second time will confirm if it be she,

She who will be a fountain of everlasting mystery,
Whose glance escaping hither and thither
Returns to him who troubles her.

This happens rarely when a man is young;
For the lusts of the young are full of universal gladness
They have no sadness of disillusioning error
But only earth's madness of thunder
And its fading bright crackle of lightning.

(305)

That is not nearly the end of the poem. It must have been a heavy blow to Pound to find himself mentioned in the same breath with the author of the lines above, and if it was Yeats's unconscious purpose to demonstrate the folly of composing in free verse, he must have felt satisfied. Turner retains the worst of Victorian sentimental rhetoric, with none of the "music"; his poem is a succession of clichés, dead metaphors, and unrealized images. The writing is so extraordinarily bad that one is tempted to invent even more malicious explanations for Yeats's having included it. Other choices of free verse are more interesting, especially those that illustrate forms based on biblical cadences, such as poems by Rabindranath Tagore and Sacheverell Sitwell. But one cannot help feeling that Yeats's unavowed intention was to prove that a great deal of the poetry written since 1914 was disastrously bad and that modernism was a monstrous mistake. The war poets he omitted entirely; his odious strictures on Wilfred Owen are well known, in which he described the poetry as "all blood, dirt & sucked sugar stick." Most selections from Eliot make that poet seem an aging reincarnation of Oscar Wilde; his comments on Eliot in the introduction could—among many other things, of course— have shocked Eliot into renewed artistic humility and the constructive efforts of *The Four Quartets,* but that was not Yeats's intention, which seems to have been to diminish Eliot's reputation and influence:

Eliot has produced his great effect on his generation because he has described men and women that get out of bed or into it from mere habit; in describing this life that has lost heart his own art seems grey, cold, dry. He is an Alexander Pope, working without apparent imagination, producing his effects by a rejection of all rhythms and

metaphors used by the more popular romantics rather than by dis-
covery of his own. (xxi)

I think of him as a satirist rather than poet. (xxii)

[A] new England Protestant by descent, there is little self-surrender
in his personal relation to God and the soul. (xxiii)

This anthology, carrying the prestige of the Oxford imprint, edited by
the most celebrated living poet, purporting to represent the modern
period, and sure of a wide and immediate sale, must have been a cause of
grief to many poets who viewed its contents. Yeats clearly believed that
much of what had been published in the previous two decades in truth
was not poetry. Once you leave the confines of meter, he argues by implica-
tion, you have crossed a prosodic Rubicon and have committed yourself
not only to the prose poem, but to prose itself. The inclusion on the
opening page of the passage from Pater, lineated as free verse, as much as
said to the reader of 1936, "My generation wrote better prose than what
you are pleased to call poetry."

My own argument may seem to parallel this view, yet I really intend
to say the opposite, namely, that the prose poem, when it is successful,
does indeed work precisely because it *is not poetry*. But it does not exist in
vacuo; the prose poem requires, for its success, not only the talent but the
works and reputation of an accomplished metricist to make it successful;
it becomes most interesting as an ironical departure from a great poet's
ordinary practice. I would not use examples of bad prose poetry or bad
free verse of any sort in order to discredit the very real achievements in
these media, any more than I would quote sentimental doggerel to prove
the viciousness of rhymed and metered poems. Bad poets of a hundred
years ago buttoned themselves up with an exactitude of scansions and
rhymes; bad writers of our time drape themselves with the mantle of
prose poetry.

Also appearing in 1936 was a new edition of *The New Poetry,* edited
by Harriet Monroe and Alice Corbin Henderson, the introduction to
which argued the case for the prosifying of poetry in the interests of
authenticity, directness, and personal cadence. As we now know, this
reaffirmed the precedents that were to govern most American poetry, for
better and for worse, for the next fifty years:

This borderland between prose and verse is being explored now as never before in English; except, perhaps in the King James translation of the Bible. The modern "vers-libertines," as they have been wittily called, are doing pioneer work in an heroic effort to get rid of obstacles that have hampered the poet and separated him from his audience. They are trying to make the modern manifestations of poetry less a matter of rules and formulae, and more a thing of the spirit, and of organic as against imposed rhythm. (xl)

Included also were the introductions of previous editions. Mingled with numerous historical and linguistic inaccuracies in the introduction to the original edition of 1917 one finds an obscure awareness that accentual meter, as opposed to accentual-syllabics based partly on French syllable-counting, was closer to the native rhythms of English. But, as with the idea of musical equivalences, this soon became lost in the efforts to identify "personal rhythm." This quest has done as much as anything else to separate poets in the latter part of the century from their possible wider audiences, putting the rhythm in the service of the poet rather than the other way around, as if the poet had invented the language itself, having first authorized his or her own existence. In particular, in employing the prose poem one usually asserts that one's individual gait is what matters rather than any acquired grace or poise.

The subject of prose poetry—like the question of just what makes a metaphor—is a happy hunting ground for critical projectors of all kinds, a topic of special usefulness to those who derive their support from the operation of scholarly vanity presses. Yet this one genre—if such it really is—has also received more thorough and competent scholarly attention than has the entire subject of free verse. The third chapter of Suzanne Bernard's monumental and (for its time) comprehensive *Le Poème en Prose de Baudelaire jusqu'à Nos Jours* (1959) occupies fifty-nine pages (out of some eight hundred), of small type and closely reasoned argument on the problem of the definition of the prose poem. Bernard's treatment is intelligent and thorough, but to many of us it is a subject the agitation of which would have helped Milton's devils forget their condition in the scholarly region of Pandemonium: a matter of endless hairsplitting. For my purposes, the prose poem is a piece of writing that falls into sentences rather than lines, that lacks regular meter or rhyme, that is printed like all other prose, and that a person otherwise known as a poet has chosen to designate as poetry; it seems to me to try to define it otherwise does not separate it from, say, a passage of gorgeous description in Conrad, or the concluding paragraphs of *Portrait of the Artist as a Young Man*. Historically, I consider only works composed since the year 1800 as candidates for prose poetry. Others, looking for precursors, have pointed to the writings that I identified in chapter 7 as belonging to the biblical-anaphoric line of free verse. As early as the seventeenth century there had been the sudden efflorescence of highly ornamented prose in English, but those who wrote it did not imagine themselves to be composing poetry. A hundred years later "Ossian" was well known on the European continent and in some quarters is—in its original or in translation—considered as prose poetry. There were other pseudotranslations imitative of or parallel to "Ossian"—supposed versions of Aztec hymns, Sanskrit chants, Inca epics, and so forth, in which a "primitive" tone and simplified vocabulary proclaimed the work of a noble savage. Poetry composed in the French Alexandrine had become insufferably stiff and formal in the eighteenth century, and to some scholars the cultivation of lyrical or impassioned prose, by Diderot (who translated "Ossian"), Rousseau, and others, qualifies as prose poetry.

Most frequently mentioned as an immediate precursor to the nineteenth-century prose poem is the collection *Hymnen an die Nacht* of Novalis, published in 1800. While I can understand the desire to place this hybrid work in some line of descent, it appears to me that the prose parts of it function mainly as a highly charged, lyrical preparation for the actual poetry. Beginning with part 4, increasingly longer pieces of rhyming and metered poetry occupy the text, until with part 6 we have nothing but poetry. It is a most interesting and, so far as I can tell, extraordinarily beautiful work, but seems to me a kind of verbal oratorio, with recitative culminating in arias. I see no evidence whatever of its connection with the French prose poem; Suzanne Bernard's 813 pages include two inconsequential references (in footnotes) to Novalis, and I accept her negligence as authoritative.

More relevant is Aloysius Bertrand's *Gaspard de la Nuit,* especially since Baudelaire stated in the dedicatory letter to his *Spleen de Paris* that he had turned over Bertrand's pages repeatedly before getting the idea of composing his own *Petits Poems en Prose*. But Baudelaire's work does not really resemble *Gaspard de la Nuit*. Bertrand clearly took biblical versets as a model for most of his poems in that series, while in Baudelaire there is none of that. Suzanne Bernard, while recognizing and documenting the considerable literature of the *style biblique* of the 1830s in France, is not prepared to associate Bertrand with those other writers, accepting instead the designation of "prosateurs," used by the literary historian, Charles Bruneau, for them. It appears that she reserves the designation "poète en prose" for those who also qualify as *poètes maudits*—that line of haunted, obsessed, and often prematurely deceased persons comprising Bertrand, Baudelaire, Rimbaud, and Lautréamont. To this list may be added Mallarmé, despite his humdrum existence as a lycée instructor. But her description of the techniques employed by biblical stylists, in the section titled "Lamennais et le style biblique," is a useful supplement to previous discussions in this book of the part played by this mode in French poetry:

> Tous ces procédés sont usuels dans la Bible, dans les Psaumes surtout; ils sont également familiers aux auteurs de Ballades ou de Chansons, en prose comme en vers: nous les avons rencontrés, notamment, dans les Chants indiens d'*Atala*. D'autres moyens, comme la division du texte en versets trés courts, les reprises de mots et la façon de faire "pivoter" l'idée sur un mot, l'emploi jusqu'à l'abus des *et* en tête de phrase, le parallélisme, font du style mennaisien [in the manner of Lamennais] un véritable pastiche de la Bible. (75)

> [All these procedures are common in the Bible, especially in the Psalms; they are equally familiar to the authors of ballads or of songs, in prose as in verse; we have encountered them, most notably, in the Indian songs in *Atala*. In other ways, such as the division of the text into very short versets, the repetition of words and the device of making the idea "pivot" on a word, the use to the point of excess of *and* at the head of a phrase, parallelism, convert the Lamennaisian style into a veritable pastiche of the Bible.]

She also puts emphasis on the prophetic manner of these writings—a quality that is missing in Bertrand.

The connection of Bertrand with Baudelaire is more a matter of mood and tone than one of style. Baudelaire mentioned Bertrand, saying that after reading him "l'idée m'est venue de tenter quelque chose d'analogue, et d'appliquer à la description de la vie moderne, ou plutôt d'*une* vie moderne et plus abstraite, le procédé qu'il avait appliqué à la peinture de la vie ancienne, si étrangement pittoresque." ["it occurred to me to try something analogous, and to apply to the description of modern life, or rather of *a* life that was modern and more abstract, the procedure that painting had applied to ancient life, so strangely picturesque.] And yet, though he did not imitate Bertrand's actual style, he did consider that a new possibility had emerged—or might: "Quel est celui de nous qui n'a pas, dans ses jours d'ambition, rêvé le miracle d'une prose poétique, musicale sans rhythme et sans rime, assez souple et assez heurtée pour s'adapter aux mouvements lyriques de l'âme, aux ondulations de la rêverie, aux soubresauts de la conscience?" (Baudelaire 281). [Who is there among us who has not, in his ambitious moments, dreamed up the miracle of a poetic prose, musical without rhythm and without rhyme, supple enough and unruly enough to adapt itself to the lyrical motions of the soul, to the undulations of the daydream, to the sudden starts of consciousness?]

A degree of cynicism permeates Baudelaire's letter to Arsène Houssaye that prefaces *Le Spleen de Paris* and from which these quotations are drawn. He opens by announcing that the work has neither head nor tail, and that one may cut it up however one pleases without any harm. He implies that this is how a poet, in his laziness and malevolence, would really like to write. Jonathan Monroe takes the point of view that this whole letter, addressed to the literary editor of a leading newspaper, was part of a scheme by Baudelaire to get the work into print, gain a larger audience, and make more money than he could by his metrical performances. Perhaps *disdainful* would fit better than *cynical* to describe the project—the idea that if the rapidly expanding bourgeois reading public could not appreciate poetry, then give them what they could handle and let them make of it what they wished. There is black humor and self-mockery in this procedure—but also moments of impulsive fellow-feeling conveyed elsewhere in verse as "Hypocrite lecteur, mon semblable, mon frère." Monroe argues this at length and convincingly in *A Poverty of Objects: The Prose Poem and the Politics of Genre,* saying of the switch from verse, "Turning the lyric's valorized self back to the world, the prose poem exposes how comic and fragmented that self really is in the context of the social reality that negates its own sublime pretensions" (27).

With admirable assiduity, Suzanne Bernard set out to identify the types of phrasing that we might expect to find in Baudelaire's *Le Spleen de Paris.* Drawing on his own introductory letter, she speaks of a "phrase heurtée"—which we might translate as "ruptured," in which sudden jolts, knocks, shocks, and transitions jerk the reader about, toying cynically with his expectations. Second is the "phrase ondulatoire"—a long, sinuous, succession of waves or meandering excursions of reverie. Third, she identifies the "phrase lyrique," which is "ascendante et dynamique, s'accordant avec des sentiments intenses, des élans joyeux ou doulouroux" ["soaring and dynamic, accommodating itself to intense feelings, to emotional impulses, whether joyous or sad"]. These varying motions, the naming of which satisfies the human instinct to categorize that goes back as far as the modes of Greek music, turn out not to be equally present in *Le Spleen de Paris*—indeed, argues Bernard, the first may not be found at all, and had to await the genius of Rimbaud to achieve realization.

As interesting and authoritative as Bernard's discussion may be, she has strayed from the central point, which is that these "petits poèmes en prose" are what they are because they are *not* poetry. Further on, Bernard begins to employ arguments and distinctions that parallel discussions of the Imagists:

> Il faut donc admettre que Baudelaire, s'il s'attache à adapter le mouvement de la phrase au mouvement intérieur qu'elle doit suggérer, s'il recherche les rythmes et les sons expressifs, se refuse à rechercher la musicalité elle-même, et à accorder une importance à la forme *en soi*. (139)

> [It is therefore necessary to admit that Baudelaire, even as he applies himself to adapting the movement of the phrase to the interior movement that it ought to suggest, even as he seeks after expressive rhymes and sounds, sets himself against musicality itself, and against allowing any importance to form *in and of itself*.]

Bernard speaks repeatedly of "cadence" also.

My own view is that if we are seriously to consider *Le Spleen de Paris* under the rubric of poetry, we are going to have to see it as an inversion of poetry, as a collection of antipoems, as a work that operates as a challenge to received prejudices of various kinds. Baudelaire, rather than loosening up the Alexandrine as had Victor Hugo and others, simply tossed the whole thing out at once. It was even more of a giant step than Mallarmé's in "Un Coup de Dés." Coming from a poet whom we now see as one of the greatest masters in all of Western literature, but who found little success in comparison with his admired contemporaries,

Hugo and Flaubert, it is a gesture of sublime irony, surpassed only by
Rimbaud's total renunciation of poetry.

My concern here is to establish the origins of the prose poem, as the
ultimate violation of prosody, in the work of the French poets of the mid-
and later nineteenth century. I shall not attempt a comprehensive survey
of their successors in France, which include even Paul Valéry, nor of all
their imitators among British and American writers. Numerous poets
have had a fling at the prose poem at one time or another, but the
results—being neither fish nor flesh—seldom find a place in anthologies
and consequently are mostly forgotten. Books written on the prose poem
differ radically in their emphases; an entire chapter in one will be devoted
to a poet who escapes mention in another. Personal preferences and inner
promptings play as large a part in the evaluation of the prose poem as in
its composition. It is unlikely that a well-established canon of prose
poetry will ever be established, resting—as Dr. Johnson would have it—
on the judgment of the common reader; the common reader has not yet
found it to be a memorable genre. Aloysius Bertrand is remembered
mostly because Baudelaire mentioned him in the prefatory letter to the
Spleen de Paris, and Baudelaire's prose poems are kept alive because of the
memorable finished poems in the *Fleurs du Mal.* French lycée students
commit to memory the "Bateau Ivre" of Rimbaud, not *Une Saison en
Enfer.*

I have mentioned how a few pieces in Amy Lowell's Imagist collec-
tions of 1915–17 were prose poems. Even earlier, and partly as another
thumbing of the nose at Victorian conventions, Oscar Wilde had pub-
lished a collection of prose poems, as had Ernest Dowson. I have already
quoted one of Wilde's, which is really a parody of biblical language; he
was closer to the French prose poem in the preface to *The Picture of Dorian
Gray* (1891), of which I quote the first half:

> The artist is the creator of beautiful things.
> To reveal art and conceal the artist is art's aim.
> The critic is he who can translate into another manner
> or a new material his impression of beautiful things.
> > The highest as the lowest form of
> > criticism is a mode of autobiography.
> Those who find ugly meanings in beautiful things are
> corrupt without being charming. This is a fault.

Those who find beautiful meanings in
beautiful things are the cultivated.
For these there is hope.
They are the elect to whom beautiful things
mean only Beauty.
There is no such thing as a moral or an
immoral book. Books are well written or
badly written. That is all.
The nineteenth-century dislike of realism is the rage of
Caliban seeing his own face in a glass.
The nineteenth-century dislike of
romanticism is the rage of Caliban not
seeing his own face in a glass.

Only four pieces by Ernest Dowson may be found in the section "In Prose," at the end of his collected poems. The best known of these is certainly "Absinthia Taetra" (1899):

Green changed to white, emerald to an opal: nothing was changed.
The man let the water trickle gently into his glass, and as the green clouded, a mist fell away from his mind.
Then he drank opaline.
Memories and terrors beset him. The past tore after him like a panther and through the blackness of the present he saw the luminous tiger eyes of the things to be.
But he drank opaline.
And that obscure night of the soul, and the valley of humiliation, through which he stumbled were forgotten. He saw blue vistas of undiscovered countries, high prospects and a quiet, caressing sea. The past shed its perfume over him, to-day held his hand as it were a little child, and to-morrow shone like a white star: nothing was changed.
He drank opaline.
The man had known the obscure night of the soul, and lay even now in the valley of humiliation; and the tiger menace of the things to be was red in the skies. But for a little while he had forgotten.
Green changed to white, emerald to an opal; nothing was changed.
(156–57)

Dowson has simultaneously captured the manner of some of Baudelaire's *Petits Poèmes en Prose* and the mood of some poems in his *Fleurs du Mal.* "Absinthia Taetra," like Eliot's "Hysteria" of 1915 (*Collected Poems* 19), is an excellent example of how an accomplished poet can produce a single distinguished prose poem as a tour de force.

A more serious effort to test the possibilities of a prose poetry loosely inspired by French models was William Carlos Williams's *Improvisations,* later known as *Kora in Hell,* which he managed to get into print in 1919. When these poems appeared, Williams was in the midst of that never-ending flurry of affiliations and repudiations, espousals and divorces, that mark his relations with his contemporaries both in theory and in practice. *Kora in Hell* counts more as part of his personal record of restless and irritable reaching after a new poetics, and as part of his perpetual rejection of received traditions, than as a document in the history of the prose poem. As he put it in the introduction that he wrote for the work's republication as a City Lights Pocket Poets book,

> But what was such a form to be called? I was familiar with the typically French prose poem, its pace was not the same as my own compositions. What I had permitted myself could not by any stretch of the imagination be called verse. Nothing to do but put it down as it stood, trusting to the generous spirit of the age to find a place for it.

With Gertrude Stein's *Tender Buttons,* first published in 1914, we are already into a self-conscious and self-congratulatory phase of prose poetry, where the writing makes a display of mimicking avant-garde fashions in poetry and in the other arts as well, a species of pseudo-modernism. It has all the charm of bad mimicry. The sort of repetition that in Wilde suggests a parable, and that in Dowson provides a haunting refrain, becomes tedious. Since we are not invited guests to the apartment on the Rue de Fleurus, we are fortunately not obliged to listen. This is of course my own dyspeptic opinion, and I can only hope that few of Stein's many admirers, such as Marjorie Perloff, come across the preceding sentences. For a more appreciative account one may turn to Margueritte S. Murphy's excellent study, *A Tradition of Subversion: The Prose Poem in English from Wilde to Ashbery.* William Carlos Williams, who was always ready to speak kindly of anyone who seemed to be bucking a

literary establishment, took Stein seriously and recognized the impor-
tance of typography to her work:

> Language being made up of words, the spaces between words and
> their configurations, Gertrude Stein's work means that these materi-
> als are real and must be understood, in letters, to supercede in
> themselves all ideas, facts, movements which they may under other
> circumstances be asked to signify. (*Embodiment of Knowledge* 17)

I am not sure what Williams meant, but to the extent that he is apprecia-
tive of Stein's achievement I would have to disagree with him. While
many of the visitants to Stein's apartment were genuinely reverent or at
least terrified into acquiescence, and while many of her subsequent read-
ers have been taken in by her own self-assessments, there are a few
dissenting votes. Allen Tate said simply that he never was able to under-
stand why anyone took either the writer or her work as seriously as they
did, as did the writer of a letter to the *Times Literary Supplement* in early
1994. Her reputation has in recent years benefited enormously from
quirks of intellectual fashion; as an influential figure and as a paradigm of
iconoclastic modernism Stein will continue to attract attention, some-
what as Byron remains the archetypal Romantic, and in her own way she
was every bit as admirable as Byron.

Early numbers of the *Little Review* include many prose poems,
some of which slip in the direction of the verset structure, and ulti-
mately toward Whitmanian anaphora. These pieces do seem to be ex-
ploring the territory on the frontiers of verse and prose. The magazine
was no doubt hospitable to these experiments because it also printed a
variety of prose genres, including short-shorts by Hemingway; *Poetry*
magazine from the same years printed only a handful of prose poems,
of which one was by Amy Lowell. Quite in the spirit of Aloysius
Bertrand was the work by Ben Hecht, of which "Dregs" (25–26) is a
good specimen. A thorough history of American prose poetry would
draw heavily on the *Little Review*. Its pages, which sometimes featured
graphics and which were much less conventional in appearance than
Poetry magazine, also bear ample evidence of new importance accorded
the typographical aspect of poetry. The teachings of T. E. Hulme were
absorbed by William Saphier, whose work leads off the April 1915
issue; the title of his selection is "Etchings Not to Be Read Aloud" and
the poems are rigorously Imagistic. In November 1916, a series of

poems by Richard Aldington appeared, entitled *Myrrhine and Konallis,*
from which I quote:

I.

The Lamp

Darkness enveloped us; I kindled a lamp of red clay to light her
beauty.

She turned her dazzled eyes away from the flame, which glowed
gently on her arms and the curve of her body.

Lamp! If you are a god, you must be broken; if a goddess we will
honour you; none but a goddess may look upon our caresses.

II.

The Wine Jar

This is a common wine-jar. The rough painter has drawn on it a
winged Psyche, fluttering in fire. She is edged with a black outline,
but the fire is red.

My soul is black with grief when you leave me, but glows red
with delight when you set your lips on my body.

III.

Red and Black

Wine is black, but red are the points of your breasts; black are the
figures of heroes on the tall wine-jars, but your lips are red. Black,
the frail sea-grass, but flushed faint red the curled shells. Red is your
life-blood, but black, deep black, the inexorable end of all.

Here we see the extreme abandonment of Victorian prosody, the quasi
classicism of early Imagism, and the effort at clarity of visual impres-
sions; yet just as with Dowson's poem there remains something of the
Pateresque iridescence, the nacreous sheen.

In all prose poetry there exists a calculated presumption on the part
of the writer that demands of the reader the attention and the reverence
customarily bestowed upon poetic masterpieces. Other varieties of free
verse are seldom so insolent. To say this is not to accuse the great origina-

tors of the mode—Baudelaire and Rimbaud—or any of their followers among the Symbolists and—in English—the Imagists, of overweening vanity. But it is to suggest that much prose poetry, sui generis, originated in the righteous disgust and outrage felt by major poetic sensibilities at the prospects open to their talent. Or, should we wish to put it unsympathetically, prose poetry is a neurotic expression of frustrated genius; it is Achilles sulking in his tent. In Rimbaud's work there is an accelerating progress from rhymed poetry of increasing looseness into versets like those of Aloysius Bertrand, then into the medley of pure prose, verset, and recrudescences of stanzas that make up *Une Saison en Enfer*—and then, silence. The typographical aspect of the prose poem is part and parcel of a sardonic claim by the poet on his reader.

In the hands of Baudelaire, Rimbaud, Lautréamont, or Mallarmé, the prose poem takes on a Faustian pathos—the transcendent genius abandoning magical powers and turning to lowly labors, to self-abasement and humiliation. It can also be an isolated tour de force or jeu d'esprit, as with T. S. Eliot's "Hysteria," but for us the prose poem achieves its greatest force and poignancy when we sense we are witnessing an abdication or renunciation of talent—temporary or permanent—that stops short of suicide. It is the simultaneously self-asserting and self-denying dignity of a profoundly outraged self-respect. It could also be an "aesthetic" protest against bourgeois expectations about poetry, a rejection of "Tennysonianness," a plangent moan of the refined but disaffected sensibilities of the decadent poet. As revived and practiced in later-twentieth-century America, however, it loses all force. One cannot make a grand renunciation of abilities that one never possessed. One does not suffer the negligence of a commercial, bourgeois culture. If anything, American academic readers are entirely too ready to accord to latter-day claimants to the laurels of Rimbaud and Baudelaire the dignities due their Gallic predecessors. The writing of prose poetry has become an avant-garde affectation or mannerism like any other, whether of lingo, diet, personal hygiene, or garb. As James Dickey once said, "If you can really write, you don't have to dress up funny."

Serious discussion of latter-day prose poetry sometimes consists of making up elaborate excuses for it in esoteric language. The work becomes an occasion for a criticism that spins webs out of itself: self-sustaining, solipsistic, and narcissistic—an exercise in Byzantine literary theology. The poet is the god, the poems are the sacred texts, and the criticism is the exegesis. As in the later stages of a religion, the exegetical part becomes an end in itself. A good example of this sort of criticism— which also serves as an additional argument for the fatuousness of theory that proposes a positive structure for any sort of free verse—is the essay by Michael Riffaterre, "On the Prose Poem's Formal Features," where we find:

> In a versified poem the formal unity is assured, if by nothing else, by the meter, that is, by an established conventional system, existing before and outside the poem itself. In a prose poem, on the contrary, the unifying factor will have to be generated by the text itself. The meaning cannot play this role, since meaning will not differentiate the poem's peculiar idiolect from language, from common usage. The unifying factor must be the significance. I propose to find the latter in a constant invariant relationship between text and intertext, in an invariable *intertextuality*. This much-abused and fashionable term designates a function involving three factors: text, intertext, and context. (Caws and Riffaterre 118)

From this point the essay, which begins with some marginally useful considerations, sinks steadily deeper into a swamp of jargon, clichés, spurious definitions, and mixed metaphors. To judge from the first sentence just quoted, the writer is unaware that bad poetry can be written in regular meters, and that a conventional form by no means assures a formally unified work of art. The fundamental banality of the discussion also betrays itself the use of the empty catchall word *factor* in three of the last four sentences quoted above. This essay, crude and insensitive to real literary values, is typical of much writing about prose poetry.

On the other hand, I find myself in entire agreement with Margueritte S. Murphy when she says of the prose poem,

> Yet it is also a genre opposed to norms, one that defies interdictions as part of its tradition. Its conception as a genre-breaking genre makes the task of definition somewhat problematic, as I hope this chapter will demonstrate. Yet it is this very tradition of affronts to tradition that gives the genre its vitality and power to continue to revise the boundaries of what is "poetry," or indeed, "literature." (61)

With a few modifications this description could be extended to all forms of free verse, and especially to the way that much free verse—through its appearance on the page—insists on drawing attention to the fact that it is not conventionally metered poetry.

Late in 1992 there appeared volume 1 of *The Prose Poem: An International Journal,* which includes a disarming and engaging introduction by its editor, Peter Johnson. After quoting the entire definition of the prose poem from *The Princeton Encyclopedia of Poetry and Poetics,* Johnson adds some phrases from Michael Benedikt's preface to *The Prose Poem: An International Anthology.* The first source emphasizes the compactness and dense texture of the prose poem; the second falls back on ideas similar to the old Imagistic criteria for free verse. Johnson then adds some reflections of his own, likening the prose poem to black humor and explaining his standards for the present collection: "I must admit that in my first reading of over 2000 poems, I often selected ones driven by a distinctive voice, a voice demanding attention, one that yelled out, 'Hey, try to ignore my vision if you can.'" Here we see illustrated in one sentence two of the grounds of free verse, the voice and vision of genius. As I have argued repeatedly, such a view of poetry comes naturally to Americans who have been conditioned by a heritage of dissent, of religions that emphasize divine inspiration and special election; this religious veneration is further enriched with organicist notions of the personal rhythm and the expressive form.

When we come to the actual texts in the *Journal,* we discover some that are not prose poetry at all, but rather a modified verset structure somewhat like the French *style biblique,* and even some biblical-anaphoric free verse. Even more remarkable is one piece that consists of short lines justified to the left-hand margin and beginning with capital letters. Perhaps this is an anti–prose poem. Of those that are printed as prose, the shorter and funnier they are, the better. The visions are, on the whole, eminently ignorable. Nina Nyhart's "Worm" is clever, and Ellen Smith's "A Parisian Dinner" is poignant—and both have an unpretentious charm remote equally from black humor and from the egocentric claims of some other pieces. Yet both of them point toward forms of perception best explored at length in prose fiction and fleshed out with plot and character development; the most we can hope for is something resembling a paragraph by Katherine Anne Porter or an isolated page by Gustave Flaubert. And for too many pieces in *Prose Poem,* the lack of discernible form is less a protest against the neglect of talent—as it was for the great French poets—than a disguise that hopes to conceal its absence. A hundred years ago the disguise consisted of never-failing rhymes and metronomically ticking stanzas, preeminently those of Henry Wadsworth Longfellow. Longfellow sacrificed nearly everything to ideals of form and euphony; the latter-day American prose poem is a typographical demolition of form, a flouting of harmony, sacrificing nearly everything to the authenticity of the personal statement.

Afterword

This survey stops short of an extended consideration of competing and conflicting theories of free verse articulated in this century. Omitted are the skirmishes and battles within and between the little magazines earlier in the century, as are numerous other comments by Pound, Flint, Lowell, Lowes, and Eliot. Nor is much room given to the manifestos by Williams, Winters, Olson, Steele, and others. All these, together with more remote religious and philosophical underpinnings of free verse, will be the subject of a separate study, *Beyond Free Verse*, in which the emphasis is more on theory than history.

Also left open is the question of where prosody may be headed in as we approach the millennium—whether Language poetry, the New Formalism, the New Narrative, the New Organicism, and whatever other avant-garde offspring may be midwived into prominence by academic studies, will prove of lasting importance. Such movements appeal more to disaffected and irritable academics than to ordinary readers of poetry; the best living poets seem innocent of these affiliations and not much interested in even knowing what they are. Nevertheless, as a continuation of the sesquicentennial American feud between genteel and rough, high modernist and populist, academic and New Grub Street, cooked and raw, these topics are of interest. Such divisions may prove as durable (and at times as deleterious) as a two-party system or a bicameral legislature.

For four hundred years the prosody of poetry in English has oscillated between formality and licentiousness, always with reference to some kind of underlying accentual regularity. There is even some evidence that for prosodists as far back as the later Roman Empire similar critical dichotomies existed. In English, the most interesting evasions of accentual meters are those that achieve their freedoms in part by taking advantage of the rich genealogy of the English language itself, with its

debts to French, Latin, Greek, Italian, Spanish, German—even to Arabic
and Japanese. In the seventeenth century, Milton availed himself of some
of these resources and took liberties in his poetry that the succeeding age
found unacceptable, partly because he was, for them, unsurpassable. Yet
Milton's artistry proceeded from a profound understanding of rhythmic
possibilities not only in English but in four or five other ancient and
modern languages. His prosody is a fusion of competing rhythms much
as his vocabulary is a synthesis of other languages with English. Not until
the publication of *The Waste Land* did another poem appear that was as
extraordinary in these respects as Milton's work had been, and once again
the author was at home in several languages—those that have contrib-
uted the most to the grammar and vocabulary of English. Too much free
verse of our own time is an effort to renounce this rhythmic and linguis-
tic inheritance, a refusal to assimilate any of it, and an attempt to replace a
shareable metric with an indefinable authenticity of personal utterance.

For both Milton and Eliot a well-established prosodic groundwork—
which threatened to become stultifyingly regular—existed. For Eliot, it
was the vacuous suavities of Swinburne and of some of Morris and Tenny-
son; for Milton, the ingenuities of Renaissance rhyming. The preface to
Paradise Lost objects to the latter, in terms that sound a little like what
Whitman and William Carlos Williams said about the metered line itself:
"The troublesome and modern bandage of rhyming," Milton argued, was
"the invention of a barbarous age, to set off wretched matter and lame
metre; graced indeed since by the use of some famous modern poets,
carried away by custom, but much to their own vexation, hindrance, and
constraint to express many things otherwise, and for the most part worse,
than else they would have expressed them."

Milton extended the frontiers of prosody beyond what anyone else
had done, but by common consent Shakespeare—whose prosodic devel-
opment paralleled and epitomized an entire age, and who both shared and
enriched a common metrical heritage—remains more of a living pres-
ence. Much else besides metrics accounts for the truth of this platitude,
but Shakespeare's ironic artistry, his refusal—unlike Milton—to promote
opinions, parallels his willingness to work with what metrics he found at
hand. In our century one might on similar grounds compare Pound and
Yeats. Robert Watson once told me of an economist whose advice was
always to make long-range predictions, since if you were wrong every-
one forgot what you had said. One can therefore safely speculate that
four hundred years from now the readers of "Homage to Sextus Proper-

tius" will be even fewer than those of Abraham Cowley's "Pindariques" are today, while "The Fiddler of Dooney" and "The Wild Swans at Coole" will continue to be read and memorized, partly because Yeats took his metrics for granted and availed himself of the shared and learnable convention. On an even grander scale, both the *Iliad* and *Hamlet* can be said to surpass *Samson Agonistes* as literary works precisely because in many respects they are less innovative than *Samson Agonistes* and more a culmination of established genres.

Free verse has been, since the English Renaissance, the most sophisticated extension of an established prosody at any given time. But the poetry that remains most vividly alive in common memory is that which works freely and unself-consciously within a convention, preoccupied neither with the disruption nor the preservation of the convention, accepting its establishment yet willing to test its limits. Emily Dickinson, Thomas Hardy, and—in our own time—Seamus Heaney are examples. Poets who work this way are not obsessed with perfection or with imperfection, knowing the one to be impossible and the other inevitable.

To see free verse as a transition toward a more complex metric is not, however, to argue the virtues of smallness and neatness. Worksheets left behind by great poets often prove that they labored mightily to make their work as good as possible, but a lapidary finish is seldom a characteristic of a great poem. Even Yvor Winters could be contemptuous of excessive smoothness, dismissing it as "parlor verse."

In the United States free verse has flourished as part of the effort at discovering a national cultural identity, with both Whitman and Williams insisting on the uniqueness of American speech. A spirit of adventure as well as experimentation animated these poets and their followers, whose vigor and informality have provided an escape from enervated imitations of British formal verse, much as Paul Bunyan and Johnny Appleseed provide a cis-Atlantic liberation from ancient European pantheons. But there is always the danger of descent into a bathetic crankiness in which the poem becomes yet one more human-interest story, advertising a formal unpretentiousness and inviting sentimental bemusement.

When we look at the extremes in contemporary poetry, we find the Language poets, who aim at what is private, transitory, and elusive in human experience, and who reject the idea that any poetry is possible that is broadly representative, universally accessible, and enduring, seeing in such poetry an acceptance of a capitalistic and commercialized society. The politics may be admirable, but the poetic fashion may well go out with the next move in hemlines. Language poetry theory and practice is, in any case, an inherently self-distracting art form, though it may survive as a way of passing one's time, as a subject for faddish scholarly studies—and most important of all as a way of life, a kind of spiritual disengagement. For a movement that claims to have been in existence for close to two decades, it has attracted few readers and is for the most part as yet unknown even to most Americans who teach and write about literature or even to young poets. Yet it may persist; Quakers have been around for several centuries, and the gentle ways encouraged by their beliefs continue to attract adherents. A good deal of New Formalist poetry may languish like well-executed but unexhibited canvases in permanent storage. From time to time, however, poets will emerge—and there are several now living—to whom rhythm and structure of some sort come naturally. Their work rejoices in a supple yet formal vitality, an immediacy that proves enduring, "news that stays news." And in every century, so long as poetry continues to be valued, new works will emerge that, like Eliot's *Four Quartets,* explore new ways of ordering human experience—even as they break away from the older ways.

Appendix

Jules Laforgue

LUNAR SOLO

(translation by Leigh Palmer)

> I smoke, stretched out, face to the sky,
> On the roof of a stagecoach
> Jolting my carcass, waltzing my soul
> Like an Ariel;
> Without gall or treacle my lovely soul flies,
> O roads, hillsides, o hollows, o vapors,
> My beautiful soul! Let's examine your papers.
>
> I loved her, madly, she loved me,
> And we broke up without a word.
> A fit of spleen against our herd
> Exiled me universally. Fine.
>
> Her eyes would say, "You understand?
> You don't understand? How come?"
> But no one wanted to make the first move;
> We longed to fall to our knees *as one.*
> (You understand?)
>
> At this hour of night, where is she?
> Perhaps she weeps . . .
> At this hour of night, where is she?
> Oh! at least take care, I beseech you!

O cool of the woods as they rise and recede,
O shawl of melancholy around my life, envied
By everything
Listening!
I ride this coach roof like a toad turned king.

Let's accrue irreparables!
Cheat our fate!
The stars outnumber shoreline pebbles
Where others have watched her body bathe;
All go to Death as a last resort.
No other port.

Years will pass by,
We'll each congeal into our own,
And often (already I see myself)
Say to ourselves, "If I had known . . ."
But even married, wouldn't we sigh
"If I had known, if I had known! . . ."?
Ah! cursed all along!
Heart gone bad on the shelf!
I've done you wrong.

Maniacally happy,
Then, what shall we do? I with my soul,
She with her fallible youth?
O sinner growing long in the tooth,
How many evenings, in your honor,
Shall I stoop to infamy!

Her eyes would blink, "You understand?
Understand? Why don't you?"
But neither of us made the first move
To fall to our knees together. So! . . .

The moon climbs its beam,
O road coiled in dream! . . .
We have left the textile mills, the sawmills,
Only kilometric markers abound,
Clouds of confectioner's rose-frills,
While a thin crescent of moon climbs,

O road in a dream, o song without sound,
In these pinewoods where since
The world commenced
The sun never shines,
What proper chambers, and profound!
Oh! for a one-night honeymoon!
And I people them, and I see myself there,
What a handsome, loving pair:
By their gestures, an outlaw bride and groom.

And I pass and abandon them,
The road turns on, and I lie,
As Ariel, down to face the sky;
Nobody waits for me; I go to no home.
I have only the friendship of hotel rooms.

The moon climbs its beam,
O road coiled in dream,
O road without end.
A station arrives,
Where they light the lanterns,
Chug a glass of milk down,
Then on, postilion!
To the crickets' round
Under the stars of July.

O light of the Moon,
Wedding of Bengalese fireworks drowning my woes,
Poplar shadow along the road . . .
Mountain stream listening
To its own tune . . .
In these eddies of Lethe, which overflows . . .

O lunar Solo,
You defy my pen.
Oh! this night on the road,
Ominous stars,
You're all there! All!
How quickly this hour withers . . .
Oh! that there were a means
For me to distill this soul for the coming Fall!

Now how cool it grows, how cool,
Oh! if at the same hour
She also runs at the forests' edge
To drown her plight
In a wedding of moonlight!
(Staying out late keeps her enthralled!)
She'll have forgotten her shawl,
She'll catch her death, in light of this hour!
Oh! take care of yourself, I implore you!
I don't want to hear that cough anymore!

Ah! that I failed to fall at your knees!
Ah! that you didn't faint at my knees!
I would have been the model spouse for you!
As the frou-frou of your gown is the model frou-frou.

References and Bibliography

Most citations in the text provide only the page numbers of the sources identified there. Additional information appears with the citation if there is any ambiguity about the author, editor, or title. All sources quoted and works consulted appear below.

Abrams, M. H. *The Mirror and the Lamp: Romantic Theory and the Critical Tradition.* New York: Oxford UP, 1953; rpt. New York: Norton, 1958.

Addison, Joseph. *The Spectator.* Vol. 1. Ed. George A. Aitken. London: John C. Nimmo, 1898.

———. *The Works of Joseph Addison.* Vol. 1. New York: Harper and Brothers, 1837.

Alaya, Flavia. *William Sharp—"Fiona Macleod."* Cambridge: Harvard UP, 1970.

Alcott, Bronson. "Orphic Sayings." *Dial,* 1, 1 (July 1840) 85–98.

Aldington, Richard. "Free Verse in England." *Egoist,* 1, 18 (Sept. 15, 1914) 351–52.

———. "Myrrhine and Konallis." *Little Review,* 3, 7 (Nov. 1916) 1–2.

Allen, Donald M., ed. *The New American Poetry.* New York: Grove, 1960.

Allen, Gay Wilson. *American Prosody.* American Literature Series. New York: American Book Company, 1935.

Andrewes, Lancelot. *Preces Privatae Quotidianae.* London: Oxford UP, 1853; rpt. New York: AMS P, 1967.

Appel, Willi. *Harvard Dictionary of Music.* Cambridge: Belknap P of Harvard UP, 1969.

Arnold, Matthew. *The Works of Matthew Arnold.* Vol. 5. London: Macmillan, 1903–4.

Ashleigh, Charles. "The Poetry of Revolt." *Little Review,* 1, 6 (Sept. 1914) 23.

Auden, W. H. *The Collected Poetry of W. H. Auden.* New York: Random House, 1945.

———. *The Dyer's Hand.* New York: Random House, 1962.

Babbitt, Irving. *The New Laokoon.* Boston: Houghton Mifflin, 1910.

Barnes, Barnabe. *Parthenophil and Parthenope.* Ed. Victor A. Doyno. Carbondale: Southern Illinois UP, 1971.

Baudelaire, Charles. *Oeuvres*. Paris: Nouvelle Revue Française, Pléiade ed., 1954.

Baugh, Albert Croll. *A Literary History of England*. New York: Appleton-Century-Crofts, 1948.

Bernard, Suzanne. *Le Poème en Prose de Baudelaire jusqu'à nos Jours*. Paris: Librairie Nizet, 1959.

Bernstein, Charles. *A Poetics*. Cambridge: Harvard UP, 1992.

Blake, William. *Complete Writings*. Ed. Geoffrey Keynes. London: Oxford UP, 1966.

Bohn, Willard. *The Aesthetics of Visual Poetry*. Cambridge: Cambridge UP, 1986.

Boswell, James. *London Journal*. New York: McGraw Hill, 1950.

Boyer, Lisa. "Some Thoughts about Free Verse." Unpublished essay, 1992.

Bridges, Robert. *Milton's Prosody*. London: Oxford UP, 1921.

Bryant, William Cullen. *The Prose Writings of William Cullen Bryant*. Vol. 1. New York: Russell and Russell, 1964.

Buffière, Félix, ed. and trans. *Anthologie Grecque*. Vol. 12. Paris: Belles Lettres, 1970.

Bush, Douglas. *English Literature in the Earlier Seventeenth Century*. London; Oxford UP, 1962.

Carroll, Paul, ed. *The Young American Poets*. Intro. by James Dickey. Chicago: Follett, 1968.

Carpenter, Edward. *Towards Democracy*. New York: Mitchell Kennerly, 1912.

Caws, Mary Ann, and Hermine Riffaterre, eds. *The Prose Poem in France*. New York: Columbia UP, 1983.

Christensen, Paul. *Charles Olson*. Austin: U of Texas P, 1979.

Clack, Jerry, ed. *An Anthology of Alexandrian Poetry*. Pittsburgh: Classical World, 1982.

Clark, Tom. "Stalin as Linguist." *Partisan Review,* 56, 3 (Spring 1987) 299–304.

Clarke, Graham, ed. *T. S. Eliot: Critical Assessments*. London: Christopher Helm, 1990.

Coffin, Robert P. Tristram, and Alexander M. Witherspoon, eds. *Seventeenth Century Prose and Poetry*. New York: Harcourt Brace, 1946.

Cohen, Milton A. *Poet and Painter: The Aesthetics of E. E. Cummings' Early Work*. Detroit: Wayne State UP, 1987.

Cohn, Robert G. *Mallarmé's Masterwork*. The Hague: Mouton, 1966.

Coleridge, Samuel Taylor. *Biographia Literaria*. Vol. 2. Ed. J. Shawcross. London: Oxford UP, 1907.

Conte, Joseph M. *Unending Design*. Ithaca: Cornell UP, 1991.

Cowley, Abraham. *The Complete Works in Verse and Prose*. Vol. 1. Ed. Alexander B. Grosart. Hildesheim, Germany: G. Olms, 1969.

———. *Poems*. Ed. A. R. Waller. Cambridge: Cambridge UP, 1905.

———. *The Works of Mr. Abraham Cowley*. 7th ed. London: Printed by J. M. for Henry Herringman, at the sign of the Blue Anchor in the lower walk of the New Exchange, 1681.

Cranch, C. P. *The Life and Letters of Christopher Pearse Cranch*. Ed. Leonora Cranch Scott. Boston, 1917; rpt. New York: AMS P, 1969.

Crane, Hart. *The Complete Poems and Selected Letters and Prose*. New York: Double-day and Company, Anchor Books, 1966.

Cummings, E. E. *Tulips and Chimneys*. New York: Liveright, 1976.

Cunningham, J. V. *The Collected Essays of J. V. Cunningham*. Chicago: Swallow P, 1976.

Cushman, Stephen. *William Carlos Williams and the Meanings of Measure*. New Haven: Yale UP, 1985.

Dacey, Philip, and David Jauss. *Strong Measures*. New York: Harper and Row, 1986.

Davidson, John. *A Selection of His Poems*. Ed. Maurice Lindsay. London: Hutchin-son, 1961.

Deloffre, Frédéric. *Le Vers Français*. Paris: Société d'édition d'enseignment Su-périeur, 1969.

Derrida, Jacques. *Of Grammatology*. Trans. Gayatri Chakravorty Spivak. Balti-more: Johns Hopkins UP, 1976.

Donne, John. *Sermons of John Donne*. Vol. 7. Ed. Evelyn Simpson and George R. Potter. Berkeley and Los Angeles: U of California P, 1954.

Dorchain, Auguste. *L'Art des Vers*. Paris: Librairie Garnier, 1933.

Dowson, Ernest. *The Poems of Ernest Dowson*. Portland, Maine: Thomas B. Mosher, 1902.

Drummond, William. *Poems and Prose*. Ed. Robert H. Macdonald. Edinburgh: Scottish Academic P, 1976.

East, James, ed: "The Correspondence of William Carlos Williams and Kenneth Burke." Dissertation in progress, 1994.

Eliot, T. S. *The Complete Poems and Plays*. New York: Harcourt, Brace, 1952.

——. *The Letters of T. S. Eliot*. Vol. 1. New York: Harcourt Brace Jovanovich, 1988.

——. *On Poetry and Poets*. New York: Farrar, Straus and Cudahy, 1957.

——. *Selected Prose of T. S. Eliot*. Ed. Frank Kermode. New York: Harcourt Brace Jovanovich and Farrar, Straus and Giroux, 1975.

——. *To Criticize the Critic*. New York: Farrar, Straus and Giroux, 1965.

Ellman, Richard, and Robert O'Clair, eds. *The Norton Anthology of Modern Poetry*. 2d ed. New York: Norton, 1988.

Emerson, Ralph Waldo. *The Complete Works of Ralph Waldo Emerson*. Boston: Houghton Mifflin, 1903–21.

Erskine, John. *The Elizabethan Lyric*. New York: Columbia UP, 1903.

——. *The Kinds of Poetry*. New York: Duffield and Company, 1920.

Faner, Robert D. *Walt Whitman and Opera*. Philadelphia: U of Pennsylvania P, 1951.

Faulkner, William. *The Sound and the Fury*. Modern Library. New York: Random House, 1956.

Ferlinghetti, Lawrence. *A Coney Island of the Mind*. New York: New Directions, 1958.

Fitzgerald, William. *Agonistic Poetry*. Berkeley and Los Angeles: U of California P, 1987.

Flint, F. S. "Contemporary French Poetry." *Poetry Review*, 1, 8 (Aug. 1912) 355–414.

———. "The History of Imagism." *Egoist*, 2, 5 (May 1, 1915) 70–71.

———. "Recent Verse." *New Age*, n.s. 3 (July 11, 1908) 212–13.

Fogle, French Rowe. *A Critical Study of William Drummond of Hawthornden*. New York: King's Crown P, 1952.

Ford, Ford Madox. *Collected Poems*. New York: Oxford UP, 1936.

———. *Memories and Impressions*. New York: Harper and Brothers, 1911.

———. *Thus to Revisit*. New York: Dutton, 1921.

———, ed. *Imagist Anthology 1930*. New York: Covici, Friede, 1930.

Fowlie, Wallace. *Mallarmé*. Chicago: U of Illinois P, 1953.

Frank, Robert, and Henry Sayre, eds. *The Line in Postmodern Poetry*. Urbana: U of Illinois P, 1988.

Fraser, G. S. *Metre, Rhyme, and Free Verse*. London: Methuen, 1970.

"Free Verse." *The New Encyclopaedia Britannica: Micropaedia*. 1994 ed.

French, David P., ed. *Minor English Poets, 1660–1780*. Vol. 3. New York: B. Blom, 1967.

Fry, Paul H. *The Poet's Calling in the English Ode*. New Haven: Yale UP, 1980.

Frye, Northrop. *Fearful Symmetry*. Princeton: Princeton UP, 1947.

Fuller, Thomas. *Thoughts and Contemplations*. Ed. James O. Wood. London: S. P. C. K, 1964.

Fussell, Paul. *Poetic Meter and Poetic Form*. New York: Random House, 1979.

———. *Theory of Prosody in Eighteenth-Century England*. New London, Conn.: Connecticut College Monograph No. 5, 1954.

Gardner, Helen. *The Art of T. S. Eliot*. 1950; rpt. New York: Dutton, 1959.

Gerber, Helmut E. "English Literature, 1820–1920: A Speculative Overview." In *ELT Special Series*, No. 3. 1985.

Gosse, Edmund. *Jeremy Taylor*. New York: Macmillan, 1904; rpt. Grosse Pointe, Mich.: Scholarly P, 1968.

———. *Seventeenth Century Studies*. New York: Dodd, Mead, 1897.

Gould, Jean. *Amy*. New York: Dodd, Mead, 1975.

Gray, Richard. *American Poetry of the Twentieth Century*. London: Longman, 1990.

Greene, Edward J. H. *T. S. Eliot et la France*. Paris: Boivin et Cie., 1951.

Grierson, Herbert J. C. *Cross-currents in Seventeenth Century Literature*. London: Chatto and Windus, 1929; rpt. New York: Harper Torchbooks, 1958.

Gross, Harvey. *Sound and Form in Modern Poetry*. Ann Arbor: U of Michigan P, 1964.

———, ed. *The Structure of Verse*. Greenwich, Conn.: Fawcett, 1966.

Hall, Donald, Robert Pack, and Louis Simpson. *New Poets of England and America*. Cleveland: World Publishing, 1957. Second Selection, 1962.

Hamilton, Scott. *Ezra Pound and the Symbolist Inheritance*. Princeton: Princeton UP, 1992.

Hardenberg, Friedrich ("Novalis"). *Journal Intime, suivi des Hymnes à la Nuit* . . . Trans. G. Claretie and S. Joachim-Chaigneau. Paris: Librairie Stock, 1927.

———. *Novalis Werke*. Munich: C. H. Beck, 1969.

Hartman, Charles O. *Free Verse*. Princeton: Princeton UP, 1980.

Hecht, Ben. "Dregs." *Little Review*, 2, 8 (Nov. 1915) 25–26.

Henley, William Ernest. *Poems*. New York: Scribner's, 1922.

Holden, Jonathan. *Style and Authenticity in Postmodern Poetry*. Columbia: U of Missouri P, 1986.

Hollander, John, ed. *American Poetry: The Nineteenth Century*. New York: Library of America, 1993.

Honan, Park. *Matthew Arnold, a Life*. New York: McGraw-Hill, 1981.

Hughes, Glenn. *Imagism and the Imagists*. Stanford: Stanford UP and London: Oxford UP, 1931.

Hughes, Langston. *Selected Poems of Langston Hughes*. New York: Vintage, 1990.

Hulme, T. E. *Further Speculations*. Ed. Sam Hynes. Minneapolis: U of Minnesota P, 1955.

———. *Notes on Language and Style*. Ed. Herbert Read. Seattle: Folcroft P, 1929; rpt. 1970.

———. *Speculations*. Ed. Herbert Read. London: Kegan Paul, Trench, Trubner and Co., 1936.

Hurston, Zora Neale. *The Sanctified Church*. Berkeley, Calif.: Turtle Island, 1983.

Jewell, Edwin Lee. "Exploring the Momentary Sublime: Frank O'Hara, John Ashbery, and the New York School of Poetry." Unpublished essay, 1994.

Johnson, James Weldon. *God's Trombones*. New York: Viking P, 1927; rpt. New York: Penguin, 1976, 1990.

Johnson, Peter, ed. *The Prose Poem: An International Journal*, vol 1.

Joll, James. "Nietzsche vs. Nietzsche." *New York Review of Books*, 40, 4 (Feb. 11, 1993) 20–23.

Jump, John D. *The Ode*. London: Methuen, 1974.

Kahn, Gustave. *Symbolistes et Décadents*. Paris: Librairie Léon Vanier, 1902; rpt. New York: AMS P, 1980.

Kaplan, Justin. *Walt Whitman: A Life*. New York: Simon and Schuster, 1980.

Kastner, L. E. *A History of French Versification*. Oxford: Clarendon P, 1903.

Kaun, Alexander S. "Futurism and Pseudo-Futurism." *Little Review*, 1, 4 (June 1914) 12–18.

Kenner, Hugh. *Historical Fictions*. San Francisco: North Point P, 1990.

———. *The Pound Era*. Berkeley and Los Angeles: U of California P, 1971.

Klonsky, Milton. *Speaking Pictures*. New York: Harmony Books, 1975.

Laforgue, Jules. *Poésies*. Buenos Aires: Viau, 1944.

Lampert, Laurence. *Nietzsche and Modern Times*. New Haven: Yale UP, 1993.

Lanier, Sidney. *The Science of English Verse*. New York: Scribner's, 1927.

Lehman, David. "A Poet in the Heart of Noise." *New York Times Book Review*, 98, 25 (June 20, 1993) 18.

———, ed. *Ecstatic Occasions, Expedient Forms*. New York: Macmillan, 1987.

Lessing, Gotthold Ephraim. *Laocoön, Nathan the Wise, Minna von Barnhelm*. London: J. M. Dent, and New York: Dutton, 1930.

Lewalski, Barbara Kiefer. *Protestant Poetics and the Seventeenth-Century Religious Lyric*. Princeton: Princeton UP, 1970.

Lewis, C. S. *English Literature in the Sixteenth Century*. New York: Oxford UP, 1954.

Lindberg-Seyersted, Brita. *Pound/Ford: The Story of a Literary Friendship*. New York: New Directions, 1982.

Lowell, Amy. "A Consideration of Modern Poetry." *North American Review*, 205 (Jan. 1917) 103–17.

———. "The Rhythms of Free Verse." *Dial*, 64 (Jan. 17, 1918) 51–56.

———. *Six French Poets*. New York: Macmillan, 1920.

———. *Tendencies in Modern American Poetry*. Boston: Houghton Mifflin, 1921.

———. "Vers Libre and Metrical Prose." *Poetry*, 3 (Mar. 1914) 213–20.

———, ed. *Some Imagist Poets*. Boston: Houghton Mifflin, 1915.

———, ed. *Some Imagist Poets*. Boston: Houghton Mifflin, 1916.

———, ed. *Some Imagist Poets*. Boston: Houghton Mifflin, 1917.

Lowes, John Livingston. *Convention and Revolt in Poetry*. Boston: Houghton Mifflin, 1919.

Macpherson, James. *The Poems of Ossian*. Ed. William Sharp. Edinburgh: John Grant, 1926.

Mallarmé, Stéphane. *Igitur, Divagations, Un Coup de Dés*. Paris: Gallimard, 1976.

———. *Oeuvres Complètes*. Paris: Bibliothèque de la Pléiade, 1945.

Malof, Joseph. *A Manual of English Meters*. Bloomington: Indiana UP, 1970.

Mariani, Paul. *William Carlos Williams: A New World Naked*. New York: McGraw-Hill, 1981.

Masters, Edgar Lee. *Whitman*. New York: Scribner's, 1937.

Matthiessen, F. O. *Theodore Dreiser*. New York: William Sloane Associates, 1951.

Mendès, M. Catulle. *Rapport . . . sur Le Mouvement Poètique Français. . . .* Paris: Imprimerie Nationale, 1902.

Metzger, Bruce, and Roland Murphy, eds. *The New Oxford Annotated Bible*. New York: Oxford UP, 1991.

Miki, Roy. *The Prepoetics of William Carlos Williams*. Ann Arbor: UMI Research P, 1983.

Miller, Perry. *The New England Mind: The Seventeenth Century*. Boston: Beacon P, 1961.

Monroe, Harriet, ed. *The New Poetry*. New York: Macmillan, 1923.

———. *Poets and Their Art*. New York: Macmillan, 1932.

———. "Rhythms of English Verse." *Poetry*, 3 (Nov. 1913) 61–68; 3 (Dec. 1913) 100–111.

Monroe, Harriet, and Alice Corbin Henderson, eds. *The New Poetry*. New ed. New York: Macmillan, 1936.

Monroe, Jonathan. *A Poverty of Objects*. Ithaca: Cornell UP, 1987.

Morris, D. Hampton. *Stéphane Mallarmé: Twentieth-Century Criticism*. University, Miss.: Romance Monographs, 1977.

Murphy, Margueritte S. *A Tradition of Subversion*. Amherst: U of Massachusetts P, 1992.

Nethercot, Arthur H. *Abraham Cowley, the Muse's Hannibal*. London: Oxford UP, 1931.

Olson, Charles. *Selected Writings of Charles Olson*. Ed. Robert Creeley. New York: New Directions, 1967.

Owen, Trevor A. *Lancelot Andrewes*. Boston: Twayne, 1981.

Patmore, Coventry. *Poems*. Intro. Basil Champneys. London: George Bell and Sons, 1906.

Perloff, Marjorie. *Radical Artifice*. Chicago: U of Chicago P, 1991.

Perry, Bliss. *Walt Whitman*. Boston: Houghton Mifflin, 1906.

Pickard-Cambridge, Arthur. *Dithyrambic Tragedy and Comedy*, 2d ed. rev. by T. B. L. Webster. Oxford: The Clarendon P, 1962.

Plato. *Works of Plato*. Four volumes in one. Vol. 3. Trans. Benjamin Jowett. New York: Tudor Publishing, 1937.

"Poetry's Banquet." *Poetry*, 4, 1 (April 1914) 25–29.

Pondrom, Cyrena N. *The Road From Paris*. Cambridge: Cambridge UP 1974.

Pound, Ezra. *Ezra Pound: A Critical Anthology*. Ed. J. P. Sullivan. Harmondsworth: Penguin, 1970.

———. *The Selected Letters of Ezra Pound*. Ed. D. D. Paige. New York: New Directions, 1950.

———. *Selected Poems*. Intro. by T. S. Eliot. London: Faber and Faber, 1928.

———. "T. S. Eliot." Review of *Prufrock and Other Observations*. *Poetry*, 10, 5 (Aug. 1917) 264–71.

Powell, Johannes U. [Latinized], ed. *Collectanea Alexandrina*. Oxford: Clarendon P, 1925; rpt. Oxford: Oxford UP, 1970.

Prince, F. T. *The Italian Element in Milton's Verse*. London: Oxford UP, 1954.

Prunty, Wyatt. *Fallen from the Symboled World*. New York: Oxford UP, 1990.

Rampersad, Arnold. *The Life of Langston Hughes*. Vol. 1. New York: Oxford UP, 1986.

Raymond, Marcel. *From Baudelaire to Surrealism*. New York: Wittenborn, Schultz, 1950.

Reed, Edward Bliss. *English Lyrical Poetry*. New Haven: Yale UP, 1912.

Reid, J. C. *The Mind and Art of Coventry Patmore*. New York: Macmillan, 1957.

Reinfeld, Linda. *Language Poetry*. Baton Rouge: Louisiana State UP, 1992.

Rexroth, Kenneth. *American Poetry in the Twentieth Century*. New York: Herder and Herder, 1971.

Roberts, Michael. *T. E. Hulme*. Manchester: Carcanet New P, 1982.

Roethke, Theodore. *On the Poet and His Craft*. Seattle: U of Washington P, 1965.

Rollins, Hyder Edward, ed. *The Renaissance in England*. Boston: Heath, 1954.

Rothman, David Jacob. "The Whitmanian Poets and the Origin of Open Form." Diss. New York U, 1992.

Rude, Fernand. *Aloysius Bertrand*. Paris: Éditions Seghers, 1971.

Russell, Bertrand. *The Autobiography of Bertrand Russell*. Vol. 1. Boston: Little, Brown, 1967.

———. *Unpopular Essays*. New York: Simon and Schuster, 1950.

Saintsbury, George. *History of English Prosody from the Twelfth Century to the Present Day*. 3 vols. London: Macmillan, 1906–10.

Sandburg, Carl. *Complete Poems*. New York: Harcourt, Brace and World, 1950.

Santayana, George. *The Genteel Tradition*. Ed. Douglas L. Wilson. Cambridge: Harvard UP, 1967.

Saphier, William. "Etchings Not to Be Read Aloud." *Little Review*, 2, 2 (April 1915) 1.

Sayre, Henry M. *The Visual Text of William Carlos Williams*. Urbana: U of Illinois P, 1983.

Schiller, Friedrich. *The Works of Frederick Schiller*. Vol. 6. London: G. Bell, 1879.

Scott, Clive. *French Verse-Art*. Cambridge: Cambridge UP, 1980.

———. *A Question of Syllables*. Cambridge: Cambridge UP, 1986.

Scott, David. *Pictorialist Poetics*. Cambridge: Cambridge UP, 1988.

Scott, Janet Girvain. *Les Sonnets Elizabéthains: Les Sources et l'Apport Personnel*. Paris: Champion, 1929.

Shafer, Robert. *The English Ode to 1660*. New York: Haskell House, 1966.

Sharp, William [Fiona Macleod, pseud.]. *From the Hills of Dream*. Edinburgh: Patrick Geddes and Colleagues, 1896.

———. *Studies and Appreciations*. New York: Duffield and Co., 1912.

Shelley, Percy Bysshe. *The Complete Poetical Works*. Ed. Neville Rogers. Vol. 1. London: Oxford UP, 1972.

Shetley, Vernon Lionel. *After the Death of Poetry*. Durham: Duke UP, 1993.

Sidney, Philip, Sir. *Poems*. Ed. William A. Ringler Jr. Oxford: Clarendon P, 1962.

Smart, Christopher. *Jubilate Agno*. Ed. W. H. Bond. London: Rupert Hart-Davis, 1954.

Smith, Egerton. *The Principles of English Metre*. London: Oxford UP, 1923.

Snodgrass, W. D. "Pulse and Impulse." *Southern Review*, 27, 3 (July 1991) 505–21.

Southey, Robert. *The Poetical Works of Robert Southey*. Boston: Houghton Mifflin, [1884?].

Starkie, Enid. *From Gautier to Eliot*. London: Hutchinson, 1960.

Stead, C. K. *Pound, Yeats, Eliot, and the Modernist Movement*. New Brunswick, N.J.: Rutgers UP, 1986.

Steele, Timothy. *Missing Measures*. Fayetteville: U of Arkansas P, 1990.

Stewart, Stanley. *The Expanded Voice*. San Marino, Calif: Huntington Library, 1970.

Stock, Noel. *The Life of Ezra Pound*. New York: Avon Books, 1970.

Storer, Edward. "Form in Free Verse." *New Republic*, 6 (March 11, 1916) 154–56.

———. *Mirrors of Illusion*. London: Sisley's, 1909.

Stovall, Floyd. *The Foreground of Leaves of Grass*. Charlottesville: UP of Virginia, 1974.

Sutton, Walter. *American Free Verse*. New York: New Directions, 1973.

Swinburne, Algernon Charles. *Letters*. Ed. Cecil Y. Lang. Vol. 1. New Haven: Yale UP, 1959.

Taaffe, James G. *Abraham Cowley*. New York: Twayne Publishers, 1972.

Taylor, Carole Anne. *A Poetics of Seeing*. New York: Garland, 1985.

Taylor, Jeremy. *The House of Understanding*. Ed. Margaret Gest. Philadelphia: U of Pennsylvania P, 1954.

Thompson, John. *The Founding of English Metre*. New York: Columbia UP and London: Routledge and Kegan Paul, 1961.

Thoreau, Henry David. "Homer. Ossian. Chaucer." and "Ethnical Scriptures." *Dial*, 4, 1 (Jan. 1844).

Traherne, Thomas. *Poems, Centuries, and Three Thanksgivings*. Ed. Anne Ridler. London: Oxford UP, 1966.

Trawick, Leonard M., ed. *Backgrounds of Romanticism*. Bloomington: Indiana UP, 1967.

Trotter, David. *The Poetry of Abraham Cowley*. Totowa, N.J.: Rowman and Littlefield, 1979.

Untermeyer, Louis, ed. *Modern American Poetry: A Critical Anthology*. New York: Harcourt, Brace, 1925.

Wagner, Linda Welshimer. *The Poems of William Carlos Williams*. Middletown, Conn.: Wesleyan UP, 1964.

Whitehead, Alfred North. *The Aims of Education*. New York: Macmillan, 1929; rpt. New York: Mentor Books, 1949.

Whitman, Walt. *Complete Writings*. Vol. 9. New York: G. P. Putnam's Sons, 1902.

———. *Leaves of Grass*. New York: New York UP, 1965.

———. *Rivulets of Prose*. New York: Greenberg, 1928.

Wilde, Oscar. *The Writings of Oscar Wilde*. Vol. 9. London: Keller-Farmer, 1907.

Wilkinson, Marguerite. *New Voices*. New York: Macmillan, 1923.

Williams, Ellen. *Harriet Monroe and the Poetry Renaissance*. Urbana: U of Illinois P, 1977.

Williams, William Carlos. *The Autobiography of William Carlos Williams*. New York: Random House, 1951.

———. *The Collected Poems of William Carlos Williams*. New York: New Directions, 1986.

———. *Embodiment of Knowledge*. New York: New Directions, 1974.

———. *Kora in Hell*. San Francisco: City Lights Books, 1957.

———. "The New Political Economy." Review of *Discrete Series* by George Oppen. *Poetry*, 44 (July 1934) 221–22.

———. *Selected Essays*. New York: Random House, 1954.

———. *Selected Poems of William Carlos Williams*. Introduction by Randall Jarrell. New York: New Directions, 1968.

Winn, James Anderson. *Unsuspected Eloquence*. New Haven: Yale UP, 1981.

Winters, Yvor. *The Early Poems of Yvor Winters*. Denver: Alan Swallow, 1966.

———. *In Defense of Reason*. Denver: Alan Swallow, 1947.

———. *Uncollected Essays and Reviews*. Chicago: Swallow P, 1973.

Wright, George T. *Shakespeare's Metrical Art*. Berkeley and Los Angeles: U of California P, 1988.

Yeats, W. B., ed. *The Oxford Book of Modern Verse*. New York: Oxford UP, 1936.

Index

Abrams, M. H., viii, 27, 34, 35, 39
"Absinthia Taetra" (Dowson), 265
Adamo (Andreini), 79
Adams, Henry, 156
Addison, Joseph, 213, 215–17, 220
Adonic measure, 161, 241
Aeneid, The (Virgil), 57, 58, 215
Aeschylus, 153, 250
African-American poetry, 44, 168–73
Akenside, Mark, 108
Alcaic measure, 215
Alcott, Bronson, 158
Aldington, Richard, ix, xii, 7, 8, 43, 230, 235, 268
"Alexander's Feast" (Dryden), 98, 102, 220
Alexandrine, 12, 113
   Blake's use of, 150
   Eliot's use of, 181, 206–8
   as French standard, 260
   Hugo's treatment of, 12, 182, 263
   Laforgue's use of, 192
   Southey on, 113
"Alisoun" (anon.), 57
Allen, Donald M., 2, 3
Allen, Gay Wilson, 160, 168
Anaphora
   African-American poets' use of, 168, 170–72
   Beat poets' use of, 175–76
   Blake's use of, 150
   British poets and, 173
   Eliot's use of, 174, 197, 201, 202, 204, 206, 208

   French poets and, 224
   Hebrew poetry and, 138, 142
   King James Bible as source of, 43, 143
   list of modern poets using, 174–75
   Pound's use of, 239
   Sandburg's use of, 136
   Whitmanian, 2, 143, 168, 173, 224, 245, 267
   Whitman's use of, 43, 100, 154, 159
Ancient-Modern controversy of seventeenth century, 89
   compared to debate over free verse, ix, 14
Andreini, Giovanni Battista, 79
Andrewes, Lancelot, 144–45
Andrieux, François, 183
Anglo-Saxon. *See* Old English
Apolelymenon, 78, 98
   as used by Milton, 78
Apollinaire, Guillaume, 231, 238
Arcadia, The (Sidney), 64
Archy and mehitabel (Marquis), 251
Aristotle, 38
Arnold, Matthew, vii, 129, 131, 229
   believes in "Ossian," 122
   Celtic literature and, 122
   as a free-verse poet, 1, 18, 19, 23, 48, 51, 63, 100, 120–23, 127, 185
   and "Pindarism," 122
   as precursor to Eliot, 180, 193
   Saintsbury's views on, 120, 122
Art of English Poetry, The (Puttenham), 218